Paying for Pollution

PAYING FOR POLLUTION

Why a Carbon Tax is Good for America

Gilbert E. Metcalf

OXFORD
UNIVERSITY PRESS

Oxford University Press is a department of the University of Oxford. It furthers
the University's objective of excellence in research, scholarship, and education
by publishing worldwide. Oxford is a registered trade mark of Oxford University
Press in the UK and certain other countries.

Published in the United States of America by Oxford University Press
198 Madison Avenue, New York, NY 10016, United States of America.

© Oxford University Press 2019

CIP data is on file at the Library of Congress
ISBN 978–0–19–069419–7

9 8 7 6 5 4 3 2 1

Printed by Sheridan Books, Inc., United States of America

For Simon and Calvin

CONTENTS

PREFACE

According to Nathanial Hawthorne, "Easy reading is damn hard writing." That is especially true when writing a book on a technical subject for a general audience. In writing this book, I have deliberately avoided the mathematical tools and conventions that economists fall back on in academic writing. Readers need not fear that they will see complicated equations, derivatives, stochastic calculus, or other high-tech tools of modern economics. Instead, I have tried to write a book that is accessible to any person interested in the issue of climate change and in how our government should respond to this threat. I took this approach to reach as wide an audience as possible in hopes of influencing debate over climate policy. At the same time, I have provided extensive endnotes and references for readers who want to see the research that underpins this book.[1]

I have carried out research on climate change policy for roughly twenty years now. Nearly all of that work informs this book. I have benefitted greatly from conversations with Joe Aldy, Dallas Burtraw, Kelly Sims Gallagher, Marc Hafstead, Ted Halstead, Kevin Hassett, Captain William Holt, USCG, Ret., Chris Knittel, Ray Kopp, Henry Lee, Billy Pizer, John Reilly, Ricky Revesz, Rob Stavins, Jim Stock, Jerry Taylor, David Weisbach, and Rob Williams, among many others. They cannot be held responsible for any of the opinions I've expressed in this book. Those opinions are mine alone. Richard Forman, Jeff Greene, and Michael Klein have read drafts of this book and provided constructive suggestions for which I'm grateful.

I wrote most of this book while on leave from the Department of Economics at Tufts University. I spent some of that time as a visiting scholar at the Mossavar-Rahmani Center at Harvard's Kennedy School of Government. My thanks to Larry Summers for extending the invitation and to John Haigh and Scott Leland for making me welcome there.

I am also grateful for a grant from the Smith Richardson Foundation that supported my writing of this book including funding part of my leave.

This book has benefitted from the thoughtful guidance of David Pervin, my editor at Oxford University Press, and the comments of two anonymous reviewers. Stefan Koester dug up data, factoids, old articles, and other useful material with impressive speed. Erika Niedowski was a superb copyeditor who helped shape and tighten my writing throughout the book. If this book is noteworthy for its readability, it is due in no small part to her exacting standards and close reading of the manuscript along the way.

Finally, I want to thank my wife, Rebecca Winborn, who has been a source of unwavering support throughout my writing of this book. She has shown great patience while I've been absorbed in this project. More than that, she reminds me every day that how we live our lives is a choice we each make; doing so in a deliberate way enriches us in many ways. I hope this book, in its own way, can help us as a society live more deliberately and enrich our world not just for ourselves but for future generations as well.

Paying for Pollution

Introduction: Why This Book?

The world is in the midst of a risky and unprecedented experiment. We are adding carbon dioxide and other greenhouse gases into the atmosphere at a prodigious rate, primarily from our burning of fossil fuels. By trapping heat in the atmosphere, these accumulated gases are pollutants that cause long-lasting, pervasive damages from higher temperatures, more extreme weather, sea-level rise, and glacial melt, among other things. Those damages are costly, not only for those of us alive today, but also for our children and our children's children. Carbon dioxide and other greenhouse gases linger for hundreds of years in our atmosphere. Like the proverbial frog in a frying pan, we need to jump out of the pan while there is still time to do so—that is, we must speed up the pace at which we move our economy away from a reliance on fossil fuels.

The best way for the United States to do that is to enact a national carbon tax. This may seem quixotic in our current political environment. But the problem is urgent and our efforts to date are not sufficiently aggressive to successfully deal with the problem. It's time for a new approach.

Why is there an urgent need to act? Every month brings new reports of record-breaking temperatures. But the problem goes well beyond high temperatures. Anyone following the news in the summer and early fall of 2017 could be excused for fearing that the apocalypse might be at hand. In August, Hurricane Harvey, a category 4 hurricane, stalled over Texas, dumping as much as sixty inches of water on the eastern part of the state. Parts of Houston, in Harris County, received over forty inches of paralyzing rain. Nearly three-quarters of the county was under at least one and a half feet of water, and the rebuilding will cost many billions of dollars.[1]

Category 5 Irma roared through the Atlantic on the heels of Harvey causing extensive damage in the Caribbean and Florida Keys only to be followed by Maria two weeks later. Maria, another category 5 storm, ravaged Puerto Rico, leaving the island's population of 3.4 million almost entirely without electricity and other basic services. At the start of 2018, over half of the island was still without power.[2]

Then came devastating wildfires that burned thousands of acres in California, destroying over 6,700 homes and killing at least forty-three people. Across the nation, over ten million acres of forest burned in 2017, making it one of the worst fire seasons ever.

The impacts of climate change go beyond immediate storm and fire damage. Climate change contributes to regional instability and conflict as well. Some researchers have linked the Syrian civil war to a severe drought most likely exacerbated by climate change. The drought—one of the worst in 900 years—spurred some 1.5 million people to migrate from rural areas to Syrian cities, cities that were ill-prepared for this massive influx. This destabilizing movement of Syrians put even greater pressure on the government to address domestic social problems. The spillovers from the Syrian conflict continue, with an out-migration of refugees that has put severe pressure on the European Union (EU) and added to tensions that contributed to Brexit, the United Kingdom's vote to leave the EU.[3]

Climate skeptics are now having a tougher time dismissing these events, though that skepticism doesn't change anything. As Neil DeGrasse Tyson puts it, "that's the good thing about science: it's true whether or not you believe in it."

It's not enough simply to recognize that climate change is a big problem. We must act. The United States is second only to China in emissions of carbon dioxide and so needs to play a key role in global efforts to reduce emissions. Our country, however, is shirking its responsibility to lead in this effort. Indeed, the current administration is backtracking on taking *any* commitments to reduce US emissions. Since then administrator of the Environmental Protection Agency (EPA) Scott Pruitt moved to withdraw plans to regulate carbon pollution from power plants, it is unlikely that the current set of policies will be sufficient to meet the US pledge made in Paris to reduce greenhouse gas emissions "26 to 28 percent below its 2005 level in 2025." That pledge, of course, has little meaning given President Trump's June 2017 announcement to pull the United States out of the Paris Agreement, an international agreement to reduce global emissions.[4]

We do have policies at the federal level to support clean energy production, such as solar and wind. But those policies are being actively undermined by the Trump administration. The decision to roll back the more stringent CAFE emission rules for cars and light trucks for model years 2022–2025 is just one more example of backtracking. And even if the policies weren't being undercut, they are inadequate given the magnitude of the challenge we face.[5]

In an encouraging sign, states are stepping up to fill the breach. Coming together in response to Trump's announcement to pull out of the Paris Agreement, the US Climate Alliance of seventeen states and federal territories now represents over one-third of the US population. The alliance members pledged state-level leadership on climate policy and committed to "showing the nation and the world that ambitious climate action is achievable."[6] There is precedence for such state leadership; under our federal system, states have long served as laboratories of democracy, testing ideas and approaches to governance.

Although state leadership is critically important, it is not a substitute for strong federal leadership, but we'll have to do better at the federal level than we've done so far. Over the past thirty years or so, federal leadership has been a mix of inefficient regulatory mandates combined with assorted tax breaks for zero-carbon energy production, while—to add to our policy incoherence—we continue to subsidize fossil fuel extraction. To paraphrase a quotation often attributed to Winston Churchill: "Americans will always do the right thing, only after they have tried everything else." We have tried just about every policy to spur the growth of green energy except the most obvious and, as any economist will tell you, the most efficient: pricing pollution. When it comes to climate policy, pricing pollution is Churchill's "right thing." And now is the time to do it.

Why is a carbon tax the right response? Markets work best when the price of a good reflects all its costs. If the price of the good doesn't include all the costs—the damages from pollution, for example—then we are effectively subsidizing that good and, as a result, will consume too much of it. Because we don't include the costs of climate change in the price of fossil fuels, we consume more of them than is good for society. Taxing carbon aligns the price we consumers see with the true costs of using these fuels. It's pretty simple. People respond to prices. If we raise the price of fossil fuels to reflect their true cost, consumption falls. When gasoline prices rise, people drive less and buy more fuel-efficient cars. Lower-carbon natural gas is burned to produce electricity in place of high-carbon coal. Factories invest in more efficient furnaces to reduce their fuel combustion—and on and on, in literally millions of decisions made by businesses and families across the country. That's the power of the market at work.

Taxing our carbon emissions is the least expensive way for our economy to cut carbon pollution. Rather than write regulations for all the parts of the economy that use fossil fuels, we simply make fossil fuels more expensive to reflect the full cost of their use. Users of fossil fuels, from the owner of a big factory to the driver of a compact car, can adjust their behavior in response to the price of energy that includes the full price of carbon. There's less waste with a price than with complex rules and regulations. A carbon tax brings to mind the slogan for the retail chain Target: "Expect more, pay less."

In addition to the pocketbook argument for cost-effective policy, there is a practical political argument. We will have greater success overcoming opposition to climate policy if we can reduce the policy's costs. We won't easily overcome opposition from groups negatively impacted by a carbon tax—owners of coal mines, for example. But we create unnecessary problems if we choose policies that are overly bureaucratic, are burdensome to comply with, and drive up costs for all Americans. As a corollary, moving away from our current emphasis on regulation, or command and control rules, as the principal tool of climate policy may resonate with those who favor a smaller, less intrusive federal government and less red tape. Recognizing that climate policy is inevitable, oil companies like ExxonMobil, Shell, and BP have come out in support of a carbon tax on the grounds that it would be better to have a simple, efficient policy like a tax rather than messy and inefficient regulations.[7]

If we're going to have a carbon tax, we'll need to decide what to do with the revenue. To avoid conflating climate policy with the question of how big the federal budget should be, a carbon tax should be revenue neutral: every dollar raised should be returned to taxpayers either through cuts in other taxes or cash grants. Republicans and Democrats have argued for years over the size of the federal government. It's a contentious argument that should not ensnare carbon policy. Revenue neutrality is important for another reason. The opposition to a carbon tax is always framed as opposition to a standalone tax, rather than to a carbon tax at the center of a broader tax reform package. Our focus needs to be on a green tax reform rather than a carbon tax considered in isolation. Any tax is burdensome and an economic drag on an economy; a carbon tax is no different. Given the need to pay for important federal services, including defense, an interstate highway system, and Social Security, however, taxation is inevitable.

It makes more sense to tax things we don't like (e.g., pollution) than things we do (e.g., employment and saving). Revenue from a carbon tax could be used to finance reforms to the corporate or personal income tax that improve the fairness of the tax code and contribute to economic growth. But there are other ways we could use the revenue to benefit every US household without expanding the federal budget. We'll need a framework for thinking about how to return carbon tax revenue to households. That's a topic I address in Chapter 9.

Greening our tax code would also better align the United States with other major developed countries. The Organization for Economic Cooperation and Development (OECD), a club of thirty-five countries with market-based economies, tracks various fiscal measures of its member countries. Among the member countries, the United States collects the smallest share of its taxes from environmental taxes. In fact, most of the twenty-one non-OECD countries that the OECD tracks also rely more heavily on environmental taxes than the United States.[8]

Finally, here is one more reason for this book. Our government is in a state of near paralysis with a level of political polarization unseen since, perhaps, the Civil War. We desperately need leadership that can bridge the divide between the two parties and return us to an era where disagreements were hammered out in a spirit of common good. In writing this book, I have focused on arguments that can appeal across the political spectrum. Using a market-based instrument to address an environmental problem should appeal to those who want less government. A carbon tax could be the basis of a bipartisan compromise that resonates with both Democrats and Republicans. And who knows, maybe we can even restore some faith in our politicians as they demonstrate that they can tackle the big problems facing our country in the twenty-first century.

CHAPTER 1

Climate Change: What's the Big Deal?

Roxy Moore, age seventy, turns on her kitchen tap to fill her coffee pot. No water comes out. The well on her rural New Hampshire property has run dry for the first time in the thirty-three years she has lived here. Bottled water is stacked on tables and in corners of her small, one-story house. Roxy ticks off the problems: "You can't do laundry, you can't do dishes, you can't flush the toilet, you can't take a bath, you can't clean your house, you can't do anything you're accustomed to doing." With no money to dig a deeper well, she is resigned to the situation. "It is what it is, you know. You've got to learn to live this way until God gives us rain."

A hundred miles south in Rochester, Massachusetts, Dawn Gates-Allen, a fourth-generation cranberry grower, prepares to dry-harvest her cranberry crop. In a normal year, cranberry growers flood their fields and gather the floating berries with booms. Wet-harvesting a two-acre field takes fifteen to twenty minutes. Dry-harvesting the same field takes two to three days, requires expensive machines, and results in a loss of 10–15 percent of the crop. The last time Gates-Allen dry-harvested a cranberry crop was over forty years ago when she was a young girl helping her grandparents on the farm. Surveying one of her fields, a bed of cracked and dry mud flats with exposed tree roots, Gates-Allen says, "It looks like a true swamp. It's hauntingly eerie."[1]

DROUGHTS AND OTHER EXTREME WEATHER

These examples highlight the impact of drought conditions affecting the northeastern states in the summer of 2016. By the end of that summer, over half of Massachusetts was in "extreme drought" conditions, the second highest of four drought designations described by the US Drought Monitor. The nearly five million affected people had never experienced such conditions since the Drought Monitor began collecting data in 1999.[2] Across Massachusetts, farmers reported over $13 million in crop losses. Impacts were wide-ranging. Farmers in western New York suffered with fires during straw removal from their fields. State extension expert Robert Hadad commented that "the two- and four-legged critters are more voracious when it's this dry. We are seeing lots of damage in new sweet corn from geese. Deer are eating everything else. It's ugly!"[3] Meanwhile, Maine beekeepers reported that many beehives in the state did not produce sufficient honey to survive the coming winter.[4] This could have knock-on effects on agriculture in New England given the importance of honey bees for pollination for many crops and fruit trees. The drought in the Northeast was unusual: according to the Drought Monitor, the extreme drought conditions are a once-in-twenty- to once-in-fifty-year event.

Depending on who you ask, California's recent drought began in 2012 or 1999, or it is the most recent episode of a "mega-drought" going on for decades. Regardless of when it started, it has been devastating. In 2016, nearly two-thirds of Californians—over twenty-three million people—experienced extreme or exceptional drought, the two highest drought ratings, and economists at the University of California, Davis (UC Davis) estimated that drought-related costs drained over $600 million from state farmers. This is good news, relatively speaking, as costs were $2.7 billion in 2015, when the drought was even more severe. Farmers left nearly eighty thousand acres of farmland fallow in 2016 due to a lack of water; this idled land led to some $250 million in lost revenue and a loss of over eighteen hundred jobs. Farmers also incurred $300 million in additional costs to pump groundwater to replace surface water lost from the Central Valley and State Water Projects.[5]

Meanwhile in the south, residents of Livingston Parish in Louisiana watched once-buried coffins float through the streets after more than twenty-five inches of rain fell in a three-day period in August 2016, flooded the parish, and saturated the local cemetery. The Louisiana deluge is an example of a five-hundred-year rainfall event: the probability of a storm of this magnitude in the state in any given year is 1/500 or 0.2 percent. But this was the eighth five-hundred-year rainfall event in the United States in just *four months*, suggesting an increase in the frequency and severity of such storms.

Just a few months earlier, the "Tax Day Flood" of April 17–18, 2016, had killed at least seven people and destroyed some 6,700 homes in the

Houston, Texas, metropolitan area.[6] Some communities experienced seventeen inches of rain in the two-day period and the Harris County Flood Control District estimated that 240 billion gallons of water fell during the storm.[7] That's enough water to fill fifteen bathtubs for every man, woman, and child in the United States.[8] It seemed like a lot, until Hurricane Harvey stalled over Texas the following year and, in four days, dumped a trillion gallons of water on the county in which Houston sits. That's sixty bathtubs worth of water per person in the United States or as much water as flows over Niagara Falls in fifteen days. Overall, Harvey dumped thirty-three trillion gallons of water on Texas, Louisiana, Tennessee, and Kentucky—enough to cover the state of Arizona with nearly one and a half feet of water.[9]

After enduring over five years of record-breaking droughts, California was pummeled with heavy rainfall and snow in early 2017. Snowpack in the winter of 2017 was over 70 percent higher than average, and the state's reservoirs were over 20 percent fuller than average. Even if the drought is over, its effects will linger as over one hundred million trees have died since the drought began and groundwaters have been depleted. "The groundwater drought is likely to linger for quite some time," observed Jay Lund, a water expert at UC Davis, "in some areas possibly permanently."[10] Depleted groundwater has long-lasting and, perhaps, permanent costs. As groundwater is depleted from an aquifer, the land can settle or "slump like a punctured air mattress," as one climate scientist described it. Parts of the western edge of the Central Valley, California's major agricultural region, which depends heavily on groundwater for irrigation, "have sunk by nearly thirty feet since the nineteen-twenties" putting roads, bridges, and other local infrastructure at risk.[11] Groundwater aquifers are a savings bank for California farmers that can sustain them during periods of low rainfall and drought. But the system can't function effectively if Mother Nature doesn't make occasional deposits to the bank. Aggravating the problem is the fact that land subsidence due to groundwater depletion reduces the amount of storage space for underground water and so diminishes the ability of the water bank to recover over time.

Climate change only makes this situation worse. California's water system depends heavily on winter snowpack to store water for gradual release in the spring and summer. The state's water infrastructure of dams, canals, and reservoirs was designed to take advantage of a large winter snowpack that would store and gradually release water throughout the year. But as more precipitation occurs in the form of rain rather than snow, the snow pack will over time be smaller and will melt more rapidly and so subject future generations of Californian farmers and residents to more frequent spring-time floods and summer-time droughts.

California's recent swing from drought to flood conditions is just one example among an increasing number of extreme weather events in the United States. Such examples of unusual weather events are helpful for visualizing the impacts of climate change. But what is extreme weather? Climatologists define *extreme weather event days*—days with very high temperatures, heavy precipitation, long-lasting drought, frequent tornados, and so on—as days that occur very infrequently. For example, consider a county that has experienced a June day with a maximum daily temperature of 100 degrees or higher fewer than ten times over the past 100 years. Climatologists might then say that this county experienced an extreme weather event on any day in June that the temperature exceeds 100 degrees, since a June day hotter than 100 degrees has occurred less than 10 percent of the time in the historic record.

This is the idea behind the Climate Extremes Index (CEI) devised by the National Oceanic and Atmospheric Administration (NOAA), which tracks the frequency of extreme weather events, defined as a day with weather conditions that occur less than 10 percent of the time in the historic weather record tracked at tens of thousands of locations across the United States. The index tracks days that are unusually hot or unusually cold and also tracks drought and extreme precipitation events. It then combines this information into a summary index of extreme events for the United States, ranging from 0 to 100. In a given month, if there are no locations with extreme weather events, the index for that month is zero; if every location has an extreme weather event during the month, the index for that month equals one hundred.

If conditions in a given month follow historic patterns, the CEI will equal twenty. Occasionally the index is lower than twenty as in 1970 when it dropped to eight. And occasionally it spikes, as it did in 1934 when the index topped thirty-eight. But what is notable is that the top three years for extreme climate were 2012, 2015, and 2016 with index values of fifty-two, forty-three, and forty-four, respectively. To put this in perspective, an index value of fifty-two for a given year means the United States is more likely to experience a day with extreme weather than a flipped coin is likely to land with heads up.

It is easy to point to examples of unusual heat spells or floods in the past few years. But for purposes of detecting climate change, trends over time are more relevant—and more troubling. The NOAA's Monthly Climate Update has been tracking temperature and precipitation since 1895. Its data show a clear trend toward hotter weather. Six of the ten hottest years on record for the continental United States have occurred since 2000 with the three hottest years occurring in 2012, 2016, and 2017. Seven of the ten hottest summers have occurred over this same period, with the summers of 2011 and 2012 surpassed only by the Dust Bowl summer of 1936.[12]

The Dust Bowl is a perfect example of extreme weather, given the combination of high temperatures and drought conditions experienced in the Midwest during the 1930s. In 1935 alone, hot, dry winds blew some 850 million tons of topsoil from over four million acres of land—enough topsoil to bury Manhattan to a depth of thirty feet. By 1938, an estimated ten million acres had lost five inches of topsoil and another 13.5 million acres had lost two and a half inches. It is difficult to quantify the economic and social costs of the Dust Bowl, but a few statistics give a sense of its magnitude. Farmland values fell by 30 percent in high-erosion counties in the 1930s and by 17 percent in counties that experienced less severe erosion. That translates into an economic loss of roughly $35 billion in today's dollars. The loss in land value was only partially recovered over the next several years, and that only came about through a massive out migration of population as many of the small farmers abandoned their homes and livelihoods in an exodus graphically portrayed in John Steinbeck's *The Grapes of Wrath*. As many as one in eight residents of counties that experienced high erosion is estimated to have moved away in search of better economic opportunities. The US experience of the Dust Bowl is a grim reminder of the potential for economic dislocation and social upheaval as climate patterns change in different parts of the world—and as we are already seeing in parts of Africa and the Middle East.[13]

Droughts, floods, and extreme temperatures are very serious. But there are even bigger concerns. Scientists are increasingly focused on abrupt and irreversible major changes—what one might refer to as catastrophic events. These include such events as the complete loss of the Greenland ice sheet or the West Antarctic ice sheet. The Greenland ice sheet is two miles deep at its center and its mass "is so great that it deforms the earth, pushing the bedrock several thousand feet into the mantle. Its gravitational tug affects the distribution of the oceans."[14] It is akin to a massive bucket of ice precariously perched on the rim of a glass of water. Drop the ice into the glass and the water rises. The complete loss of the Greenland ice sheet would raise sea levels by over 22 feet, a sea level rise that, in the absence of any steps to protect themselves, would entirely inundate a number of major cities including Norfolk, Virginia, home of the largest naval complex in the world. Even more cities would be partially flooded. Over three-quarters of Savannah, Georgia, would be flooded and even Washington, DC, would be partially flooded, with the complete flooding of Reagan National Airport and, across the Potomac from the airport, US Joint Base Anacostia-Bolling (formerly the Anacostia Naval Support Facility and the adjoining Bolling Air Force Base).[15]

Meanwhile in Antarctica in early 2017, scientists began tracking a growing crack in the Larsen C ice shelf. The crack extended to over a hundred miles long and was growing at a rate of five football fields a day. In July, a giant iceberg the size of Delaware and capable of covering the United States in nearly five inches of ice broke off the ice shelf and drifted off into the Southern Ocean where it will eventually break up into smaller bergs.[16] This floating berg will not itself raise sea levels, since the ice shelf was already floating in the ocean. But it removes a cork, in the words of Eric Rignot, a glaciologist at the University of California, Irvine (UC Irvine), which is holding back land-based glaciers that would raise sea levels should they break up and slide into the seas around Antarctica.

Other concerns include the sudden release of massive amounts of methane (a potent greenhouse gas) locked up in ice formations in Arctic permafrost, that is, permanently frozen soil. Methane release is an example of a vicious spiral where higher temperatures lead to permafrost melt and methane release which, in turn, lead to even higher temperatures, more melt and methane release, and so on. Especially worrisome are the very large amounts of methane locked up in permafrost and ocean seabed formations (so-called clathrates), given methane's much more potent global warming impacts relative to carbon dioxide—some thirty-four times more over a century.[17]

Such changes are hardly limited to the United States, and evidence from throughout the world reinforces confidence in the fact that climate change is not only happening but accelerating. Each of the past three decades has set a record for global average temperatures with the global average temperature increasing by one degree Celsius since 1900.[18] Land temperatures are rising, as are sea temperatures.

A one-degree temperature increase doesn't seem like a big deal. But consider the Great Barrier Reef, the largest structure made by living beings on the planet—larger than the states of Wisconsin and Minnesota combined. Reefs are constructed by corals, tiny tube-shaped animals that live in colonies in the reefs. The Great Barrier Reef corals feed on photosynthesizing algae that they capture and maintain. The algae, however, are highly temperature sensitive and produce toxins in response to higher temperatures. Corals respond by expelling the algae and then turn white, a phenomenon known as coral bleaching. If the temperature drops, the corals can gather new algae and recover. If the temperature stays high enough for long enough, they will die. Record temperatures in 2015 and 2016 have led to the third occurrence of mass coral bleaching in the Great Barrier Reef since 1998.[19]

The most recent high temperatures at the Great Barrier Reef led to one-third of the corals being exposed to between fourteen and thirty *degree heating weeks* (Fahrenheit). A measure of fourteen degree heating weeks means an ocean area experienced some combination of higher temperature for a number of weeks (e.g., two degrees Fahrenheit above normal for seven weeks or one degree above normal for fourteen weeks). Scientists estimate that an exposure of fourteen degree heating weeks will lead to 80 percent of reefs experiencing coral bleaching, and thirty degree heating weeks will lead to near 100 percent bleaching. Global sea temperatures have increased by about 1.5 degrees Fahrenheit since the end of the nineteenth century, with the temperature increase higher in tropical areas. The concern is that more frequent and intense bleaching episodes will kill off the coral permanently. Even if coral populations recover, slower growing coral will be crowded out by faster growing coral, leading to diminished diversity of coral populations in tropical reefs. However you may feel about coral, keep in mind that the Great Barrier Reef supports some seventy thousand tourism jobs in the region and creates billions of dollars of economic activity in northeast Australia.[20]

Rising sea temperatures contribute to the melting of both sea ice and land-based ice, and the implications of rising sea levels are among the most troubling. While the negative impacts of climate change are most often the focus of attention, there can be localized benefits as well. Melting sea ice in the Arctic Ocean means the Arctic waters will become navigable over longer periods of time, thereby opening new sea routes and potentially shortening transit times. This melting also opens this region to new economic activity including increased fishing, oil and gas drilling, and undersea mineral extraction.

These economic benefits have led to an Arctic land rush. Russia, for example, staked a claim in 2015 to nearly half a million square miles of the Arctic Ocean including the sea bed under the North Pole, an area larger than the combined areas of Texas and California. If accepted, this claim would give Russia control over all economic activity there including fishing, mining, and oil and gas drilling. Russia is not alone in this Arctic "land" rush: Canada, Norway, and Denmark have also filed claims to areas in the Arctic region.[21] But let's be clear. The existence of localized benefits should not lull us into inaction. Offsetting any benefits of Arctic ice melt are the costs of disruptions to animal habitats and the destabilization of the economies of local indigenous people. Melting sea ice also has implications for national security. As Secretary of Defense James Mattis told Congress during his confirmation hearings, "the Arctic is key strategic terrain . . . . Russia is taking aggressive steps to increase its presence there. I will prioritize the development of an integrated strategy for the Arctic."[22]

Melting Arctic ice has no impact on sea levels for the same reason that a melting ice cube in a glass of iced tea does not raise the level of tea in the glass. Melting glaciers, which are based on land, do on the other hand, contribute to sea-level rise, just as adding additional ice cubes will raise the level of the tea. The evidence is that glaciers across the world are shrinking, which means that an increasing amount of water is eventually reaching the seas. The best estimates are that since 1971 there has been an average ice-loss of 226 billion metric tons per year. The rate of loss is accelerating and now tops 301 billion metric tons per year, enough ice to bury the state of Kansas five feet deep.

That is a lot of ice cubes. To say that the seas and oceans are like big glasses is to state the obvious. Nonetheless, since the beginning of the twentieth century, global average sea levels have risen by roughly eight inches, with the rate of rise increasing in recent years. Depending on global emissions of greenhouse gases over this century, the global average sea level could rise between one and two feet in the best-case scenario—over three feet in the worst-case scenario—making coastal areas more vulnerable to land erosion and flooding.[23] In the United States, over half the population lives near the coast and over half of our economic activity is generated in coastal areas.[24] Hurricanes Katrina and Harvey illustrated the vulnerability of coastal cities to major storms and the impact of flooding on low-lying areas. How future sea level rise will affect coastal areas depends critically on how well we can adapt. Adapting will require investment in infrastructure that is resilient to the impacts of more intense coastal storms, rising sea levels, and higher temperatures. Climate-resilient infrastructure includes such things as more durable seawalls, elevated highways in some areas, land set asides for wetland preservation, and other costly investments. Adaptation will also require our putting systems in place to protect the urban poor, who tend to congregate in the most vulnerable areas in coastal cities, and fixing the mispricing of coastal and flood insurance, which doesn't accurately reflect the risks of living in coastal areas.[25]

CLIMATE CHANGE OR WEIRD WEATHER?

The first Alaskan forest fire of 2016 broke out in February with a second one following eight days later. In contrast, the first forest fires in 2015 didn't start until May.[26] By April 2016, New Mexico had experienced twice as many fires as in the whole of the previous year. Meanwhile that same month, the *New York Times* reported that fires along the Colorado River between Arizona and California were burning so intensely that flames were leaping over the river, forcing an evacuation of two RV parks.[27] The early start to the fire season in 2016 was a sign of the increased severity and duration of wildfires. By one measure—the elapsed time between the first and last large fire in a year—the fire season in the West has increased by seventy-eight days since the 1970s. The 10 million acres burned in the United States in 2015 were the most burned in any year since the 1950s.

Meanwhile, 2017 shaped up as one of the worst forest fire seasons ever recorded. By mid-October, over 8.8 million acres had burned and over 10,000 firefighters were struggling to bring six large fires in California under control. At its peak, over 25,000 firefighters, National Guardsmen, and active-duty soldiers were fighting the blazes. The October fires in California damaged or destroyed over 21,000 homes, 2,800 businesses, and 6,100 motor vehicles. Even more tragic, forty-three people died. The California Department of Insurance reports more than $9.4 billion in insurance claims for those fires.[28]

Wildfires have clear costs to taxpayers and nearby residents. US Forest Service fire suppression costs alone topped $2.7 billion in 2017, making it the most expensive firefighting year on record. In the United States, twice as much acreage burns now as did thirty years ago, and the six worst fire seasons since 1960 have all occurred since 2000. Indeed, some of the western states have recently witnessed the largest wildfires they have ever seen. The increased size and severity of fires has consumed an ever-growing share of the US Forest Service budget. Whereas 16 percent of the Forest Service budget was spent on wildfire costs in 1995, over half of its $6.5 billion budget in 2015 was devoted to wildfire-related costs. US Secretary of Agriculture Sonny Perdue noted that "we end up having to hoard all of our money that is intended for fire prevention, because we're afraid we're going to need it to actually fight fires. It means we can't do the prescribed burning, harvesting, or insect control to prevent leaving a fuel load in the forest for future fires to feed on. That's wrong, and that's no way to manage the Forest Service."[29]

The rising cost of fighting fires is putting pressure on the Forest Service budget. But suppression is just one of the costs of wildfires. Loss of homes and tax revenues, rehabilitation, and other costs in the aftermath of a fire raise the total cost. An analysis of six wildfires since 2000 shows that the total costs can be many multiples of the costs of firefighting alone. A 2003 fire in the Santa Ana watershed of Southern California illustrates the additional costs. While fire suppression itself cost $61 million, homeowner and business losses, land rehabilitation, and water costs drove the total costs of the fire to $1.2 billion—roughly twenty times the cost of suppressing the fire.[30]

The key question is not whether wildfires are more common now. Rather it is whether this spike in fires is a fluke or a sign of climate change. This is a core question for scientists. Climate change refers to longer-term, permanent changes in temperature, precipitation, and other climatic conditions. What complicates detecting the long-run permanent changes in climate are short-run weather fluctuations. But scientists are making progress in disentangling the impacts of climate change from those due to random weather fluctuations. One study finds that human-induced climate change was responsible for over half of the increased forest fires in the western United States since 1970 and for an increase in burned areas since 1984 equal to the combined areas of Massachusetts and Connecticut. Climate change, the authors of the study concluded, also added nine additional days, on average, of high-fire potential in the West.[31]

THE KEELING CURVE

The increase in forest fires is one indicator of the impact of our continued burning of fossil fuels. The greenhouse gases released as we burn fossil fuels linger in the atmosphere for decades and even for centuries. Since climate change results from that atmospheric build-up of gases, it makes sense to measure and track that accumulation over time. The Keeling Curve does precisely that.

In 1958 a young scientist named Charles (Dave) Keeling stood on the upper slopes of the Hawaiian volcano Mauna Loa, over 11,000 feet above sea level, inspecting his newly installed carbon dioxide monitoring equipment. Starting in March of that year and continuing to this day, Keeling's equipment has silently sniffed the air hourly and recorded carbon dioxide concentrations.[32] Long before climate change became a focus of many scientists, Keeling understood the importance of accurately measuring the accumulation of carbon dioxide in the atmosphere. His former colleague, John Chin, recalled, in a *New York Times* profile, "the painstaking steps he took, at Dr. Keeling's behest, to ensure accuracy. Many hours were required every week just to be certain that the instruments atop Mauna Loa had not drifted out of kilter."

Nor was Keeling's passion for detail and precision limited to the instruments. His son Ralph recalls mowing the lawn as a young boy and his father instructing him to edge the lawn to exactly two inches. "It took a lot of work to maintain this attractive gap," Ralph recalled, but his father believed "that was just the right way to do it, and if you didn't do that, you were cutting corners. It was a moral breach." The scientific result of Keeling's meticulousness is sixty years of continuous data, unchallenged by other scientists.[33]

Keeling's climate record is even more impressive when you consider how sensitive his equipment had to be. Greenhouse gases accumulate in the atmosphere where they persist for decades or centuries depending on the gas. It is the stock of gases that matters for thinking about climate impacts and damages. The stock of gases in the atmosphere is a bit like the money in a savings account that was deposited in steady increments over time. Each year as fossil fuels are burned, we add to the stock of gases in the atmosphere just as annual deposits add to a savings account's balance over time.

The stock of greenhouse gases in the atmosphere is measured as the amount of carbon dioxide in parts per million (ppm). Pre-industrial age concentrations of carbon dioxide in the atmosphere averaged around 280 ppm. At 280 ppm, the amount of carbon dioxide contained in an empty Olympic-size swimming pool would fit in a three-foot square box just over two and a half feet high.

The concentration of carbon dioxide in the atmosphere has steadily grown since Keeling began taking measurements. By the time he installed his equipment on the Hawaiian volcano, in 1958, concentrations had already grown from 280 ppm—at the end of the nineteenth century—to 315 ppm, and that box, three-foot-square and just over two and a half feet high had grown to just over three feet high. By 2018, concentrations topped 406 ppm, and the box is now nearly four feet high. That inexorable upward trend over the past sixty years that has taken us over the 400-ppm threshold is illustrated in figure 1.1 in what has come to be called the Keeling Curve.

The Keeling Curve illustrates another important feature of the earth's atmosphere: its distinct sawtooth pattern demonstrates the atmosphere's sensitivity to natural and human activity. Because trees and plants, disproportionately located in the Northern Hemisphere, absorb more carbon dioxide as they grow, there is a reduction in atmospheric carbon dioxide levels during the Northern Hemisphere summer months. This is represented in the valleys in figure 1.1. In the winter, plants go dormant and absorb less carbon dioxide, indicated by the peaks. After Keeling and his co-authors showed, in 1996, that the sawtooth pattern of carbon dioxide concentrations was becoming more pronounced, climate scientist Rhys Roth remarked that the earth is "breathing deeper."[34] While the sawtooth pattern is interesting, it is the sharp upward trend of the curve that is especially worrying.

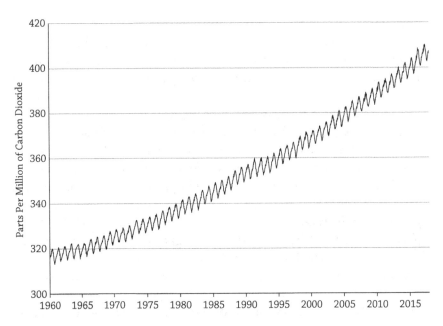

Figure 1.1. Keeling curve
Source: Scripps Institution of Oceanography and NOAA Earth System Research Laboratory

As impressive as it is, Keeling's data records atmospheric carbon dioxide concentrations only over the past sixty years. This is a limited amount of data and drawing from it alone the relationship between rising carbon dioxide concentrations and more extreme weather conditions risks confusing correlation with causation. Put differently, it might be sheer coincidence that carbon dioxide concentrations are rising in the atmosphere as we experience higher temperatures and more extreme weather. We need more data to draw the conclusion that the rising carbon dioxide concentrations are driving these changing climate conditions.

Fortunately, there are other sources of evidence to add to the Keeling data. Data from ice samples in Antarctica tell the story of fluctuations in carbon dioxide concentrations over the past four hundred thousand years. By analyzing tiny air bubbles trapped in the ice, scientists have shown that carbon dioxide concentrations fluctuated between 180 and 280 ppm in the pre-industrial age. Periods with high carbon dioxide concentrations tend to be warming periods in Earth's history while periods with low concentrations of carbon dioxide occur during cooling periods and ice ages. This historic record demonstrates two important facts. First, carbon dioxide concentrations have fluctuated over earth's history, but only within a narrow band roughly half the present-day concentrations.

Second, scientists have shown a remarkable correspondence between temperature change and carbon dioxide concentrations.[35] As carbon dioxide concentrations rise, so do temperatures.

What caused the recent increase in carbon dioxide concentrations—from 280 ppm to over 400? Energy-related carbon dioxide emissions—from our cars and trucks, the burning of fuel at power plants, the manufacture of many of the goods we consume today—account for roughly three-quarters of global greenhouse gas emissions. There has been a massive increase in global energy-related carbon dioxide emissions between 1980 and 2013, as is clear from figure 1.2. Global emissions have risen by nearly 80 percent over that period. The world's two largest emitting countries have been the United States, which led in emissions until 2005, and China, the current world leader in carbon dioxide emissions. Chinese emissions grew by a factor of six over this period while US emissions were essentially flat. This pattern for these two countries mirrors that for developed and developing countries as a group. Historically, developed countries were the largest emitters, but that has changed, and the fast-growing developing countries now lead. Developing country emissions are growing so rapidly that their cumulative emissions will surpass cumulative emissions from developed countries before the end of the decade. This fact doesn't let developed countries off the hook. After all, our historic emissions that contributed to our growth and current prosperity are, for the most part, still circulating in the atmosphere and remain a major reason the Keeling Curve has broken through the 400-ppm barrier.

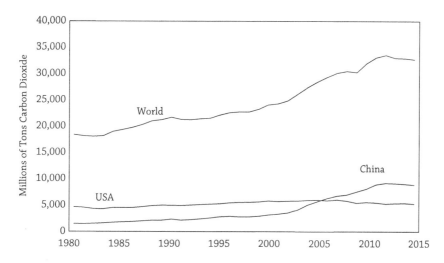

Figure 1.2. Energy-related carbon dioxide emissions
Source: Energy Information Administration

What explains the difference in trend rates of developed and developing countries? Annual greenhouse gas emissions are the product of four factors: 1) emissions per unit of energy used; 2) energy use per dollar of gross domestic product (GDP); 3) GDP per capita; and 4) population. The first factor, known as emissions intensity, tracks activities to reduce emissions per unit of energy. Switching from coal to natural gas for electricity generation or to wind or solar power reduces our emissions intensity. The second factor, known as energy intensity, measures our energy use per dollar of economic activity, as measured by GDP. Improvements in energy efficiency through new technologies and greater energy conservation can reduce our energy intensity.

GDP per capita is a rough measure of a country's prosperity. As economies grow both in population and in per capita income, emissions will rise. This explains the dramatic growth in emissions in fast-growing economies like China. But as economies get wealthier, they begin to turn away from dirtier forms of energy to cleaner forms. Thus, emissions per unit of energy start to fall. At the same time, their greater income gives them the wherewithal to invest in more efficient capital. As a result, energy use per dollar of GDP also begins to fall. These two factors help explain why emissions in the United States and other developed countries have plateaued since the beginning of this century.

FROM EMISSIONS TO CLIMATE CHANGE

Central to understanding the effect on climate change of accumulating stocks of carbon dioxide in the atmosphere is a scientific parameter known as *climate sensitivity*. Climate sensitivity measures the increase in temperature arising from changes in the stock of greenhouse gases in the atmosphere. Just as the glass roof of a greenhouse traps solar radiation and raises the temperature inside the greenhouse, carbon dioxide and other greenhouse gases trap solar radiation in our atmosphere and raise the planet's temperature. Hence the reference to "greenhouse gases" and the greenhouse effect of climate change. How fast the temperature rises in response to an increase in the stock of greenhouse gases depends on the climate sensitivity parameter.

Over one hundred years ago, Sweden's Svante Arrhenius, a childhood math prodigy and Nobel Prize-winning chemist, made the first estimates of climate sensitivity in his 1906 book, *Worlds in the Making*, translated into English in 1908. Arrhenius estimated the value of the climate sensitivity parameter to be four degrees Celsius—that is, a doubling of greenhouse gases leads to an increase in temperature by four degrees Celsius (just over seven degrees Fahrenheit). He made this calculation notwithstanding the very early state of climate science and lack of current, let alone historical, data on temperature and greenhouse gas concentrations. Arrhenius's estimate of climate sensitivity is remarkably durable. Despite the complexity of modeling climate sensitivity, modern estimates are in the ballpark of Arrhenius's one-hundred-year-old estimate.

The Keeling Curve is helpful for distinguishing the costs of our past burning of fossil fuels and other releases of greenhouse gases from the costs related to future greenhouse gas emissions. The build-up of carbon dioxide from 280 to 406 ppm is the result of our historic emissions. Even if we were to stop all greenhouse gas emissions today, the stock of gases in the atmosphere would take centuries to dissipate to pre-industrial levels. We will have to confront the damages from climate change from our past emissions—Arrhenius's climate sensitivity parameter is key to understanding how the higher stock of gases in our atmosphere from past emissions raises temperatures and contributes to climate change. But unless we act to curtail our current emissions, the greenhouse gas concentrations in the atmosphere will continue to rise, and those increased concentrations will cause additional damages. Our challenge is twofold: find ways to cope with the damages arising from our past emissions and simultaneously avoid further damage by working to cut our future emissions.

CHAPTER 2

Business as Usual: What Are the Costs?

Climate change is happening now and we're already coping with its impacts. But what's done is done. Short of a new technology that somehow inexpensively soaks up and removes greenhouse gases from the atmosphere (no, it doesn't exist), there's nothing we can do to reverse the build-up of greenhouse gases in the atmosphere from the emissions that have already spewed from our tailpipes and smokestacks. We may regret having incurred costs that are irreversible, but there's no sense worrying about them. As the saying goes, "don't cry over spilt milk."

Future emissions are a different story. Those we can control. People who oppose acting on climate change often cite the high cost of reducing emissions. But our "business as usual" path of overreliance on fossil fuels also has significant costs. Changing nothing about the way we live means that atmospheric greenhouse gas concentrations will increase and we will see hotter and more extreme weather conditions more and more frequently. And because carbon dioxide and other greenhouse gases persist for hundreds of years in the atmosphere, our business as usual path will not affect just us; it will also affect our children, grandchildren, and even our grandchildren's grandchildren.

DAMAGES AND ADAPTATION

The costs of continuing on our present path fall into two categories. The first category is damages from on-going emissions, such as the value of labor productivity lost during hotter weather, the loss of beachfront property as sea levels rise, higher mortality rates in developed and developing countries, destruction of natural habitats like coral reefs, among other damages. The second category of costs includes all those actions we take to cope with hotter or more extreme weather, such as increased investment in air conditioning to cope with hotter summers, in sea walls to reduce flooding as sea levels rise, and in more expensive infrastructure that can handle more extreme weather. These are examples of *adaptation*, that is they are actions we will need to take to respond to the increased threats and damages from climate change.

Let's consider a specific example to understand how climate change has costs that reflect both damages and adaptation: flooding in New York City and surrounding areas from violent storm surges made worse by rising sea levels. This is no abstract threat, as Hurricane Sandy made clear. Sandy hit New York City in late October 2012 and brought the city to its knees for days. Its storm surge peaked on the evening of October 29 at nearly fourteen feet, six feet higher than the average high tide at the Battery tidal station at the lower end of Manhattan. Six feet of water surged through the streets of Brooklyn's Red Hook neighborhood. The lights went out over much of lower Manhattan as well as the Jersey shore, parts of Brooklyn and Queens, and most of Long Island. Millions of people were left in the dark, some for weeks. There were gasoline shortages and rationing was imposed—something not seen since the first oil shock in 1973. One week after the storm, three-quarters of gas stations in New York City were still closed, and the army trucked in emergency fuel. Residents huddled around temporary cellphone charging stations, while their phones struggled to connect to an overtaxed network. Storm damage was estimated at $21 billion in New York City alone and $62 billion in the New York–New Jersey metropolitan area.

The combination of rising sea levels and more extreme weather from our continued carbon pollution is likely to make storms like Sandy more common, resulting in more destruction and higher costs up and down the East and West coasts as well as in the Gulf of Mexico. How costly are these storms and how much will the cost rise if we continue our consumption of fossil fuels?

As with all uncertain events, we can only talk about the risks of something occurring and its expected damages or costs. Most years will see little or no flooding in Manhattan and other parts of the New York–New Jersey harbor region. But occasionally more damaging floods will happen.

Very damaging floods will still be rare, but will be less rare than they are now: our ongoing greenhouse gas emissions will—over time—contribute to higher sea levels and more extreme storms. Assuming no action to cut emissions, scientists estimate that we can expect a more than twenty-fold increase in risk to property and life if sea levels rise by three feet over the next sixty years. Based on this increased risk, it is estimated that storm-surge-related costs for the region, from the continued emission of greenhouse gases between now and the end of the century, will increase by an average of $2 billion per year.[1]

That estimate assumes the region does nothing to protect itself against more intense storms and higher risk of flooding. Presumably, New York City will take steps to protect itself against higher waters and storm-induced flooding. That is, it will adapt. Whatever the region spends to protect itself against storm-related flooding counts as a cost of our failure to reduce emissions. One proposal to confront a massive storm surge pushing water up New York Harbor and into low-lying areas is to strategically place storm surge barriers in the harbor—similar to the barrier the United Kingdom (UK) placed on the Thames River near London. Engineers have studied the costs and benefits of building barriers across New York's outer harbor—from Sandy Hook in New Jersey to the Outer Rockaways in Queens—and in the East River at its opening to Long Island Sound. Additionally, some especially vulnerable infrastructure inside the barriers (such as electricity transformers) would be physically raised to remain above high-water levels in the Hudson River during major storms. This project would cost around $13 billion and require annual maintenance costs of roughly $120 million.[2]

This project may or may not be a good idea. But it illustrates in a very concrete way how our on-going carbon pollution has costs that include both damages and adaptation. The infrastructure costs are an example of an adaptation cost. Putting in a storm-surge barrier system would reduce but not eliminate all the damages from our on-going emissions. Once the system is in place, the region would still face expected damages of $1 billion per year.

TRADING OFF TODAY VERSUS TOMORROW

The costs for the New York storm-surge barrier system occur at different points in time: after the initial investment to build the system, there is the ongoing maintenance cost. Is there a way to combine the future and current costs? That is, how should we think about annual maintenance costs of $120 million that occur fifty, seventy-five, or a hundred years from now? Clearly, we shouldn't treat a cost of $120 million today the same as a cost of $120 million in fifty years.

To answer that question, consider the following two, no-risk investment opportunities. The first pays $1,000 immediately; the second is a government note that pays $1,000 in twenty-five years. The note pays no interest; all it does is guarantee a $1,000 payment at a future date. Pretty much anyone offered this choice would prefer the investment opportunity that pays $1,000 right now. After all, it could be invested in an insured savings account today and, at an annual interest rate of 4 percent per year, more than double in twenty-five years due to the power of compounding. At 4 percent interest, $1,000 grows to $1,040 in one year, to $1,082 after two years and to $1,125 after three years—all the way to $2,666 in the twenty-fifth year. Clearly a note that pays $1,000 in twenty-five years is less valuable than a payment of $1,000 today.

How much less valuable? Assuming an annual return of 4 percent, the note is worth only $375. That is because a deposit of $375 in a savings account earning 4 percent per year will grow to $1,000 in twenty-five years.

The interest rate plays an important role in any calculation of the present value of future costs. The interest rate used to compare money across time periods (e.g., today versus twenty-five years from now) is called the *discount rate*. The discount rate is like the rate of return on a college savings fund. It tells you how to think about the value of future dollars in today's dollars.

As with a college fund, the higher the discount rate, the less a saver needs to set aside today to hit a target of $1,000 in twenty-five years. At a 7 percent rate, one need set aside only $184. At a lower discount rate, more will need to be set aside to ensure enough money in the college fund in twenty-five years. Specifically, at 2 percent, $610 would be needed today. The expression *present discounted value* refers to a future sum (the $1,000 in twenty-five years) *valued* in today's dollars (in the *present*) given the interest (or *discount*) rate.[3]

Let's get back to New York Harbor and the cost of our continued emissions. One cost is the $13 billion to build the surge barriers and other infrastructure improvements. That is a cost incurred immediately. The annual maintenance costs over the next century is an additional cost. Consider the maintenance costs one hundred years from now. Assuming a 4 percent discount rate, the present discounted value of $120 million in a hundred years is $2.4 million today. But we also need $120 million for maintenance ninety-nine years out. The value today of that $120 million is $2.5 million.

Then we need funds worth $2.6 million today for the maintenance in ninety-eight years. And so on for every one of the hundred years of the next century. Adding it all up, the value in today's dollars of the maintenance costs for each of the coming hundred years is $2.9 billion.

The total cost of the infrastructure—measured today—is the $13 billion cost of the project itself and the ongoing maintenance costs, valued today at $2.9 billion, for a total of $15.9 billion today. That is the cost of adaptation required to deal with our continued carbon pollution over the century for this one particular threat.

But that's not the total cost of our on-going carbon pollution with regard to storm-related flooding in the New York area. The storm-surge barrier project reduces but does not eliminate the annual expected damages. The expected damages remaining after building the storm-surge barrier system is $1 billion each year for the century. The present discounted value of these damages over the century is computed in the same way as the present discounted value of the annual maintenance costs was calculated and comes to $24.5 billion.

Adding up the adaptation and damage costs, the storm-surge related flood costs for the New York–New Jersey area due to our business-as-usual path of continued emissions is $13 billion + $2.9 billion + $24.5 billion = $40.4 billion.[4]

PAYING TO AVOID RISK

The example just presented ignores an important element of the damage costs. While the expected damages are $1 billion a year, actual damages in any given year could be much higher—as Hurricane Sandy demonstrated. In general, people don't like risk and we should take that into account when considering the costs of our business-as-usual path. Once we account for risk, the damage costs go up. Here's why.

Consider a bet with a fifty-fifty chance of winning some amount equal to 10 percent of your income or losing an amount equal to 10 percent of your income. On average anyone taking this bet wins as much as they lose. Even though this is a fair bet, most people would decline it. For someone earning $60,000 a year, the pleasure of winning $6,000 is more than offset by the pain of losing $6,000. Economists and psychologists call this *loss aversion*—the sadness or regret that comes with a loss of a given amount outweighs the happiness of gaining the same amount. (Loss aversion and the related concept of risk aversion—a desire to avoid risky outcomes—explain why people buy insurance.) For most people, even though this fifty-fifty bet has an expected cost of zero, it involves significant risk and the possibility of a painful loss. So, focusing on the expected cost in a risky situation understates the full impact on people.

Consider this hypothetical risky situation. Most of the time (ninety-five times out of a hundred), nothing happens. But occasionally (five times out of a hundred), the person loses $10,000. People frequently face risks like this one: your house could suffer a serious fire, or someone could run into your car in a supermarket parking lot. For this risky situation, on average, the cost is $500 [(0.05 × $10,000) + (0.95 × $0)]. Most people would like to avoid this risk and would pay to avoid it. How much they would pay depends on how much they dislike losing $10,000. Anyone disliking risk would probably gratefully pay $500 to avoid it. After all, the payment would replace the risk of a $10,000 loss with a zero-risk outcome with the exact same loss on average. Someone who especially wants to avoid risk might, in fact, pay as much as $575 to avoid this potential loss. In that case, the real cost of this bet is not the expected loss of $500 but rather $575 as this takes into account the fact that the loss of $10,000 is especially painful.

This is exactly how insurance operates. People are willing to pay a known annual premium to avoid a risky loss that could be quite large. Those premiums are higher than the average expected loss.[5] People's willingness to buy insurance at a price that exceeds the expected losses drives home the point that focusing on average losses can understate the loss people experience in risky situations.

How does this relate to our example of flooding in New York? After investing in storm-surge barriers, the region still faces annual expected damages of $1 billion if nothing is done to reduce emissions. This is an average loss, akin to the expected loss of $500 in the risky situation just outlined. But in any given year, the actual damages will not equal exactly $1 billion. In most years, there will be no flooding or maybe modest flooding that is, at worst, an inconvenience. But occasionally a storm like Hurricane Sandy causes billions of dollars of damage. It's rare, but when it happens it is very costly. While $1 billion may be a reasonable estimate of the average damages in dollar terms, the example presented here suggests New York and New Jersey residents would be willing to give up some amount more than $1 billion to avoid this risk. How much more depends on attitudes toward risk and the ability to insure against bad outcomes. But the bottom line is that the $1 billion expected loss likely underestimates the damages people will face.[6]

The storm surge barrier project highlights one example of the costs of our failing to act on climate change. There are many more. After all, two-fifths of the US population live in coastal zones with economies accounting for nearly one-half of US economic activity. Anyone living near the coast understands that ignoring the risks of damages from rising oceans and more intense storms is foolish. The residents of Sunset Harbour in Miami Beach certainly understand that. As this low-lying neighborhood experiences increased flooding during high tides around the full moon, neighborhoods are increasingly under water. As a stop-gap measure, the city has adapted by raising streets three feet above the neighboring sidewalks and storefronts. Raising the streets is reminiscent of Chicago's massive initiative to raise streets and buildings in the mid-1850s to combat the filth and mire of muddy, disease-ridden streets flooded by Lake Michigan.[7]

Raising Florida streets won't keep stores from flooding, but at least the traffic can still flow, if only to evacuate residents during increased periods of flooding. Building dykes around Miami Beach to cope with flooding— as the Dutch have done to great success in the Netherlands—won't help matters. The bedrock underlying the area is limestone and water flows through it as if it were Swiss cheese—build a dyke atop this bedrock and high water will simply flow underneath.[8] Elevating roads is an example of adaptation and illustrates how infrastructure can blunt the impact of storm-induced flooding. But it will be costly. And it won't eliminate *all* damages. It will only reduce them.

MORE COSTS OF OUR BUSINESS-AS-USUAL EMISSIONS

Damages from flooding and extreme storms are not the only cost of our failure to cut carbon emissions. High temperatures kill, especially temperatures above ninety degrees Fahrenheit. And just as costly sea walls can reduce the damages from the increased risk of flooding, investing in air conditioning can protect against higher temperatures. The United States saw a dramatic fall in the mortality rate on days with temperatures above ninety degrees between 1960 and 2004, a drop on the order of 95 percent. This was a time when residential air conditioning began to be widely adopted. While only one in eight homes had air conditioning in 1960, seven out of eight homes had air conditioning by 2004. That's at the national level. While one in four homes in the South had air conditioning in 1960, essentially all homes in this region had it by 2004. The data show that the penetration of residential air conditioning has contributed to a decline in deaths at high temperatures on the order of roughly 20,000 lives per year in the United States.[9]

Clearly, air conditioning has huge benefits. Besides lowering death rates on very hot days, it enhances comfort levels on hot and humid days, contributes to worker productivity at the office, and has made the South and Southwest much more livable, contributing to the economic development of these regions. But it also comes with costs. There is the cost of all those air conditioners installed in people's homes. Then there is the electricity required to power them. Air conditioning is responsible for about 6 percent of all electricity consumption in the United States and about 117 million tons of carbon dioxide emissions each year.[10] The global growth in air conditioning will put even greater demands on our electricity grid. Air conditioning in China's cities is now ubiquitous and its penetration in India, Brazil, and other developing countries is proceeding rapidly. One study estimates that household ownership of air conditioners will rise from 1.1 billion units in 2016 to over 4 billion units by 2050. The electricity needed to power those new air conditioners exceeds the current electricity consumption in Germany and the United States.[11] While air conditioning is a great adaptation to rising temperatures, it risks creating a vicious climate spiral if we power those air conditioners with electricity generated by burning coal or natural gas. Moreover, air conditioning is not an adaptation available to all. The poorest people in China, India, and other developing countries do not have air conditioning nor do they have any prospect of getting it anytime soon.[12]

This last fact is a good reminder that the costs of our ongoing emissions will disproportionately affect low-income families. Often it is the poor who live in areas most sensitive to the impacts of climate change. That was certainly the case for the mostly black residents of the Lower Ninth Ward in New Orleans who suffered some of the most devastating impacts of Hurricane Katrina. But even when they don't live in areas especially vulnerable to climate change, they can be impacted. In Miami, for example, poorer blacks have historically lived in neighborhoods far from the ocean, a legacy of discriminatory lending and rental practices. But as sea-levels rise, these neighborhoods, which are at higher elevations, are likely to increase in value. As recounted in a 2017 news article on gentrification and climate change, "historically black communities on higher ground are increasingly in the sights of speculators and investors. Real estate investment may no longer be just about the next hot neighborhood, it may also now be about the next dry neighborhood." The article quotes a local resident, "'Oh, Miami Beach is going under, the sea level is coming up. So now the rich people have to find a place to live. My property is fifteen feet above sea level, theirs is what? Three under? So OK,' he said, taking on the voice of a rich developer, 'let's knock down the projects, and we move in and push them out.'"[13] Equity issues matter in public policy. Politicians often put considerable weight on how new policies impact vulnerable groups, including the poor. Similar concerns matter when considering the failure to act on climate change.

PASCAL'S WAGER AND CLIMATE SKEPTICS

The recurring message in this chapter is that our on-going carbon pollution is costly. Despite the compelling and growing body of evidence that our burning of fossil fuels is a major contributor to the build-up of greenhouse gases in the atmosphere, some still doubt the evidence. This is clearly a minority view among scientists. A survey sent to members of geoscience departments listed in the American Geophysical Union's membership directory found that 90 percent of respondents believed that average global temperatures have risen compared to pre-industrial age levels and 82 percent felt that human activity is a "significant factor" in changing average global temperatures.[14] But what about the 18 percent of scientists who disagree with the importance of human activity in driving climate change? Should we simply ignore these outlying views? Or should we somehow take their skepticism into account when considering climate policy? To answer these questions, it is helpful to turn to the seventeenth-century French philosopher, Blaise Pascal.

Pascal struggled with the question of whether he should believe in God or not. He resolved this question with what has come to be known as *Pascal's Wager*. Here's how it works. Either God exists or God does not exist. Upon dying, Pascal argued, we would learn whether God existed or not. But meanwhile, we are living and must choose whether to believe in God or not. Believing in God requires one to make certain sacrifices that have a cost while one is alive. If our belief is correct, then the reward is infinite salvation in the afterlife. If one does not believe, then one can party, skip church, and otherwise enjoy the moment. But if God exists, failing to believe is very costly: an eternity of damnation. For Pascal, the choice to believe or not is really the choice of which side to take in a wager: to believe or not to believe? Pascal resolved the question as follows. As long as there is some chance that God exists, the infinite rewards of heaven far outweigh any minor inconveniences of religious devotion. On the other hand, the pleasures and freedom of being an atheist cannot counterbalance an eternity of damnation if Pascal bets wrong. Given this logic, Pascal chose to believe.

Pascal's decision-making process is an example of what might be called the *worst outcome* decision-making criterion.[15] The worst-outcome approach says to look at the worst possible outcome for a given choice (believe or not believe) and then choose the action that gives the best result among these worst outcomes. If Pascal chooses to believe, the worst outcome is to believe when there is no God, and he forgoes some earthly pleasures needlessly. If, on the other hand, he chooses not to believe, the worst outcome is eternal damnation if it turns out that God exists. By the worst-outcome rule, believing is better than not believing. Believing—at worst—leads to minor inconveniences, an outcome that pales in comparison to an eternity of suffering.

In considering climate policy, we are in a similar situation to Pascal when contemplating the existence of God. Scientists cannot point to a piece of evidence—a smoking gun, if you will—that proves with 100 percent certainty that our carbon dioxide and other greenhouse gas emissions are driving climate change. Their models are compelling and corroborative data are piling up. But the nature of scientific inquiry is such that scientists generally cannot "prove" a theory definitively, whether it is climate change induced by our fossil fuel consumption or Einstein's theory of general relativity. They can find evidence consistent with the theory; or they can find evidence that contradicts the theory—in which case the theory needs to be adjusted or possibly replaced with an entirely new theory.[16]

Our inability to definitively prove the existence of climate change driven by our use of fossil fuels should not paralyze us, however. Here's where Pascal's approach can be helpful. Consider the following thought experiment. Imagine two states of the world. In one, our greenhouse gas emissions are making climate change worse, with rising damages. In the other state, our emissions are not causing any damages. As one measure, we can consider how global GDP is affected in these two states of the world when we act to curtail emissions or when we don't. Table 2.1 provides the relevant information.

Payoffs in the table are percentage changes in global GDP relative to a baseline, which is global GDP if human-induced climate change is occurring

Table 2.1. PAYOFFS FROM PASCAL'S CLIMATE WAGER*

	Majority of Climate Scientists Are Correct (% change in global GDP)	Climate Skeptics Are Correct (% change in global GDP)
Act to Reduce Emissions	+17%	+34%
Don't Act to Reduce Emissions	0	+41%

* Payoffs are a percentage of global GDP relative to global GDP when the majority of climate scientists are right and no climate policy is in place. Estimates from van der Ploeg and Rezai (2017).

and we don't act to reduce emissions. The baseline is in the lower left corner of the table with the entry zero. If most climate scientists are correct about human-induced climate change, then global GDP will be 17 percent higher if we reduce emissions (upper left entry in table). In other words, given that climate change is real, reducing emissions boosts global GDP by 17 percent.

If, on the other hand, the skeptics are correct and our burning of fossil fuels is not increasing global temperatures, then we don't have to worry about climate change creating damages that hurt economic growth. In that case, global GDP will be 41 percent higher than in the baseline case (lower right entry in table). Global GDP is higher since temperature is not going up and we aren't suffering climate-related damages. Spending money on mitigation when the skeptics are right cuts the GDP gain some. In that case, global GDP will be only 34 percent higher (upper right entry in table).

This looks a lot like Pascal's Wager. We have to act now (limit emissions or not) before we know which world we're in (human-induced climate change or random fluctuations). The urgency is driven, in part, by the essential irreversibility of our actions. Given how long greenhouse gases persist in our atmosphere, we cannot realistically undo our burning of fossil fuels at the scale with which we are consuming coal, oil, and natural gas. We are stuck with these gases for centuries to come.[17]

Consider the worst outcome decision-making criterion. If we act to reduce emissions, global GDP is either 17 or 34 percent higher than the baseline case (temperature rising and no action taken) depending on whether the skeptics are wrong or right. The worst outcome when we act is a 17 percent increase in global GDP relative to the baseline. This occurs when we curtail emissions unnecessarily. If we don't act to reduce emissions, global GDP is either unchanged from the baseline or 41 percent higher. Now the worst outcome is the baseline case (a change of zero) where we didn't act when we should have. The worst-outcome approach says to choose the action that gives the highest payoff among these worst possible scenarios. In this case, we should reduce emissions. Following the worst-outcome approach and reducing emissions today is an insurance policy against bad outcomes.

Another way we could decide whether to reduce emissions or not is to focus on avoiding regret. The *regret avoidance* approach focuses on the cost of making a mistake and chooses an action that will leave you with the least regret if you are wrong.[18] If human-induced climate change is indeed happening, then we will regret not reducing emissions. Global GDP is 17 percent higher if we reduce emissions than in the case where we don't reduce them. If the skeptics are correct, then we'll regret having reduced emissions when we didn't need to. In that case, global GDP is 7 percent higher by avoiding an unnecessary cost. A 7 percent reduction in GDP is something to regret but much less painful than the 17 percent loss if we don't reduce emissions when we should have. Regret avoidance also points to the value of reducing emissions.

It is not productive to simply dismiss anyone who challenges climate models or other evidence of climate change as a "climate denier." Scientists who raise questions about the science or modeling may be in the minority, but they may not be wrong. This is not to say that we should accord the same weight to climate skeptics that we do to climate change scientists. If four out of five scientists think human-induced climate change is happening, giving equal time to both sides gives skeptics undue airtime. But our policies can and should account for the possibility that skeptics are right. We can account for that possibility by adopting a worst outcomes or a regret avoidance approach to our climate policy. Both these approaches emphasize the value of acting now to reduce emissions. We will not act because we are certain the climate models are correct. Rather, we will act because we understand the high cost of failing to cut our emissions when the models are correct.

The analogy to Pascal's wager only goes so far. It illustrates how to think about policymaking in an uncertain world. But let's not push the analogy too far. After all, whether one believes in God or not is a matter of faith that cannot be resolved by science no matter how much data you collect. Scientists, on the other hand, have accumulated a host of data that have allowed them to refute any number of alternative explanations for our hotter temperatures, melting ice caps, and more extreme weather. As the data accumulate, the message is increasingly clear: our carbon pollution is a major contributor to climate change. And the longer we wait, the higher the costs. The question is not whether climate change is real but rather how best to cut our emissions starting now.

CHAPTER 3

Why Do Economists Like a Carbon Tax?

Given the costs of not reducing future carbon pollution, we need to do something to protect ourselves and future generations. It would be great if the efforts of individuals could achieve this goal, but in reality, governments will need to get involved. Why? To answer this question, let's take a little detour through history to the nineteenth-century English court case *Sturges v. Bridgman*.

RONALD COASE AND THE CASE OF *STURGES V. BRIDGMAN*

In the 1860s, a confectioner named Bridgman had a shop at 30 Wigmore Street just off Cavendish Square in London where he and his father had been producing candy for more than sixty years. He used two mortars, built into a brick wall in the kitchen at the back of the house, to pulverize loaf sugar and other ingredients with two large wooden pestles. In 1865, a doctor named Sturges bought a home at 85 Wimpole Street, an adjacent side-street, where he opened a medical practice. In 1873, Dr. Sturges built a consulting room at the end of his garden, using a common wall with Bridgman's shop. That common wall also served as the back wall of Bridgman's kitchen and the supporting structure for the candy maker's mortars and pestles.

Not surprisingly, the noise and vibration from the pounding of the pestles interfered with the doctor's practice. After complaining to Bridgman without success, he brought suit to restrain Bridgman from using the mortars and pestles. The candy maker responded that there had been no issue during the eight years before the new consulting room was built and that the problem would have been avoided altogether had the doctor built the consulting room with a separate back wall rather than using the common wall.

This obscure court case is recounted in one of the most important and highly cited articles in economics and is a major reason its author, Ronald H. Coase, was awarded the Nobel Prize in Economics in 1991.[1] Coase was an unusual economist who, by his own admission, was weak in mathematics and formal theory. The son of a post-office worker, Coase was raised in a decidedly unacademic household where the major interest was sports. Coase had "weak legs" (as he recounts in his Nobel Prize autobiography), necessitating his wearing leg braces and prompting him to turn to more cerebral pursuits. At age eleven, he was examined by a phrenologist who told him, "You are in possession of much intelligence, and you know it, though you may be inclined to underrate your abilities." The phrenologist continued, "You will not float down, like a sickly fish, with the tide . . . you enjoy considerable mental vigor and are not a passive instrument in the hands of others. Though you can work with others and for others, where you see it to your advantage, you are more inclined to think and work for yourself. A little more determination would be to your advantage, however." Whether or not Coase needed more determination, he clearly did not "float down like a sickly fish."[2]

Coase recounts the court case of *Sturges v. Bridgman* to make an important point about *externalities*. An externality occurs when one person's action has some impact on another person that is not reflected in the costs borne by the first person. That impact can be beneficial (a positive externality) or, as in this case, harmful (a negative externality). Here, the externality is the noise and vibration coming from Bridgman's candy making, which has an adverse impact on the doctor who is not able to use his consulting room when the pestles are pounding away. The damages suffered by the poor doctor are not reflected in Bridgman's costs of candy production.

Pollution is a classic negative externality, and carbon pollution is central to the problem of climate change. The burning of fossil fuels adversely impacts others through the accumulation of greenhouse gases in the atmosphere. In the case of burning fossil fuels, the costs of burning coal in an industrial boiler include the costs of mining and transporting coal to the factory. The costs, however, do not include the damages from the carbon dioxide emissions.

Key to the problem of pollution is the distinction between *private costs* and *social costs*. The costs to firms burning fossil fuels are private costs. Private costs reflect the costs borne by the firms as they decide whether and how much oil, natural gas, or coal to burn. These are costs that the firm accounts for as it seeks the profit maximizing level of activity. Social costs, in contrast, are the total costs of burning fossil fuels and include both the private costs as well as the damages from the accumulated greenhouse gases in the atmosphere.[3] The difference between private and social costs is the damage done by the polluting activity. Firms do not take into account the damages to others as they make their production decisions, including the amount of fossil fuels to consume. To be clear, this is not a value judgment on firm behavior. Firms cannot be expected to include in the costs of running their business the damages from greenhouse gas emissions, especially when those damages may impact people far away from the firm or people not yet born. Publicly owned firms have a fiduciary responsibility to maximize profits for their shareholders. They can't, of course, fall back on that fiduciary responsibility to justify reckless or illegal behavior. But burning fossil fuels is not illegal. And if costs of burning fossil fuels don't include the full social costs of their use, that's a failure of public policy, not of the firm's ethical and fiduciary obligations.

In the absence of public policy to reduce pollution, markets will overproduce goods or services associated with pollution because the producer does not pay the full cost of its inputs. If the factory owner doesn't need to pay for the costs of the carbon dioxide added to the atmosphere from burning coal, then he will make decisions about how much coal to burn relying on an artificially low coal price. The price is artificially low because it does not reflect the damages from the carbon dioxide emissions flowing from the factory's smokestack. If the price reflected the true social cost of burning coal, then the factory would likely burn less coal. The higher price of coal provides the right incentive to factory managers to fine tune their equipment to reduce energy consumption, buy more energy efficient machines, and otherwise cut down on its coal consumption.

Let's consider the issue of private and social costs for our two nineteenth-century London neighbors. For Bridgman, using the mortar and pestle to grind ingredients and make candy is essential for his business. Let's assume that if he operates the machine for two hours a day, he can make a small amount of candy that will earn him, after all his costs for ingredients and labor, £50. That's £25 for each hour of operation. If he operates more hours, he can produce more candy but he may need to lower the price a bit to sell it all. Table 3.1 shows Bridgman's hourly profits for each hour of the day. Adding more hours of operation adds to his profits but at a diminishing rate. By the tenth hour, his profits go up only by £5 for that last hour of operation. Clearly it is profitable for Bridgman to operate his mortars and pestles ten hours a day. Presumably that's what he had been doing before Dr. Sturges complained.

Table 3.1. HYPOTHETICAL COSTS OF PRODUCING CANDY
IN BRIDGMAN'S SHOP

Mortar and Pestle Operation (hours)	Additional Profit to Confectioner (Pounds Sterling)	Additional Damage to Doctor (Pounds Sterling)
1	25	0
2	25	0
3	15	5
4	15	5
5	15	5
6	8	10
7	8	10
8	5	15
9	5	15
10	5	15

Source: Author's figures based on *Sturges v. Bridgman* as recounted in Coase (1960).

But now let's consider the doctor's situation. If the machines operate for just two hours a day, he can rearrange his activities so that he is not inconvenienced and thus does not suffer any damages. But his damages (in the form of lost profits) increase as the machines are used for more of the day. Lost profits rise from zero to £15 per hour. Table 3.1 reports damages to Sturges in the final column.

Bridgman's machines create pollution in the form of noise and vibration that interferes with the doctor's practice. We typically think of pollution as some contaminant of air or water. But the vibration from the candy maker's machines is also a form of pollution, albeit not a pollutant that would be regulated today by the US Environmental Protection Agency (EPA). The damages from that pollution are the loss of profits to the doctor. This simple example of the doctor and the candy maker illustrates a number of points that are important for thinking about negative externalities like pollution, the difference between private and social costs, and the socially optimal level of pollution.

Polluters do not have an incentive to voluntarily reduce their pollution. By operating his machinery for ten hours a day, Bridgman could earn profits of £50 + 45 + 16 + 15 = £126 a day. He clearly has no incentive to cut back on his use of the machines. Even reducing the use of his machines by one hour would reduce his profits by £5.

Unrestricted pollution generally is not socially optimal. What is privately optimal is not necessarily socially optimal. Bridgman and Sturges are each focused on what is privately optimal for himself. Whatever maximizes each person's profits is privately optimal. From society's point of view, what matters is the welfare of everyone. In the case of Bridgman and Sturges, social optimality is achieved by maximizing the sum of profits to Sturges and Bridgman. Since no one else is harmed if Bridgman and Sturges arrange their affairs in a way that makes their joint profits as large as possible, everyone is made better off if we can make the two of them better off. Any increase in the sum total of their profits could be shared in a way that makes both of the two neighbors better off.

Dr. Sturges faces maximal inconvenience and loss of work when the machines are in constant use over the ten-hour work day. While Bridgman's profits fall by £5 if he cuts back the use of his machines by one hour, a single hour of respite from the machines for Dr. Sturges would result in some very high-value work in his office that is worth £15. The gain to Sturges from a reduction in the use of the machines of just one hour is triple the loss in profits to Bridgman. Considering the profits of the two of them together, total profits rise by £10 if the machines are run for one hour less a day.[4] Cutting back the use of Bridgman's machines—and the consequent reduction in pollution—reduces Bridgman's profits (a private loss) but increases the sum of their profits (a social gain).

Zero pollution generally is not optimal either. By suing Bridgman, Dr. Sturges hoped to shut the candy maker's machinery down which means that no candy would be produced and Bridgman, his workers, and his customers would all suffer damages. But consider what happens if Bridgman were allowed to use his mortar and pestle two hours a day. He would earn £50 profits. And the loss to Dr. Sturges? Zero. He can rearrange his work in a way so he is not inconvenienced in any way for the two hours the machines are operating behind the common wall. The joint profits of the two businessmen would be increased if even two hours of candy making activity were allowed.

There is a socially optimal level of pollution. Operating the confectioner's machines for five hours a day will maximize the sum of profits of the doctor and confectioner. The machines operating for two hours generated profits of £50 for the confectioner at no cost to the doctor. Operating three more hours adds £45 to the confectioner's profits but costs the doctor £15. Total joint profits rise by £30 by expanding the hours to five. That's as far as they should go. Adding one more hour of machine use earns the confectioner only £8 but loses the doctor £10. Total joint profits start to fall once we run the machines more than five hours.

To determine the optimal amount of time for the machines to operate, we start at zero and increase the number of hours until the sum of profits for the two businessmen peak.[5] Joint profits of Sturges and Bridgman are maximized at some intermediate level of pollution. Running the machines all day or shutting them down entirely leads to lower total profits for the two men. The optimal level of pollution, in general, will vary from case to case. If the damages from the first bit of pollution were higher than the benefits from that first bit of pollution, then it would be optimal to ban all pollution. Similarly, if the benefits from allowing the last bit of pollution were higher than the damages from that last little bit, then restricting pollution would not be socially desirable. For most pollutants—including greenhouse gas emissions—it is not socially desirable either to ban pollution entirely or to allow an unrestricted amount.

Did the judges take these economic principles into account when they passed down their ruling in *Sturges v. Bridgman*? Alas, no! The judges weighed the candy maker's rights to continue operating as he (and his father) had for some sixty years against the doctor's rights to use his property in peace. In the end, they sided with the doctor and ruled that Bridgman must stop operating his machinery.

Coase's analysis went a step further, however, to deal with the fact that the doctor was awarded the right to a quiet workplace environment. This right to a quiet work environment is a property right and the assignment of this right to the doctor created an opportunity for Sturges and Bridgman to negotiate among themselves to ensure the socially optimal level of pollution occurs. This is Coase's key insight, enshrined as the Coase Theorem (although Coase himself never set down the rigorous conditions that would elevate his insight to the level of a theorem).

By winning the lawsuit, Dr. Sturges had been granted the right to be free from the nuisance of Bridgman's machinery. Coase observed that this is a right that the doctor would be free to exchange (in part or the whole). Assuming Bridgman and Sturges are focused only on the profitability of their respective businesses, a deal could be struck that would make them both better off. Bridgman could come to Sturges and say, "My dear Dr. Sturges. Shutting my machinery down entirely is very costly to me. What if I were to pay you £35 daily for the right to run my machinery five hours a day?" Sturges thinks to himself, "Hmmm, I will be slightly inconvenienced to the tune of £15 but my neighbor is willing to pay me more than double that amount. We definitely can make a deal to allow him to use his machines for five hours in return for a payment." After some negotiation, they settle on a payment and Bridgman goes back to his candy making albeit only for five hours a day.

Coase's analysis made clear that we cannot predict what the actual payment would be between the two businessmen. The best we can do is put bounds on it. Since the doctor's profits fall by £15 when the machines operate for five hours a day, £15 is the minimum payment that would be acceptable to him. For Bridgman, his profits equal £80 when he can operate the machines for five hours a day. If he can't operate the machines, his profits are zero. So Bridgman would be willing to pay some amount up to £80 for the right to use his machines. The actual payment will be between £15 and £80 with the precise amount depending on the relative bargaining skills of the two men.

Coase's analysis goes further. Consider if Dr. Sturges had lost the lawsuit and Bridgman continued to use his machines for ten hours a day. After stewing for a few days and drinking many glasses of port, Sturges could approach Bridgman saying, "Mr. Bridgman. You have won the lawsuit and have the right to use your machines as you wish. I will pay you £40 a day if you cut back your use of them from ten to five hours. What say you, sir?" Bridgman is a reasonable man and thinks, "Well, my profits will go down by £5 an hour for each of the first three hours I cut back and an additional £8 pounds an hour for the next two hours. That's a loss for me of £31. But my neighbor is offering me £40. We definitely can make a deal where I cut back my use of the machines to five hours in return for a payment." After some negotiation, they settle on a payment and Bridgman goes back to his candy making albeit only using his machines for five hours a day.

As above, we can only put bounds on the payment. Since Bridgman's profits will fall by £31 per day if he reduces his machine use to five hours a day, he will only entertain offers of at least £31. Sturges's profits go up by £65 when the machine use is curtailed. Recall that for the first three hours of respite from the pounding, Sturges could see high-value patients that would earn him profits of £15 per hour. That's £45 total. For the next two hours of peace and quiet, he could earn £10 per hour. That's an additional £20 for a grand total of £65. The most Dr. Sturges would pay for five hours of peace and quiet during the day is £65. So whatever deal is struck will include a payment from Sturges to Bridgman between £31 and £65 a day.

For Coase, the key to ensuring the optimal level of pollution is the clear establishment of property rights. When Sturges wins the lawsuit, he has been granted rights to a quiet and peaceful office space and Bridgman must make an overture to the doctor to obtain permission to use his machinery. If Bridgman wins the lawsuit, he has been granted rights to the free and unfettered use of his machines and it is Dr. Sturges who must make an overture to obtain a few hours of peace and quiet during which he can run his medical practice.

In both scenarios, the doctor and candy maker settle on the level of machine use that maximizes their joint profits. Coase argued in his famous paper that this is precisely what would happen. Let's assume that after the trial, Bridgman makes an offer to Sturges that allows him to use his machines for four hours a day and Sturges accepts the offer. After making that agreement, it is easy to see that there is an opportunity for a mutually beneficial trade that they are passing up. Sturges might come to Bridgman and say, "I understand that if you were allowed to use your machines for one more hour a day, your profits would go up by £15. My profits would fall by £5. Pay me an additional £10 and I'll let you use your machines for five hours a day instead of four." Since Bridgman's profits (after the payment) will rise by £5, he agrees and Bridgman uses his machines for five hours a day.

At any number of hours of operation other than five, there is some payment between the two neighbors that would increase each of their profits if the machine use can be raised or lowered to five hours a day. But the same is not true when the machines are operating for five hours a day. Increasing to six hours would raise the confectioner's profits by £8 but cost the doctor £10 in lost profits. There is no payment that is acceptable to both parties to increase the machine use from five to six hours. Similarly, reducing from five to four is not mutually beneficial. Doing so lowers Bridgman's profits by £15 but gains the doctor only £5. Again, there is no payment acceptable to both parties to decrease the machine use from five to four hours.

For a generation of economists schooled in the tradition that government intervention is the only way to address pollution, Coase's argument that private parties could efficiently deal with pollution on their own left them dumbstruck. Coase included the argument in a paper about the Federal Communications Commission that he submitted to the *Journal of Law and Economics*, the premier academic journal focused on the application of economic principles to legal analysis published by scholars at the University of Chicago. The economists at Chicago—one of the top economics departments in the world—could not believe that "so fine an economist could make such an obvious mistake," in the words of George Stigler, himself a winner of the Nobel Prize in Economics. In a sign of how economics was done in the old days (the late 1950s), they invited Coase to visit Chicago and discuss his paper over dinner at the home of Aaron Director, editor of the journal and himself a renowned economist. As Stigler recounted later, "In the course of two hours of argument, the vote went from twenty against and one for Coase, to twenty-one for Coase." Coase was asked to elaborate his arguments in a paper that became "The Problem of Social Cost." That was not the end of it. Coase was subsequently invited to join the Department of Economics at Chicago where he spent the rest of his illustrious career.[6]

Coase's insight is that excessive pollution results from a failure to assign clear and enforceable property rights. Assigning and protecting property rights is a key role of government. But that can be easier said than done at times. And so, there is one more insight from his theorem that is critical for thinking about greenhouse gas emissions.

The Coase Theorem requires low barriers to negotiation. A key condition for Coasian bargaining to lead to an efficient outcome is that it can't be too difficult for the affected parties to work out a deal among themselves. Bridgman and Sturges were neighbors and knew each other. Only the two of them were affected by the use (or non-use) of the machines. Moreover, each knows (or has reason to believe) the change in profits for the other party as machine use is changed and that any offer made by either of the parties is credible and will be upheld.

The Coase Theorem is often dismissed as just the sort of writing that would come from economists at the University of Chicago, the bastion of conservative economic thinking and free-market principles—think Milton Friedman, another Nobel Laureate, self-avowed libertarian, and author of the wildly popular book *Free To Choose*—a manifesto of sorts in the Reagan era with its call for less government intervention in the economy.

That dismissive argument is unfair to Coase. Coase was responding to the conventional view among economists at the time: If there is an externality, then government regulation is called for. Coase's view was more nuanced. Clearly, the sort of bargaining imagined between Bridgman and Sturges is utterly unrealistic for a situation where billions of people are responsible for pollution that in turn affects billions of others. Coase acknowledged as much in his paper. He wrote that in the "standard case of a [pollutant] which may affect a vast number of people engaged in a wide variety of activities," private negotiations to optimally reduce the pollutant are impossible. In such a case, Coase argued, the solution may well be government regulation or a tax.

The notion of applying Coasian bargaining at the individual level to reduce greenhouse gas emissions is a fanciful idea. How would we do it? Consider a neighboring natural gas fired power plant generating electricity. With whom would the plant owners negotiate? Climate change has global impacts; it would be impossible to coordinate dealmaking between the world's population and this plant. Moreover, because carbon remains in the atmosphere for centuries, many of the damages will be suffered by future generations. Who is going to negotiate for them? An obvious answer is the government. But this would be very cumbersome, especially since there are nearly two thousand natural gas and about four hundred coal fired power plants in the United States. There are also another two hundred and sixty million vehicles on the road burning gasoline or diesel fuel.[7] There must be a better way to reduce emissions optimally. There is. And for that we can thank another great twentieth-century British economist, Arthur Pigou.

USING PRICES TO INTERNALIZE THE EXTERNALITY

Born in 1877 on the Isle of Wight, Arthur Cecil Pigou entered King's College, Cambridge, in 1896 where he took a first class in the history tripos—the undergraduate exams given at Cambridge—followed by a first in the moral sciences tripos in 1900. He came to economics rather late, having first submitted a thesis on "Browning as a Religious Teacher" in an unsuccessful bid for a fellowship at King's College. He had better luck in economics: he began lecturing in economics at King's in 1901 and in 1908 took the chair of political economy previously held by the great economist Alfred Marshall, arguably the developer of modern neoclassical economics. Pigou's reputation was not assured at first. In a short biography, David Collard (2004) writes that Pigou's "publications record at the time [of his appointment to the chair] was respectable though not substantial; he was certainly appointed very much on promise rather than performance." Collard notes that Pigou "loved practical jokes . . . and often affected a silly high-pitched voice. He was an enthusiastic rock-climber and led parties of undergraduates both in the Alps and in the Lake District." But he had a serious side as well. A committed pacifist, he volunteered as an ambulance driver in World War I and frequently put himself in danger on the front lines.

A brilliant debater and highly organized lecturer, Pigou made his mark with his 1920 book *The Economics of Welfare*, in which he emphasized the critical distinction between private and social benefits from which arises the modern idea of an externality. But Pigou went beyond articulating the idea of an externality. He came up with an elegant solution to the problem of externalities that harnessed the power of markets.

Pigou had the following insight. Pollution creates a cost for someone that is not paid by the polluter. That cost is the damages caused by pollution and the adaptation expenses to cope with the impacts of climate change. If pollution creates a cost, argues Pigou, then government should impose a tax on the polluting activity. Return to the example of Bridgman and Sturges and imagine that Pigou was the judge in the case. Given the facts, he might have ruled as follows: "It is neither fair to subject Dr. Sturges to unrestricted pollution nor is it fair to deprive Mr. Bridgman of his right to operate his business. I will set a tax on Bridgman's use of his machines that balances his profits from using the machines against Dr. Sturges's loss of profits from their use. I will set a tax of £10 per hour of machine operation. Revenues from the tax will be used to lower the city property tax."

How does Bridgman react to this tax? Bridgman's costs of using the machines have just risen by £10 for each hour of operation. Bridgman now does a mental calculation: he earns £25 in profits for each of his first two hours of machine use. Even after paying the tax, he will earn a profit. His hourly profit for the next three hours of use is £15. He still earns a profit by expanding his machine use from two to five hours. But if he runs the machines another hour, he'll earn an additional £8. This won't be enough to cover the £10 tax he'll have to pay, so it's not worth running the machines the extra sixth hour. Rather, he runs the machines for five hours and pays a total tax of £50. The noise and vibration pollution from the pounding mortars and pestles has been reduced to the level that maximizes the total profits of the two businessmen.

Applying a tax in *Sturges v. Bridgman* is a bit silly. But it illustrates how a tax can be used to reduce pollution to the socially optimal level. For greenhouse gas emissions in general and carbon dioxide emissions in particular, a carbon tax can nudge polluters to the optimal level of emissions by confronting fossil fuel users with the full social costs of burning these fuels. Those include the private costs of mining coal or drilling for natural gas or oil, processing and transporting the fuels, storing them, and finally burning them. The full social cost also includes the damages to our planet from burning those fuels and adding more and more greenhouse gases to the atmosphere.

Part of the appeal of a carbon tax is that it uses markets to solve the pollution problem. Rather than mandating new carbon-free technologies or subsidizing clean-burning fuels, a carbon tax acts as a price on pollution that steers millions of people toward activities and purchases that reduce our carbon footprint. As the carbon tax raises the cost of burning fossil fuels, people react by buying more fuel-efficient cars and investing in more home insulation and higher efficiency furnaces, among other things. Factories purchase more fuel-efficient boilers and source less energy-intensive intermediate goods used in production, along with a host of other activities.

Conservatives often talk about the power of markets and the way that Adam Smith's "invisible hand" leads us to efficient outcomes. Where pollution is involved, Pigou's insight ensures that the invisible hand has a green thumb!

A carbon tax has costs. That should not be surprising. After all, the payoff to the carbon tax is a cleaner environment and reduced damages to future generations. We should not expect to get those benefits for free. Those costs include investments in new energy-efficient technologies, shifts in modes of transportation (e.g., to electric or hydrogen-powered motor vehicles), potentially higher fuel costs, and so on. But, it is important to emphasize that the cost to society of the carbon tax is *not* the tax payment itself. The tax itself is a transfer from one group of people to another group. A tax applied to the *Bridgman v. Sturges* case illustrates the point.

Imagine the government levies Pigou's tax on Bridgman for every hour of machine use and uses the revenue to lower London's property tax. The £50 collected from Bridgman benefits all London property tax payers, including Bridgman, by lowering their aggregate taxes by the same amount. This is a pure redistribution from one group to another. While the £50 is clearly a cost to Bridgman, it is not a cost to London taxpayers as a group since the net amount of taxes collected is unchanged.

The economic cost of the tax is the reduction in Bridgman's profits as he curtails the use of his machines five hours a day, a loss of profits equal to £31.[8] What about the benefits to Dr. Sturges in being able to use his examining room. With the tax in place and the machine use reduced from ten to five hours a day, the doctor's profits increase by £65, more than outweighing the loss of profits to Bridgman. The increase in the doctor's profits is the benefit of the tax. What this example shows is that the *net benefit* (benefit minus cost) of the tax is positive. The tax has no aggregate social costs at all! If it is optimal to limit pollution, then society will be better off by doing so. That is, net benefits to society will rise. That is the whole point of imposing the tax.

Why do we say that taxes are costly then? For one, taxes are clearly costly to the taxpayer. Consider how Bridgman would feel if subjected to a Pigouvian tax to get him to reduce his machine use to the socially optimal amount of time. Not only does he pay £50 in taxes, his profits fall by £31 relative to when he operated for a full ten-hour workday. It is cold comfort to Bridgman that the £50 tax bill itself makes London property taxpayers better off (even if he himself also benefits in a small way from a lower property tax). He cares about his taxes, not any tax reduction enjoyed by others. Plus, he might argue, the tax reduction for others is miniscule in comparison to the tax he has to pay. All this is true but the fact remains that overall tax collections are unchanged: Bridgman's taxes went up while taxes for others went down. It is easy to forget this. People paying a tax tend to be especially vocal in their opposition to it, while those who benefit by only a small amount are not likely to speak up—it's too small a sum to get exercised about.[9]

Accounting for how tax proceeds are used is especially important for a carbon tax. A carbon tax of $50 per ton of carbon dioxide would raise approximately $200 billion annually.[10] If simply given back to every man, woman, and child in the United States through an income tax cut, a family of four would receive $2,500 as a "carbon dividend." One could justify such a tax rebate as a Coasian property rights payment to citizens for the use of the atmosphere to store accumulating greenhouse gases. Such a rebate would more than offset the higher costs of goods and services due to the carbon tax for some 70 percent of US residents. While a potentially politically appealing bargain, the rebate is spread across millions of people while the impact of the tax is concentrated on a much narrower group of people, those who own, or work in, energy-intensive industries including, for example, the roughly fifty thousand workers employed in coal mining.

That a Pigouvian tax applied to Bridgman's candy business improves societal welfare is clear in our simple example because we can easily account for the costs (lost profits to Bridgman) and benefits (increased profits to Sturges) from reducing pollution. It is much more difficult to sum up all the costs and benefits of a carbon tax. While the costs of reducing emissions are reasonably straightforward to calculate, it is difficult to measure the full benefits. For one thing, many of the benefits—avoided permafrost melt in the Arctic region, avoided sea-level rise around the world—are difficult to monetize. What is the value of the loss of polar bears, for example, if the Arctic region is fundamentally changed? Will polar bears go extinct? What about the disruptions of sea-level rise? To the extent that sea-level rise leads to shifts in living patterns and mass migrations, it is extraordinarily difficult to measure the dollar value of these disruptions. Moreover, the bulk of benefits from reducing emissions will go to unborn generations. This complicates the task of measuring the benefits of reducing greenhouse gas emissions now.

Because of the difficulty in measuring the benefits of reducing emissions, economists have focused considerable attention on the question of whether there are benefits to carbon taxes other than emission reductions. This has given rise to the so-called *Double Dividend* literature. The idea of a double dividend is straightforward. The first dividend from a carbon tax is the environmental improvement from reducing pollution. The second dividend is the revenue from the carbon tax that can be used to lower income tax rates. Our income tax discourages work and savings by individuals, encourages people to take out mortgages to buy homes (or subsidizes larger mortgages to buy larger homes), and affects firms' investment decisions. These are examples of what economists call tax distortions. A vast literature exists on the shortcomings of our tax system and how it distorts the behavior of taxpayers as they engage in various activities to reduce their tax burden.[11] Having a tax system that discourages activities we like (e.g., jobs, saving, and investment) means there is the possibility of a second benefit (or dividend) from a carbon tax. If the carbon tax revenue is used to lower a distorting tax, then we can offset some of the costs of our tax system. In fact, if the tax system is especially messed up, then it is possible that you could get a *strong double dividend*, where the reductions in costs by lowering especially distorting taxes are greater than the costs to firms from the carbon tax. Then a carbon tax makes society better off *even when we ignore the environmental benefits*. Alas, while an appealing idea, there is little evidence to support the idea of a strong double dividend from a carbon tax.[12]

While the strong double dividend might not exist, it is certainly true that using the carbon tax revenue to lower those taxes that are especially distorting could contribute to stronger economic growth. The most distorting taxes, in general, are taxes on capital income (e.g., the corporate income tax and taxes on dividends and capital gains). For the largest possible double dividend, we'd use carbon tax revenue to cut taxes on capital income. But cutting taxes on capital income disproportionately benefits high income people. From a fairness point of view, we may feel that carbon tax revenue should benefit a broader group of individuals than those at the top of the income and wealth heap. This illustrates the political trade-off between economic efficiency and fairness. It is worth noting, moreover, that any argument for lowering the US corporate income tax has become even less persuasive after the 2017 tax cut lowered the top corporate rate from 35 to 21 percent, its lowest level since 1937.[13]

FROM THEORY TO PRACTICE: CARBON TAXES IN ACTION

It is one thing to advocate a carbon tax in theory. It's another to see how it operates in practice. Carbon taxes have been used by countries and subnational governments for more than twenty-five years. In 2017, sixteen national or subnational carbon taxes were in effect with another three added in 2018.[14] There have been two waves of carbon tax enactments: a Scandinavian wave starting in the early 1990s saw carbon taxes legislated in Denmark, Finland, Norway, and Sweden, among other countries. By 2000, seven countries had a carbon tax. A second wave in the mid-2000s saw carbon taxes put in place in Switzerland, Iceland, Ireland, Japan, Mexico, and Portugal. In addition, the Canadian provinces of British Columbia and Alberta have enacted carbon taxes.

The carbon taxes in Sweden and British Columbia are worth a closer examination as they reveal quite a bit about how a carbon tax might affect the US economy. Sweden enacted its tax in 1991 with a "standard" rate that applied to households and the commercial sector. Industry and agriculture were taxed at a lower rate, given concerns about international competition. The general tax rate in 2018 is just under $130 per metric ton of carbon dioxide, and the industry discount has been eliminated.[15]

A 2016 report by the Heritage Foundation that analyzed a carbon tax in the United States at one-third the rate paid by Swedish industrial firms argued that the tax would have "devastating economic costs."[16] Has Sweden been devastated by its carbon tax? Hardly. Prior to enacting the tax, Sweden's economy grew between 1961 and 1990 at an annual rate of 2.9 percent while the US economy grew at 3.7 percent. The gap between the Swedish and US growth rates fell after the tax was enacted. Sweden's GDP grew between 1991 and 2015 at an average annual rate of 2.1 percent, just a bit lower than the US growth rate of 2.4 percent. This is not to argue that Sweden closed the gap between its growth rate and the US growth rate *because* of its carbon tax. But it is hard to argue that the country has been devastated by its carbon tax. In fact, Sweden's growth rate has exceeded the US growth rate since 2000.[17] Sweden's carbon tax accounts for 1.6 percent of total tax collections—equivalent to two-thirds of 1 percent of GDP. Based on its share of GDP, Sweden's carbon tax revenue would be comparable to a US carbon tax that raised $120 billion annually.

Why has Sweden thrived despite having the highest carbon tax rate in the world? Part of the success of the Swedish carbon tax is its use of revenue. From its beginnings, the carbon tax was part of a broader tax reform that reduced labor taxes through increases in taxes on energy use, including the carbon tax. This green tax shift contributed to economic growth and a decoupling of economic growth and emissions. Decoupling refers to the breakdown of the historic link between economic growth and carbon emissions. As economies grow, so do emissions. But as countries get richer, the demand for environmental quality grows and the growth–emissions link can be broken.[18] The link has clearly been broken in Sweden's case. Figure 3.1 shows that while real GDP grew by three-quarters between 1990 and 2016, Sweden's emissions fell by one-quarter.

Sweden is just one example. An example closer to home is the Canadian province of British Columbia, where the carbon tax is closer in structure to what the United States might consider. Sweden's carbon tax applied only to

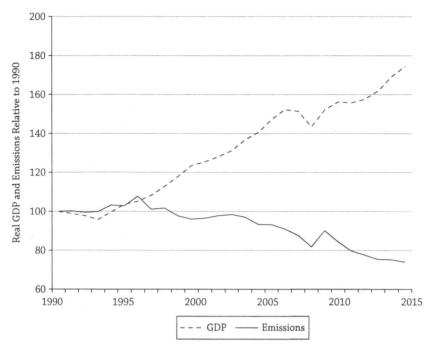

Figure 3.1. Decoupling of economic growth and emissions in Sweden, 1990–2016
Source: World Bank and Statistics Sweden

fossil fuels used by the residential sector plus industrial firms not subject to carbon pricing by other means.

As part of a broader package of tax reforms, British Columbia enacted a broad-based carbon tax in 2008 starting at $10 (Canadian) per metric ton of carbon dioxide and increasing by $5 per year to its current $35 in Canadian dollars (as of 2018). That's equivalent to $27 in US dollars.[19] The tax is scheduled to increase by $5 (Canadian) per year until it reaches $50 per ton in 2021. The tax is a broad-based tax on the carbon emissions of all hydrocarbon fuels burned in the province. Given the existing federal and provincial taxes already in place, the carbon tax raised the overall excise tax on gasoline by roughly one-fifth.

The tax collects over $1 billion annually—over 5 percent of provincial tax collections—and all the revenue is returned to businesses and households through a combination of tax-rate reductions, grants to businesses and households, and other business tax breaks. Worried that the new carbon tax would disproportionately affect low-income households, policymakers included several elements in the tax reform to offset adverse impacts on them. One element was a low-income climate action tax credit of $115.50

per adult plus $34.50 per child, which reduced taxes by $300 for a low-income family of four. In addition, tax rates in the lowest two tax brackets were reduced by five percentage points. Also, in the first year of the carbon tax, there was a one-time "climate action dividend" of $100 for every BC resident. This equal-sized dividend represents a greater share of the disposable income of low-income households than of higher income households.

Meanwhile, business tax rates were cut. The tax rate for small businesses, for example, was cut from 4.5 percent to 2.5 percent in 2008. As the carbon tax rate rose from $10 to $20, there was more carbon tax revenue to rebate, much of which was channeled to businesses in the form of new business tax credits.

British Columbia's carefully constructed policy package to return tax revenue to its residents and businesses balanced concerns about distributional impacts and economic growth. Targeting tax cuts to low-income households ensured the burden of the tax wouldn't fall disproportionately on those households. And the focus on small business emphasized the importance of supporting economic growth.

The evidence strongly supports the conclusion that neither economic growth nor employment were adversely affected by the tax. One analysis comparing economic growth in British Columbia to that of other provinces finds that growth was unaffected by the tax after controlling for differences across the Canadian provinces. Another study found that overall employment increased given the growth in the service sectors stimulated by the increase in consumption by BC residents upon receiving carbon rebates.[20] While jobs were shed in energy-intensive sectors, those lost jobs were more than offset with new jobs in sectors that use little energy (services, for example). This is precisely what the carbon tax's price signal is expected to do: redirect jobs away from carbon polluting sectors to nonpolluting sectors. The reallocation of new jobs in British Columbia is an example of the power of prices to reshape an economy.

Balancing the carbon tax with decreases in personal and corporate income tax rates helped counteract any negative economic impacts of the tax. The evidence for the tax's impact on reducing the use of fossil fuels is even more clear-cut. British Columbia experienced a sharp drop in fossil fuel consumption at a time when per capita fuel consumption was rising in the rest of Canada.[21]

The evolution of public attitude toward the tax has been documented by the Canadian political scientist Kathryn Harrison. She shows that attitudes toward the carbon tax have swung sharply from majority opposition to support since the middle of 2011. Harrison (2013) notes a few factors that may have contributed to this swing of opinion including 1) growing acceptance that the tax was "here to stay"; 2) less media attention on the tax; and 3) a growing recognition that eliminating the tax would create a budget shortfall of roughly 3 percent that would be difficult to make up. She also notes that over time the rebated tax revenue has shifted from rebates to people (and especially low-income households) to tax reductions that favor "more specific, and presumably more attentive, subpopulations" such as business groups receiving special tax breaks. This suggests a coalition is emerging to support maintaining the tax.

British Columbia's carbon tax is a case study of a *revenue neutral* tax reform where the revenue is used to lower other taxes so that overall tax collections are unchanged. It was a politically savvy approach since BC residents couldn't argue that the tax would simply increase their overall tax burden. In returning the revenue in a visible and transparent way, policymakers undercut a potential opposition to the tax.

British Columbia's experience with a carbon tax informed Canada's roll-out of a national carbon policy. In October 2016, the Canadian federal government extended carbon pricing to all Canadian provinces. Each province is free to establish a carbon pricing approach as it sees fit so long as it satisfies criteria laid out in the federal pricing system. Specifically, pricing has to apply broadly and be at or above a federal benchmark of $10 per metric ton (Canadian) in 2017; the benchmark rises by $10 a year until it hits $50 in 2022. Provinces that don't adhere to federal guidelines are subject to a federal carbon levy so that carbon pollution is priced in every province.[22] The federal approach honors Canada's commitment to its federal structure and provincial rights while ensuring national action is taken and consistent pricing achieved across Canadian provinces.

Taxing carbon pollution is an idea solidly grounded in economic theory. A tax on carbon pollution uses the power of markets to shift behavior, encourage energy savings, incentivize clean energy innovation, and raise money that we can use to good purpose elsewhere in the federal budget. Despite all this, it's clear that people have a visceral dislike of taxes. This dislike can be traced to various factors, including the complexity of the current tax code and a sense that others are not paying their fair share of taxes.[23] The question, however, is how best to achieve the goal of reducing our carbon emissions and avoiding the damages from those on-going emissions. The best policy is the policy that balances simplicity, efficiency, and fairness. Pointing to the problems with taxes without looking at the drawbacks of the alternatives is unfair to tax policy. Or as Winston Churchill noted in another context, "[m]any forms of government have been tried . . . Indeed, it has been said that democracy is the worst form of Government except for all those other forms that have been tried . . ."[24]

CHAPTER 4

Isn't There a Better Way? (No, There Isn't)

Doing nothing to curb emissions will impose serious costs on current and future generations. Simply as a matter of prudence, we should act to reduce emissions. While doing nothing is costly, reducing our emissions will also be costly. Less costly than doing nothing, to be sure, but there is no free lunch when it comes to climate policy.

Since many polices can reduce emissions, we need some criteria to evaluate them against a carbon tax. Let's start with the most basic: the policy should actually *reduce emissions*. That seems so obvious that it doesn't seem necessary to mention. But some policies may look good on paper but not actually reduce emissions. Next, the policy should be *cost-effective*. A policy is cost-effective if it reduces emissions at the lowest possible cost to society. In other words, the policy gives us the biggest bang for the buck.

The policy should also *encourage innovation*. We need to lower the cost of zero-carbon energy to make it affordable and avoid raising energy costs as much as possible. Innovation will be key to developing new and affordable clean energy sources that are the foundation of a thriving carbon-free economy.

A good policy will be *simple* to administer and comply with and should be *transparent* in its operation. Simplicity lowers government's implementation and administration costs and firms' compliance costs. Transparency helps people understand the policy, which helps build and sustain political support, otherwise, it may look like government interfering in people's lives for no good reason. Transparency (along with simplicity) is also important to minimize political meddling that favors certain groups or individuals while raising costs to consumers. The more complex the policy, the more opportunities for politicians to game the policy to benefit special interests. One important form of transparency is distributional transparency. Who actually bears the cost of the policy? Clarity on distributional impacts is important for two reasons. First, opponents of a new environmental policy often object on the grounds that it will hurt low-income households. Many times, those arguments are overstated or simply incorrect. A clear understanding of the distributional impacts helps to clarify the true cost impact. Second, for groups adversely impacted by a policy, a clear sense of the distributional impacts can inform discussion about how to address those concerns. If policymakers don't understand that a policy hurts low-income households, they can't shape policy elements to offset the adverse impact on those households.

On every one of these criteria, a carbon tax stands head and shoulders above the alternative policies. A carbon tax is the most direct way to cut our carbon dioxide emissions. It treats all sources of emissions equally and uses prices to change behavior by harnessing the power of markets in support of our clean energy goals. Policies that are often touted as an alternative to a carbon tax generally are either much more expensive than a carbon tax or unlikely to lead to enough emission reductions to deal with our climate problem.

That's a strong claim. To see why it's true, we need to look carefully at the alternatives to a carbon tax. One alternative is the carbon pricing policy called *cap and trade*. The cap and trade policy has different issues than alternatives that don't price carbon and is the focus of the next chapter. Setting cap and trade aside for the moment, our choices include writing regulations to mandate pollution reductions, lowering the cost of activities we'd like to encourage, or using persuasion and voluntary actions to reduce emissions. How do they stack up against a carbon tax?

REGULATION

Regulation can take many forms. Basically, it is a set of rules that require firms and individuals to behave in certain ways. Mandating changes in technologies or limiting product choice (e.g., requiring appliances to satisfy a minimum level of efficiency) is a form of regulation. For example, the Obama Administration's Clean Power Plan is a mandate to reduce carbon pollution from existing electric power plants to comply with air quality standards under the Clean Air Act. The US Corporate Average Fuel Economy (CAFE) regulations mandate minimum miles per gallon (mpg) standards for passenger cars and light trucks. Since electricity production and transportation together account for three-quarters of energy-related carbon dioxide emissions in the United States, it's worth looking at the Clean Air Act and CAFE in closer detail.

The Clean Air Act dates to 1970 and the Nixon Administration. Anticipating a presidential run by Maine's Edmund Muskie, an environmental champion in the US Senate, Nixon announced in his 1970 State of the Union Address that he would put forward "the most comprehensive and costly program [to curtail pollution] in America's history." Sounding every bit the environmental economist, Nixon continued, "We can no longer afford to consider air and water common property, free to be abused by anyone without regard to the consequences. Instead, we should begin now to treat them as scarce resources, which we are no more free to contaminate than we are free to throw garbage into our neighbor's yard. This requires comprehensive new regulations. It also requires that, to the extent possible, the price of goods should be made to include the costs of producing and disposing of them without damage to the environment."[1] Nixon's proposed legislation was quickly passed by the House of Representatives in June. Senator Muskie's Senate Subcommittee on Air and Water Pollution toughened the standards and the Senate passed the new version in September. After a conference committee to reconcile the House and Senate versions of the legislation, the Clean Air Act was passed and signed into law by the end of the year.[2]

The Clean Air Act required the EPA to set air quality standards for air pollutants such as particulate matter (e.g., soot), nitrogen dioxide, carbon monoxide, lead, ozone, and sulfur dioxide (so-called *criteria pollutants*), allowing states to develop their own plans to ensure the standards were met.[3] That way, each state could customize its approach to meeting the Clean Air Act's targets based on its individual circumstances. Counties within a state that did not meet the air quality standards were subject to more stringent regulation until air quality improved.

In addition to air quality standards, the Clean Air Act set emission rates (or performance standards) for new, stationary sources of pollution (e.g., new electric generating plants) based on the state of technology (*best system of emission reduction* that has been adequately demonstrated, in regulatory-speak).[4] A system would be judged on its ability to reduce emissions, taking into account cost as well as any ancillary benefits beyond air quality improvement (including possible energy savings). Setting a performance standard (e.g., a limit on the pounds of nitrogen dioxide allowed per ton of coal burned) on the basis of some technology standard is a central feature of many regulatory approaches. Given all the uncertainties about how technologies perform and the risk of inadvertently violating the performance standard, the prudent firm will use the technology on which the regulatory standard was based. After all, if there is a problem, the firm can say "we used the technology you recommended; if it failed to perform as promised, you should have thought of that before setting a standard on its basis." That's a harder argument to make if the firm uses another technology to meet the performance standard, even if that alternative technology is better suited to the factory and likely to perform better or at lower cost.

Technology mandates—whether explicit or implicit as in the case of regulations based on best available control technologies—rarely give firms the most "bang for the buck." After all, if government mandates a technology, firms have no incentive to find better and cheaper alternatives to achieve the same pollution reductions.

Moreover, the nature of mandates suggests a scientifically driven process that can obscure political meddling by Congress. A case in point was a provision in the 1977 Clean Air Act Amendment designed to reduce sulfur dioxide emissions from new power plants. Burning coal to produce electricity is a major cause of sulfur dioxide emissions. Power plants can reduce those emissions in two main ways. They can install flue gas desulfurization technology to remove sulfur dioxide from the exhaust gas of power plants on all coal fired power plants. Scrubbers, as this technology is commonly known, are extremely expensive. For a 300-megawatt coal plant, a scrubber could cost upward of $50 million to install and $5 million to operate each year. An alternative way to reduce sulfur dioxide emissions is to switch from high-sulfur coal—typically found in the East—to low-sulfur coal from the West, especially from the Powder River Basin in Wyoming and Montana. If a power plant in the East burned high-sulfur coal from the Appalachian region with a sulfur content of 2.8 pounds per million BTUs of energy, the scrubber would reduce emissions to 0.28 pounds per million BTUs (at the 90 percent standard). But low-sulfur coal from Wyoming's Powder River Basin has a sulfur content before scrubbing of 0.28 pounds per million BTUs. Logically, a coal fired power plant should be allowed to burn low-sulfur coal from Wyoming instead of being required to install a costly scrubber.

But sometimes politics wins over logic. To protect Eastern coal mines and their high-sulfur coal, Congress mandated that all power plants reduce sulfur dioxide emissions by between 70 and 90 percent *regardless* of the sulfur content of the coal. As a result, a power plant using low-sulfur coal still needed to scrub the stack emissions; the provision undercut any incentive to replace Eastern coal with Western Powder River Basin coal.[5]

This technology mandate violates the cost-effectiveness criterion since it requires firms to use expensive technology when it might be less expensive to switch to lower-sulfur coal. It's also an example of how complex rule-making can hide a policy choice designed to benefit one group (owners of Eastern coal mines) at the expense of others (owners of Western coal mines and consumers who must pay for more expensive electricity).

The scrubber example illustrates one problem with mandates: they often force firms to use expensive pollution abatement despite the availability of less expensive alternatives. Mandates can also raise costs, even when written in ways that appear fair. Suppose Congress passes a mandate that all fossil fuel power plants reduce carbon dioxide emissions by 10 percent. Mandating the same percentage reduction for all firms seems fair. But, it ignores the wide variation in costs of power plants and the fact that some might be able to reduce pollution more easily (and cheaply) than others.

Here's why the uniform percentage reduction rule would be more costly than necessary. Consider two power plants, Edison Power and Insull Electric, that differ in their ability to reduce their carbon pollution. Let's say it costs Edison Power $100 per ton to reduce its carbon emissions. The cost for Insull Electric is $40 a ton. Imagine they each currently release 40,000 tons of carbon dioxide a day burning coal to produce electricity. This uniform emissions reduction mandate requires each plant to reduce its emissions by 10 percent or 4,000 tons per day. Each plant might cut emissions through a combination of energy-efficiency improvements to their boilers as well as energy-efficiency incentives for their customers to reduce electricity consumption. Assuming each plant cuts emissions by the required 10 percent, the total cost of overall emission reductions is $100 \times 4,000 + $40 \times 4,000 = $560,000 a day. But we could get the same reduction in emissions more cheaply if Insull Electric cut its emissions by 8,000 tons a day. The cost now is $40 \times 8,000 = $320,000, a savings of $240,000. A uniform mandate to cut emissions is not cost-effective. In this example, it raises the cost of a given reduction in emissions by 75 percent.

Your attitude might be "Too bad. Just because Edison Power's costs are higher doesn't get them off the hook. They should cut their emissions just like Insull Electric." That attitude is understandable but a policy based on that view simply drives up the cost of regulation. Shifting some of the emission reduction from Edison to Insull reduces the overall costs of cutting pollution.[6]

This is a general principle. Assuming the damages from pollution do not vary by location of the pollution—as is the case with greenhouse gas emissions—any policy that after enactment means firms have different costs for reducing emissions is not cost-effective. We can achieve the same reduction in pollution at lower cost if the firm with higher costs per ton cuts pollution a bit less while the firm with lower costs cuts pollution a bit more. A policy cuts pollution at minimum cost to society only when the cost of the last ton of pollution reduction is the same for everyone.

A carbon tax guarantees that every firm cuts its carbon emissions to the point where the next ton of emissions reduction is the same for every firm. That's because each firm reduces its costs by reducing carbon emissions wherever the cost per ton of eliminating the emissions is less than the tax rate. To minimize costs, a firm will reduce emissions until the cost of the next ton reduced equals the tax rate. Since every firm faces the same tax rate, the cost for the next ton of emission reduction is the same for all. Regulations in general don't guarantee that the cost of emission reduction for the last unit will be the same for all regulated firms. This can make regulation very expensive relative to policies that put a price on emissions, as much as doubling the cost of cutting emissions.[7]

The CAFE standards for cars and trucks are another example of a regulatory mandate. CAFE requires automobile manufacturers to meet fleet-wide average minimum fuel economy (mpg) for passenger cars and, separately, for light trucks (e.g., sport utility vehicles, or SUVs, and pick-up trucks) and, more recently, for larger trucks.

Fuel economy standards were first motivated by a desire to reduce dependence on foreign oil after the 1973 Arab oil embargo, when petroleum accounted for 46 percent of overall energy consumption in the United States and 96 percent of transportation energy use. A strong energy-security argument could be made for increasing fuel economy and reducing dependence on oil. There's no question that CAFE along with other efforts to reduce petroleum use has been successful. Today, the share of oil in US energy consumption has fallen by ten percentage points and the average fuel efficiency of cars and SUVs has risen by one-half.[8]

The 1975 Energy Policy and Conservation Act initiated a first round of fuel economy standards: 1978 model-year passenger cars were required to achieve a fleet-wide fuel economy target of 18 mpg with the target rising to 27.5 mpg by model-year 1985. The initial increase was modest: the fleet efficiency of cars on the road in 1975 was 14 mpg and the new standard would apply only to new cars. Lower standards were set for light trucks.

The light truck loophole shows how regulations that are influenced by political considerations and unexpected changes in tastes can help undermine environmental policy. In the early 1970s, SUVs were a tiny part of the automotive market. Originally designed literally for off-road use (e.g., agricultural and back-country driving), the SUV market was initially dominated by the American Motors Jeep and International Harvester Scout vehicles.

Neither a truck nor a family car, these were rugged vehicles popular with a small group of drivers for their ability to travel through mud and across rocky terrain. Nobody predicted how popular SUVs would become. After all, pick-up trucks and SUVs together accounted for only one sale in five in the United States in the early 1980s and most of these sales were pick-up trucks. As Congress pushed to enact fuel economy standards in the 1970s, it wanted to avoid harming an already fragile economy reeling from the 1973 Arab oil embargo. With the unemployment rate hitting 9 percent in May 1975, there was little appetite in Congress for what opponents termed "job killing" regulations. The common perception was that pick-up trucks were used by workers and small businessmen. Given the high unemployment rate, Congress was sensitive to charges that it would hurt struggling workers if it imposed new rules that increased costs for hardworking pick-up truck owners.

Matters came to a head in Detroit in 1977. Worrying that higher costs due to stringent fuel economy regulations would cut sales, Chrysler threatened to shut down a truck assembly plant in Detroit unless less stringent fuel economy standards were enacted for light trucks. This sparked loud protests from African American leaders in the city given the number of well-paying jobs at the Chrysler plant, a major source of jobs for African Americans in the area. In response, Congress directed the Department of Transportation to set lower fuel economy standards for light trucks.[9]

Light trucks are rather different from SUVs, so how did SUVs get thrown in with light trucks and made subject to a less stringent fuel economy standard? Here again politics played a role. American Motors was the baby brother to the big three US automakers: General Motors, Ford, and Chrysler. By the mid-1970s, the company was losing money on nearly all its product lines, except its Jeep line. Since the Jeep was built on a chassis for light trucks, Congress and the Carter Administration saw a simple way to help American Motors stay afloat and avoid the charge that it was writing job-killing environmental rules: apply the less stringent light-truck fuel economy rules to the Jeep and other vehicles built on a light-truck chassis. With few SUVs on the road, this seemed like an inexpensive tweak in a car market dominated by sedans and station wagons.

Congress and the Department of Transportation did not foresee the shift in consumer tastes as baby boomers traded the boring station wagons of their parents for rugged, sporty SUVs with names like Bronco, Blazer, Pathfinder, Cherokee, Durango, and Navigator. And lest you think that the rugged SUVs were designed for workers, even Jeep phased out its classic military-style line in favor of the Wrangler, which had shock absorbers designed to avoid the bone-jarring rides of the earlier Jeeps. It wasn't just

US automakers who had to adjust to the change in US tastes. Japanese automakers—an increasingly major player in US auto markets—were caught by surprise as well. Distributors of Japanese cars in the United States started making requests that mystified their Japanese manufacturers. As one US Suzuki executive noted, "When we asked for power steering and cloth seats [for our SUVs], the Japanese at first said to us, 'Are you crazy? These things are for plumbers.' But the US is an affluent market and people want a vehicle that gives them some individualism."[10] CAFE imposed serious restrictions on automakers to improve fuel economy and the light-truck loophole became increasingly important as SUVs took a larger and larger share of the automotive market. The light-truck share of sales doubled from just under one quarter in the mid-1970s to over half by 2000 and rose to over two-thirds by early 2018.[11]

While fuel economy standards were historically driven by concerns with oil imports and energy consumption, increasingly, the concern became carbon dioxide emissions from using oil in transportation. A 2009 EPA decision to treat carbon dioxide as a pollutant subject to federal regulation meant that EPA now teamed with the Department of Transportation to set fuel economy standards to reduce greenhouse gas emissions from the transportation fleet as well as petroleum consumption. If CAFE is one of the tools to reduce our carbon pollution, we should assess it against the criteria set out at the beginning of the chapter. Right away it fails the cost-effectiveness criterion. To start, CAFE doesn't equate the incremental cost of the last ton of emission reductions across all vehicle types and manufacturers. In addition, CAFE applies only to the transportation sector. Reducing emissions in the electricity or industrial sector is far less expensive than reducing emissions in transportation. If a factory or power plant shifts its fuel source from coal to natural gas, for example, it cuts its carbon dioxide emissions in half, given the higher energy-to-carbon content of natural gas versus coal. Making a fuel switch is much less expensive than re-engineering an entire line of automobiles or pick-up trucks.

Here's another problem. Mandates like CAFE do reduce fuel consumption and greenhouse gas emissions but they are prone to the law of unexpected consequences that can undermine those energy savings and emission reductions. Policymakers did not anticipate the shift in consumer tastes from station wagons toward SUVs. While SUVs were bound to become popular as baby boomers started families, the CAFE loophole that allowed SUVs to meet lower fuel economy standards and so kept their costs down accelerated the shift from cars to SUVs.

Another problem with fuel economy standards is *rebound*. I love my new Chevy Volt, a plug-in hybrid. It drives between fifty and sixty miles on a battery charge, which is more than enough to get me to work and back with a stop or two for errands. When the battery drains, a small gasoline engine kicks in to generate electricity for the electric motor. On gasoline, I get about 42 mpg. Compared to a conventional gas-powered car that gets the same mileage, the hybrid is cheaper to drive at gasoline prices of $2.00 a gallon or greater given what I pay for electricity at home.[12]

But the real comparison should be to the car that we sold when we bought the Volt. That was a 2007 Subaru Forester, which got between 23 and 28 mpg, depending if I was driving more in the city or on the highway. Let's call it 25 mpg on average. At $3.00 a gallon, $20 would buy enough gas to drive 165 miles. That same $20 would pay for enough electricity to drive 310 miles in my Volt. It is roughly half as expensive to drive a mile in my Volt as in my old Subaru.

Now that it costs 50 percent less to drive my Volt, the temptation to hop in the car to do a quick errand goes up. That is the rebound effect. A mandated increase in fuel economy lowers the cost of driving each mile. But as the price of driving per mile goes down, people drive more. Rebound is not a bad thing, per se. Those extra miles I'm driving because the cost of driving per mile went down give me some benefits; after all, if the extra driving wasn't beneficial, I wouldn't have driven those miles.[13] But it has increased the cost of meeting any given goal for fuel or pollution reduction. That cuts into some of the fuel savings from a regulation like CAFE that mandates higher fuel efficiency. Estimates of rebound suggest that doubling fuel economy standards will reduce gasoline consumption by only about 35 to 40 percent rather than cutting consumption in half—the fuel savings we'd get if driving behavior didn't change. Because of rebound, CAFE standards must be ratcheted more tightly to get a given reduction in oil consumption and carbon dioxide pollution. Tightening the standard raises the cost of reducing our emissions.

An additional problem with fuel economy standards is that they only apply to new cars. As a result, it will take years for higher fuel economy to permeate the entire fleet of cars and trucks on the road as owners only slowly replace their used cars with new cars. Worse, the standards raise the price of new cars relative to used cars and so create an incentive to keep older, more polluting vehicles on the road longer. This cuts the fuel savings from fuel economy standards by roughly 15 percent, an effect as big as, if not bigger than, the rebound effect.[14]

Taking all these considerations into effect, how much more expensive is it to cut emissions by CAFE relative to other approaches? Researchers at Resources for the Future (RFF), a highly respected environmental research group in Washington, DC, estimate that the cost of reducing a ton of carbon dioxide through CAFE is $85, whereas the cost of reducing emissions through a carbon tax is $12 a ton.[15]

There's one more problem with fuel economy standards. They are regressive, meaning their costs fall disproportionately on lower-income households. This last point is worth emphasizing for a couple of reasons. First, while policymakers are very conscious of the distributional impacts of tax proposals and often go to great lengths to shield lower-income households from being disproportionately burdened, policymakers are less focused on the distributional impacts of regulations. But, just as the costs of regulation are real, so too are the distributional impacts. The second reason to emphasize the distributional impact of fuel economy standards is the counterintuitive nature of the result. Fuel economy standards initially drive up the cost of *new* cars and light trucks. Higher-income households tend to purchase more new vehicles. On that basis, one might expect that the costs of fuel economy standards fall disproportionately on higher-income households. This, however, ignores the spillovers from new car markets into used car markets. If new cars are more expensive, people hold on to their current vehicles longer. With fewer used cars available for sale, their price goes up. Lower income households then must pay more for a used car. Because of the large stock of used vehicles still in use, the impact on lower-income households through more expensive used cars and trucks more than offsets the impact of costlier new vehicles on higher-income households.[16]

SUBSIDIES

Subsidizing activities that compete with the polluting activity can reduce pollution and is particularly attractive to politicians. After all, subsidies generally lower costs for their constituents. The problem, however, is that someone has to pay for the subsidy. This is easy to forget. After all, the benefits of a subsidy are clear to the small number of people who receive it while the costs are spread over many people. While the aggregate cost of the subsidy might be large, the cost to any individual may be too small to notice.

Subsidies can take many forms. Renewable Portfolio Standard (RPS) programs are popular policies at the state level and are a blend of regulation and subsidy. An RPS policy mandates that a certain fraction of the electricity sold in the state must come from renewable sources such as wind or solar. In 2014, Massachusetts, for example, required that 9 percent of the electricity sold in the state be generated by specified renewable

sources with the share to rise to 15 percent by 2020 and increase one percentage point each subsequent year. Massachusetts is one of twenty-nine
states with some form of RPS.[17] Every private company selling electricity in
Massachusetts in 2020 must prove it has satisfied its 15 percent RPS obligation. Companies demonstrate compliance by submitting *renewable energy
credits* (RECs) to the state each year. RECs are like vouchers that the state
gives to renewable electricity producers for every megawatt-hour—1000
kilowatt-hours (kWhs)—of electricity the renewable facility generates. The
owners can then sell those vouchers to electricity distribution companies
that buy as many RECs as they need to comply with the state law. The payment from the company that sells electricity to retail customers is a payment over and above the payment for the electricity that the renewable
generator sold into the system. An owner of a commercial solar farm selling
electricity into the grid might get paid between two and ten cents per kWh
depending on the time of day the power is sold. The owner could also sell a
REC to some utility that needs it to comply with the RPS rule. That might
bring another twenty-five to twenty-eight cents per kWh (based on solar
REC prices in 2014 in Massachusetts). That's a very attractive deal for solar
farm investors. Who pays for the REC? The cost of the REC gets folded in
to the cost of generation and passed on to ratepayers.[18]

While the REC costs get passed on to ratepayers, the cost increase is
blunted to some extent by the fact that wind and solar have very low (essentially zero) operating costs. As a result, electricity prices don't go up
as much as when a tax is imposed. That may be appealing to a politician
who wants to avoid painful price increases but it creates its own problems.
Keeping prices down discourages firms and individuals from investing in
energy efficiency to reduce consumption. And while a tax increase may be
unpopular, it does raise revenue that could be returned to ratepayers in a
way that preserves the energy-saving price signal while also offsetting the
income loss from higher electricity rates. Blunting the price signal raises
the cost of RPS emission reductions relative to a carbon tax. A recent study,
for example, found that the cost of cutting carbon emissions in the electricity sector by 10 percent was over six times higher with an RPS program
than with a carbon tax applied to fuels used to generate electricity.[19]

Rather than have the ratepayer pay for the subsidy as in RPS programs,
we can have taxpayers finance it. Since the first energy crisis back in
the 1970s, Congress has provided tax breaks to encourage various energy technologies, including breaks for developing and using renewable
technologies.[20] Historically, the biggest tax breaks have been tax credits
for projects that generate electricity from solar, wind, geothermal, or other
renewable sources. Currently, solar electricity and solar hot water projects

are eligible for a 30 percent *investment tax credit* that allows a homeowner who installs a $20,000 solar rooftop system to take a tax credit worth $6,000 (30% × $20,000). The credit lowers the homeowner's taxes by $6,000. A 30 percent investment tax credit is a 30 percent price discount on the purchase, pure and simple, courtesy of Uncle Sam.[21] This credit is available for residential rooftop solar panels as well as utility-scale solar projects (e.g., a solar farm). No wonder that utility-scale solar generation has increased by a factor of 600 between 2007 and 2015!

The tax subsidy for wind operates differently. A wind project that began construction in 2016 can earn a *production tax credit* of 2.3 cents per kWh of electricity generated during its first ten years of operation. That is over and above the revenue it gets from selling electricity into the grid. Consider the Marshall Wind Energy project in Beattie, Kansas. It is a 72 million-watt (MW) project. Given wind patterns in Kansas, the project will produce around 250 million kWhs of electricity each year. At 2.3 cents per kWh of electricity produced, the production tax credit cuts $5.8 million off the firm's tax bill each year it is eligible for the credit. That's $5.8 million that goes right to after-tax profits.[22]

Subsidies to clean energy are problematic. The first and most obvious problem is that subsidies *lower* the price of energy rather than *raise* it. In Texas, a wind-rich area with lots of installed wind capacity, generators have willingly accepted a *negative* price for their electricity when demand was very low, say in the middle of the night. That's because the wind generators have next to zero operating costs and can collect 2.3 cents in production tax credits for every kilowatt-hour they sell! Even if they have to pay a penny to provide electricity, they are still earning 1.3 cents on each kWh sold after cashing in on the production tax credit.[23]

Lowering consumer prices encourages more energy use. It also means consumers buy fewer energy-efficient appliances and factory owners invest less in energy-efficient equipment. Subsidies are also expensive. Production and investment tax credits reduce federal tax collections by about $3 billion a year. That $3 billion must be made up by tax rate increases or spending cuts.

Subsidies have other problems. They pick winners and losers among competing technologies—thus violating what's known as technological neutrality. If our goal is to cut carbon emissions, we should reward technologies that cut emissions regardless of how those technologies work. That will help us meet our goal of cost-effective policy. It sounds straightforward and sensible but policymaking doesn't always work that way. Consider a tax credit for purchasing hybrid cars included in the Energy Policy Act of 2005. The purchaser of a 2009 Ford Escape hybrid, for example, got a $3,000 tax credit. The credit might seem reasonable given that this hybrid got 32 mpg. But the purchaser of a gasoline powered Toyota Corolla that gets 31 mpg—essentially the same as the Ford Escape—gets no tax credit. Why not? Because the Corolla has an internal combustion engine. The hybrid tax credit is picking winners (hybrids) and losers (the internal combustion engine). Supporters of hybrid tax credits argue that the preferential treatment of hybrids is necessary to jumpstart the industry. But if the subsidy were available to the purchasers of all cars that met some aggressive fuel economy standard, perhaps automotive engineers would use their creative ingenuity to soup up the Corolla to get 60 mpg. They'd certainly have every incentive to do that if car buyers could get a tax credit for buying those super-efficient cars. After all, if the credit lowers a new car's purchase price, demand goes up. If demand goes up, automakers can raise prices and reap some of the credit's benefits for themselves.

Another problem with subsidies is that they are wasteful. Consider the federal tax credit to purchase plug-in hybrid cars. The maximum credit is $7,500. I received the $7,500 credit when I purchased my 2016 Chevy Volt. Tesla purchasers also receive this $7,500 federal credit, as do purchasers of the 2017 Mercedes-Benz B-Class electric car. Many of the people purchasing a Tesla or a Mercedes-Benz would likely buy the car regardless of the $7,500 federal tax credit. I would have likely purchased my Volt without the credit, but the extra $7,500 incentive made it a no-brainer.

When tax credits go to people who would have bought the car anyway as well as to those for whom the tax credit "seals the deal," the cost to the federal budget for every car sale motivated by the subsidy goes up. Let's say that half the plug-in hybrid car buyers would have purchased their cars regardless of the subsidy. In that case, the effective cost of the subsidy per vehicle is $15,000. That's because for every car that the $7,500 subsidy induces someone to purchase, an additional $7,500 is paid to someone else who was going to buy the car anyway. If the subsidy induces only one in five people to buy a plug-in hybrid, then the effective cost is five times the subsidy or $37,500—more than the cost of my Chevy Volt!

The problem is that we can't target the subsidy to the prospective car buyer who will be motivated to buy only because of the subsidy. So, every buyer gets it. We don't really know whether 50 percent of the sales would have occurred without the subsidy or 80 percent. For newer innovative technologies, 50 percent may be the right proportion. But for more common technologies, like energy efficient windows and appliances that have been subsidized through the tax code, a rule of thumb that four out of five of the sales would have taken place anyway is more reasonable.[24]

Giving subsidies to people who don't need them simply takes money from taxpayers to help someone buy a car they were going to buy anyway.

And when we're talking about expensive hybrid cars, that subsidy is primarily going to someone with a high income. This is a regressive subsidy. A 2016 analysis of tax returns show that 10 percent of energy tax credits go to the bottom 60 percent of the income distribution while nearly 66 percent go to households in the top 20 percent.[25] Now, maybe this sort of redistribution is an acceptable price to pay to jumpstart new energy-saving technologies, but it is doubtful that many policymakers understand the subtle redistributions at work through regulations like this one.

Subsidies can also interact with regulations in unexpected ways. For example, policies that appear complementary can actually undercut each other. Consider the federal tax credit for plug-in hybrids and electric cars. This credit makes it more attractive to buy electric cars and plug-in hybrids. Meanwhile, automakers are subject to fleet-wide fuel economy standards under the federal CAFE program. If I buy a Chevy Volt in Massachusetts in part because of the federal credit, I've now made it possible for General Motors to sell a gas-guzzling car to someone elsewhere. After all, my purchase of the Volt bumps up the overall fuel economy of the fleet, and General Motors is subject to a nation-wide mandate on the overall fuel economy of the vehicles it sells.[26]

INFORMATION AND VOLUNTARY PROGRAMS

Energy experts and policymakers have increasingly focused on the potential for carefully packaged information to reduce energy consumption. Homeowners in many parts of the country now receive monthly or quarterly reports with their utility bills telling them how their electricity consumption compares to that of their neighbors—a simple bar chart or a graph might show electricity usage over the past year.

The idea behind such reports is that consumers respond to what their neighbors are doing (an example of peer effects). If they see they are using more electricity, they might look for ways to cut consumption. Combine these reports with "smart meters" and consumers have quite a bit of information. Smart meters can provide information wirelessly to utilities on a near-continuous basis. Consumers, in turn, can themselves observe their electricity usage in real time. Perhaps you've heard about *vampire appliances*—appliances that continue to use electricity even though they are not on. You may wonder how much electricity your TV set and TiVo recorder use when you are not watching TV. In many cases, smart meters allow you to track electricity consumption from specific appliances you thought were "off."

Information is a good thing. After all, you can't manage what is not being measured. Generally speaking, more information is better than less (though behavioral economists have pointed out the problems of information overload). The beauty of information programs like the utility bill report is that they are very inexpensive. And if we use less electricity, then we burn less coal and natural gas and carbon emissions fall.

But is this approach a viable climate policy? One study by leading economists shows that programs that provide reports over a two- to four-year period cost less than two cents per kWh saved. Every kWh of electricity saved is a kWh that doesn't have to be generated. If it costs four cents per kWh to produce electricity to sell to a customer, spending two cents to cut demand by a kWh is good for everyone. The program lowers the utility's costs, reduces consumption of fossil fuels, and cuts carbon dioxide emissions. You might be concerned, however, that once you stop sending the reports, people just revert to their old habits. Or that people just ignore them over time. The study shows, however, that the energy-saving habits stick. On a cost effectiveness basis (i.e., the cost per kWh saved), these programs look pretty good.

Cost effectiveness doesn't tell the whole story, though. This study also shows that these programs yield about a 2 percent savings in energy— helpful, but not an approach that is going to get us to a zero-carbon economy! Moreover, other studies have shown that people react differently to these reports. One study shows that information reports are more effective with politically liberal households. That study showed that political conservatives actively disliked the reports and were more prone than liberals to opting out of receiving them. As the authors point out, "What works in California may not work in Lubbock, Texas."[27]

This is not to say that information programs are a bad idea. They can be useful even if they are not going to produce major reductions in carbon pollution. And certain information programs can be very useful for businesses. For example, big companies like ExxonMobil, BP, and AEP, a major energy supplier, have instituted internal carbon pricing to track their carbon emissions and plan for the day when carbon pricing policies are enacted in the United States and more stringent carbon pricing policies are implemented in Europe and elsewhere. Information programs are sometimes paired with internal carbon pricing programs. Microsoft sets an internal carbon tax that it assesses on its business units and uses the revenue to pay for emission reductions elsewhere. While the revenue is useful as a source of funds to invest in carbon-reducing activities, Microsoft sees a more direct benefit. As Tamara DiCaprio, Microsoft's senior director of environmental sustainability, put it, "When we started talking about carbon emissions not in metric tons, but in terms of dollar amount, the business people could understand it. We're all speaking the same language now: What is the cost to my group?" In other words, Microsoft employees respond to price incentives.[28]

There's certainly much more we can do on a voluntary basis. Microsoft, for example, uses some of the revenue from its internal carbon tax to purchase and retire RECs, which means the RECs can't be used by a utility to demonstrate compliance with a state's RPS program. A REC represents one thousand kWhs of renewable electricity generation. If Microsoft buys and retires 100 RECs, an additional 100,000 kWhs of renewable electricity must be generated to create 100 new RECs, since utilities need the RECs to comply with the state's RPS program.

Microsoft also uses some of its carbon tax revenue to buy offsets. A carbon offset is a payment someone can make to a company to reduce emissions to offset the buyer's own emissions. Offsets are popular with eco-conscious travelers. Someone who flies often, for example, can buy carbon offsets to compensate for her flight-related emissions. Carbon offset programs are common. For about $20, you can buy an offset that promises to reduce a ton of carbon dioxide emissions. Let's say you're considering a round trip from Chicago to Paris. That trip generates about three tons of carbon dioxide per passenger.[29] For $60, a traveler can buy offsets for her share of flight-related emissions.

But what are travelers buying with those offset payments? Ideally, the money goes to someone who, in return, will plant trees in the Amazon, for example. For each $20, the landowner would need to plant enough trees to soak up one ton of carbon dioxide over the lifetimes of the trees. For trees planted in the tropics, one offset program estimates that five trees need to be planted to ensure that enough trees live long enough to soak up a ton of emissions.[30] So the $20 offset payment should be enough to plant five trees and provide cultivation and care after planting.

That's the ideal world. But one should approach offsets with a healthy skepticism. The first question to ask is whether there actually is a real farmer who will plant trees in return for that payment. In other words, we need some way to verify that the offset action will take place. We also need to make it enforceable. Otherwise, what's to stop the farmer from taking the $20 but not planting the trees? And even if the farmer does plant the trees, we need to make sure he doesn't come along six months later and plow up the seedlings and plant a crop. All this requires a certification service to monitor and guarantee the quality of the offsets over the life of the trees.[31] That adds to the cost of the program.

Sounds like a lot of work, doesn't it? But that's the easy part! The hard part is determining if you are paying someone to do something they wouldn't have otherwise done. After all, if a farmer was already planning to plant trees on a lot in the Amazon region, the $20 offset payment won't lead to any additional trees being planted. The certification service could ask the farmer, but presumably the farmer will swear up and down that he will only plant trees in return for a payment. Clearly, we need something better than that. Let's say the certification service comes up with a clever way to deal with that problem. There's one last thing to check. Let's say that the offset company arranges to pay the farmer to plant trees in a particular field. Maybe the farmer has another field that he had been planning to return to forest. We need to make sure he doesn't now change his plans for that other field once he's agreed to put the first field into forest.[32] All in all, it is very difficult to know whether carbon offset payments lead to real carbon reductions.

But, ultimately, there's a bigger problem. Can we undertake enough real, verifiable, additional measures that reduce emissions to offset our consumption of fossil fuels for this to be a viable policy approach? After all, global carbon dioxide emissions from burning fossil fuels and producing cement equaled 36 billion metric tons in 2015. Offsets are one form of carbon trading that takes place in voluntary carbon markets. The volume of voluntary trades tracked and recorded in 2015 totaled 84 million metric tons.[33] That's 1 ton of traded carbon dioxide for every 430 tons of emissions. Most of these trades are not offsets designed to compensate for an offset buyers' emissions but rather are payments for carbon-free energy (wind, hydro, etc.). Tree planting itself accounted for only 3 million metric tons of offsets. That's 1 ton of carbon dioxide soaked up by new trees for every 12,000 tons of emissions. We would need many more offsets than are currently available to put a dent in our climate emissions.

How about incentives for zero-carbon electricity? Wind projects accounted for nearly 13 million tons of voluntary carbon trades in 2015. These are transactions where businesses or individuals contract to buy wind-generated electricity. In the Boston area, consumers can contract for 100 percent "nationally sourced renewable electricity" at a price of 10.79 cents per kWh. That's nearly a penny higher than the standard electricity price in Boston.[34] These programs can work in a variety of ways, but one common way is for the extra penny to go to purchase and retire RECs rather than have them be used to satisfy state-level RPS obligations.

Let's say Sam, a Rhode Island resident, buys 100 percent renewable electricity from a company called Green Electricity. Green Electricity might turn around and buy and retire RECs from California's RPS program equal in amount to the electricity Sam consumes. As noted above, when Green Electricity retires a REC, additional renewable electricity will have to be generated in California to create new RECs needed by utilities in that state to comply with its RPS program. Just to be clear, when Sam buys "green" electricity, that doesn't mean that his electricity necessarily comes from a wind or hydro project. All it means is that he has paid a bit extra to incentivize additional renewable electricity production somewhere in the country equal to the electricity kWh he consumes.

Unlike offsets, which may or may not lead to real emission reductions, buying and retiring RECs clearly reduces emissions. But just as tree planting won't solve the climate problem, neither will voluntary green energy purchases. Global voluntary purchases of renewable energy total about 24 million tons of avoided carbon dioxide emissions. That's 1 ton of carbon dioxide emission reductions for every 1,500 tons of emissions. You may sleep better purchasing green electricity, but don't be under any illusion that this is going to solve the climate problem. It's a useful first step, and we should not dismiss its value, but it is not a substitute for strong and effective carbon pricing.

RESEARCH AND DEVELOPMENT

Moving to a zero-carbon economy will require the invention of new zero-carbon energy technologies and that will take significant research and development (R&D). Energy firms spend a lot on R&D but there are considerable barriers that lead to less spending than is optimal. Consider what holds back investment in R&D. For one thing, investors like a quick return on risky investments. But power plants last for a very long time, so investors will have to live with their bets on new technologies for many years. Moreover, the risk of failure for new technologies is high. The new technologies may not perform as expected. The regulatory environment might change in ways that undercut the return on new technologies. Or consumers may not adopt the new technologies. Given the high cost of energy capital, all these risks impede private investment.[35] The failure of private investors to carry out the socially optimal level of R&D provides a strong rationale for government spending on R&D. It's an example of government spending that provides considerable bang for the buck. Unfortunately, politicians don't always appreciate its value.

On the day that Rick Perry testified at his nomination hearing for secretary of energy that "I am committed to the continuation of using brilliant scientists, the private sector and universities in collaborating on finding solutions to [energy] challenges," the Trump Administration released a budget dramatically cutting the department's budget, including zeroing out various R&D programs and departments. The rationale was that the private sector was better suited to carry out these activities.[36]

There are two problems with the logic behind Trump's budget cuts. First, zero-carbon technologies will have a tough time competing with traditional coal, oil, and natural gas so long as fossil fuel prices do not reflect the costs and damages from carbon dioxide emissions. That's where a carbon tax can help level the playing field. By driving up the cost of fossil fuels, it increases the return on new carbon-free technologies and makes it more attractive for firms to do the R&D to develop those technologies.

The other problem with Trump's budget cuts is that the private sector and the federal government spend very little on energy R&D. And much of what they do spend goes to fossil fuels. Energy companies reinvest about 1 percent of revenue into R&D, a share much lower than the 10 to 15 percent invested by pharmaceutical and computer-technology firms.[37] Meanwhile, federal spending on energy R&D was only about $6.4 billion in 2016. That's less than one-half of one percent of what we spend on energy each year. It's also less than we spend on potato and tortilla chips annually![38] Given the inherent risks of making bets on expensive and unproven new technologies that will be with us for decades, it's hard to see why the private sector would make the big R&D bets on zero-carbon energy. It's even harder to see how the small spending on energy R&D from the US government is going to make zero-carbon technologies competitive so long as we continue to ignore the costs of carbon pollution.

Putting a price on emissions is a clean, market-based approach that incentivizes homeowners, factory owners, investors, and millions of people across the country to make informed decisions that align the benefits of our fossil fuel use with its full costs, including damages to people, as well as our economy, infrastructure, and natural resource base. A carbon tax sets a price in a particularly straightforward fashion. As noted at the beginning of this chapter, there's another way to price emissions. That alternative policy is called cap and trade. Let's see how it stacks up against a carbon tax.

CHAPTER 5

Cap and Trade: The Other Way
to Price Pollution

W hen free markets create too much pollution, policymakers can improve welfare by taxing that pollution. Raising the cost of pollution leads firms and individuals to pollute less. But taxes are politically
unpopular. There are other ways, however, to raise the cost of pollution.
President George H. W. Bush may have put his foot in his mouth by
vowing "read my lips: no new taxes," but he was true to his word when
it came to pollution. He signed the Clean Air Act Amendments of 1990
establishing the Acid Rain Program to cut sulfur dioxide pollution from
coal fired power plants. Sulfur dioxide mixes with moisture in the atmosphere to create acid rain that contributes to the acidification of lakes and
ponds in the eastern parts of the country, as well as damage to forests,
buildings, and other infrastructure. As one perhaps symbolically important example, acid rain has eaten away at the marble columns of the
Jefferson Memorial. The National Park Service began restoration work
in 2004 and placed ties around the volutes—the scrolls at the top of the
columns—to prevent their falling off.[1] This illustrates the problem with
externalities. Some power plant in the Midwest burned coal that released
sulfur dioxide into the atmosphere and damaged the Memorial. Not surprisingly, the power plant did not take into consideration the fact that
its coal burning would cause damage to a national monument that would
require costly repairs.

The Acid Rain Program reduced pollution through a clever market-based mechanism called *cap and trade*. Cap and trade systems have three elements. The first is the cap, or the limit on pollution. This is set out in legislation. The Acid Rain Program was designed to cut sulfur dioxide emissions in half over a decade. The cap is enforced by requiring plants regulated under the program to have an allowance for every ton of sulfur dioxide that they emit. Every year, firms that release sulfur dioxide must report their emissions to the government and surrender an allowance for each ton of emissions. If the cap is sixteen million tons of sulfur dioxide in a year, sixteen million allowances are created. The cap cuts pollution to a level below what emissions would otherwise be.[2]

The second component is a process to allocate the allowances. The government could sell them, auction them, or give them away according to some formula.[3] The last component of the system is a provision for trading, in which producers can buy and sell allowances. Plants that reduce emissions below the number of allowances they have can sell their extra allowances on the open market. Meanwhile, plants wishing to pollute beyond the allowances they have in hand must buy more. Creating allowances and distributing them in effect creates property rights in emissions. People often object to buying and selling allowances on the grounds that government is granting a "right to pollute." But any program to limit pollution generally allows some amount of pollution. The question is not whether firms have a "right to pollute," but rather what is the most cost-effective way to reduce pollution to the level that society deems appropriate.[4]

The "trade" in cap and trade is the novel element of the program, as it creates a market for the buying and selling of rights to emit sulfur dioxide. The market establishes a price on emissions that creates the incentive to reduce pollution. If a firm wants to burn high-sulfur coal in its power plant, it will need allowances to cover its sulfur dioxide emissions. If it doesn't have allowances on hand, it will have to buy them. That's a cost the firm can avoid by cutting its pollution. Perhaps the plant can switch to low-sulfur coal or invest in a scrubber to capture the sulfur dioxide. Any action that cuts pollution at a cost per ton less than the price of an allowance is worth doing. The allowance trading creates a market that puts a clear price on the emissions: if a sulfur dioxide allowance is going for $300 a ton of sulfur dioxide in a sulfur dioxide trading market, $300 per ton is the price of emissions to the firm.

But what if the firm already has allowances on hand, perhaps allowances that were given to them by the government for free as part of the allocation process? Won't that mean the firm can continue to pollute for free? No. Even if firms get allowances for free, it will be costly to release sulfur dioxide pollution. After all, if a firm doesn't use its allowances, it could sell them and bank the revenue. This is an example of *opportunity cost*, the highest alternative value of a resource used by a firm. Here the resource is the allowance. The firm can "use it up" by releasing sulfur dioxide into the atmosphere and surrender the allowance to the government. The allowance is valuable as it allows the firm to release a ton of sulfur dioxide into the atmosphere. But what's the alternative? The firm could sell the allowance at the market price of $300. That's the "highest alternative value" and represents the opportunity cost of using the allowance. By taking actions to reduce its pollution (perhaps by switching from a high- to a low-sulfur coal), the firm could have sold some of its allowances. Every ton of sulfur dioxide emissions is costly, then, as it either requires the firm to buy an allowance or use one that it otherwise could have sold.

In the US Acid Rain Program, emissions trading put a price on pollution and was a cost-effective way to reduce pollution. The program's environmental goal was met: sulfur dioxide emissions were cut in half over the decade as the program intended. And it saved money while cutting pollution. Studies of the Acid Rain Program have shown that the cap and trade mechanism cut the cost of reducing pollution by more than half compared to well-designed command and control regulations.[5]

Why does emissions trading cut costs relative to regulation? Let's say a regulation requires two power plants each to reduce sulfur dioxide emissions by 100 tons a month. It might cost one company $340 for each ton it reduces. Meanwhile, the other plant can reduce sulfur dioxide emissions at a cost of $200 a ton. This cost difference—$340 for one plant and $200 for another—creates an opportunity for a deal that can benefit both. Absent trading, the cost of this regulation to the two firms is $54,000 ($340 × 100 + $200 × 100). But if the firm with higher costs could pay the other firm to cut its sulfur dioxide emissions further than the regulation requires, the overall cost falls. If the lower-cost firm cuts emissions by 200 tons a month so that the higher cost firm needn't cut emissions, total emissions fall by the amount required by the regulation. But now the cost is $40,000 ($200 × 200). As long as the cost of cutting pollution differs across firms, there is always a way to reallocate the responsibility to cut pollution in a way that provides the same amount of pollution reduction but at lower cost. In other words, we can find a more cost-effective way to cut pollution.

A cap and trade program facilitates those cost-effective trades in a simple and transparent way. Imagine each of the two plants has been allocated 100 fewer allowances in a cap and trade program than its current monthly emissions. Absent buying or selling allowances, the two firms must cut emissions just as much as a regulation that simply mandated a 100 ton per plant reduction. The cap achieves the same environmental outcome as the regulation. But that's where the similarity between the command and control regulation and a cap and trade program ends.

Under the cap and trade program, each plant manager now has a decision to make. He either has to reduce emissions (switch to a lower-sulfur coal or install a scrubber) or buy 100 allowances so his plant can continue to operate as it has been operating. If the manager of the high-cost plant could buy 100 allowances at $300 per allowance, he would save his company some money. After all, paying someone $300 for an allowance is cheaper than paying $340 to reduce a ton of sulfur dioxide emissions. A cost-minimizing plant manager at this high-cost plant would willingly pay $30,000 to buy 100 allowances so it could continue operating as it had been. Paying $30,000 to purchase allowances is cheaper than spending $34,000 a month to reduce emissions.

Meanwhile, the manager of the low-cost polluting plant would be willing to sell some of its plant's allowances for $300 each. That manager can cut its sulfur dioxide emissions at a cost of $200 a ton. Selling 100 allowances yields $30,000 in revenue that more than covers the $20,000 in costs to cuts its emissions by an additional 100 tons. If the two plant managers could get together and make a deal to exchange allowances, they can both cut their overall costs.

In practice, these trades are made on markets. The two plant managers would get on their computers and log into one of the websites for companies that facilitate trading allowances among electric utilities. Companies such as Cantor Fitzgerald serve as brokers matching buyers and sellers, determining market clearing prices, and facilitating trades for modest fees. This also allow firms to maintain their anonymity. The high-cost firm buys allowances and the low-cost firm sells allowances.

This may sound reminiscent of the trading that Ronald Coase imagined for the nineteenth-century London neighbors, Sturges and Bridgman, once property rights were established in the case of the pounding pestles and the doctor's office. The underlying principle is the same. So long as costs differ between two parties, there are potential gains from trade. In the bargaining world that Coase imagined, individuals would have strong incentives to seek out potential trade opportunities. For the Acid Rain Program, brokers act as middlemen and cut the transaction costs of finding possible trading partners.

While the idea of a pollution tax goes back over a hundred years, the idea of a cap and trade system is much newer. It is attributed to the late

Canadian economist John Dales who sketched out the idea in his 1968 book *Pollution, Property, and Prices.* Dales, a professor of economics at the University of Toronto, had no great aspirations to influence public policy. According to his son, Dales "was a man who lived in his mind more than anywhere else." Dales's book did not make much of a stir outside, or even inside, the profession. A few years after the book's publication, the Canadian professor took early retirement and turned to "bird watching and plant watching," as his son recalled.[6] It wasn't until the 1990s when the Acid Rain Program was established and it became clear that cap and trade had broad potential to address pollution that people began to take note of Dales's now out-of-print book. With its reissue in 2002, Dales's reputation was assured.

CAP AND TRADE AROUND THE WORLD

The Acid Rain Program was the first large-scale cap and trade program to reduce pollution. In the United States, subsequent cap and trade programs were instituted to reduce nitrogen oxide and sulfur dioxide emissions in Southern California, to reduce nitrogen oxide emissions from power plants in the Eastern United States, and to reduce carbon dioxide emissions in Eastern power plants and in California. Internationally, the EU's Emission Trading System (ETS) is the largest carbon dioxide cap and trade system in the world; it was developed as the tool for the EU to meet its obligation under the 1997 Kyoto Protocol to reduce greenhouse gas emissions. Cap and trade systems to reduce greenhouse gas emissions have also been implemented in Ontario, Quebec, and South Korea. China is in the process of implementing a national cap and trade system that builds on a set of pilot cap and trade programs in various cities and provinces that began in 2013.[7]

Cap and trade was not the EU's first choice to control emissions. A prior effort in the early 1990s to institute an EU-wide carbon tax foundered because EU rules require any fiscal instrument—including a tax—to be unanimously approved by the member countries. Not all member countries supported an EU-wide carbon tax, so this approach had to be abandoned. A cap and trade system, in contrast, is considered a regulatory instrument under EU rules, requiring only majority approval of member countries. The unique institutional framework of the EU led it to adopt a cap and trade system as opposed to any inherent preference for cap and trade. Ironically, it was the United States that pushed forcefully for allowance trading in the Kyoto Protocol negotiations despite strong EU opposition. Having pushed for the inclusion of cap and trade as permissible under Kyoto over the resistant EU, the United States subsequently failed to ratify the Kyoto Protocol. The EU, meanwhile, embraced cap and trade and established the first multi-national trading program in carbon pollution.[8]

In the United States, nine Northeast and Middle Atlantic states established the Regional Greenhouse Gas Initiative (RGGI), a cap and trade system for greenhouse gas emissions.[9] Beginning in 2009, RGGI capped carbon emissions from the electric power sector. The annual cap started at 188 million tons of carbon dioxide and has gradually been tightened; the cap for 2020 is 78 million tons.[10] Nearly $3 billion has been raised from allowance auctions, with the proceeds designated to fund energy efficiency and renewable investments in the participating states. Power plants covered under the RGGI program account for roughly one-quarter of greenhouse gas emissions in the region.

California established a cap and trade system in 2012 as part of a statewide initiative to reduce greenhouse gas emissions by 80 percent from 1990 levels by 2050. Initially covering electricity and emissions from large manufacturers, it was expanded to cover motor fuels in 2015 so that 85 percent of California's emissions were brought under the cap. The initial program was designed to reduce emissions by 2020 to 1990 emission levels. The law was renewed in 2017 with a goal of reducing emissions by 2030 to 40 percent below 1990 levels.[11]

CHOOSING BETWEEN TAXES AND CAP AND TRADE SYSTEMS

While economists agree that either a tax or cap and trade is better than more traditional regulation, the agreement ends there. In one sense, these two approaches are the yin and yang of pollution policy. A tax sets a price on pollution and lets the market determine how much pollution occurs in response to that price. The higher the price, the lower the pollution levels. A cap and trade system sets the allowable amount of pollution and lets the market determine the price of that pollution through allowance trading. In a world with no unexpected shocks that change the demand for allowances or the costs of reducing emissions, the economic impacts of the two instruments are identical. If a $300 per ton tax on sulfur dioxide emissions cuts sulfur dioxide emissions to ten million tons a year, then a cap and trade system that issued allowances for ten million tons a year of emissions would have a market clearing price of $300 a ton.

In the real world, however, the two approaches differ in a number of important ways, in particular with regard to *uncertainty and price* volatility, administrative complexity, distributional concerns, and adverse policy interactions. Let's take each one in turn.

Uncertainty matters given what the two instruments control. A tax controls the price and emissions adjust in response to the price signal. Cap and trade sets a limit on emissions, and the price is determined through allowance trading that balances demand and supply. What is controlled matters in a world with uncertainty. By uncertainty, I mean unanticipated events such as recessions, housing market crashes, and train derailments, among many other things.

Train derailments, you may ask? Nearly half of US coal comes from the Powder River Basin (PRB) in Wyoming and Montana. PRB coal is mined in massive open pit mines and is particularly desirable because it has a very low sulfur content relative to Eastern coal. Nearly all of the PRB coal is transported by rail, much of it along the Joint Line, a 103-mile-long railroad owned by the Burlington Northern Santa Fe (BNSF) and Union Pacific railroads. In 2005, these two railroads transported all the coal out of the PRB. In the mid-2000s, the Joint Line was the busiest freight railroad in the world, with 130 trains a day going into or out of the PRB area. A loaded coal train can weigh 19,000 tons or more and stretch for well over a mile in length.

A mile-long train full of coal can blow off a good deal of coal dust, and railroads work hard to keep caked and hardened dust from accumulating on the tracks. This is a major problem for the Joint Line given the traffic density going in and out of the PRB. In April and May 2005, heavy rain saturated the stone bed under the railroad ties and mixed with heavy accumulations of coal dust. On May 14, the buildup of coal dust caused fifteen cars on a BNSF train to jump the track just north of Bill, Wyoming, damaging the track. The next day, a Union Pacific coal train derailed twenty-eight cars just a few miles north of the first derailment. With a third derailment that day, the Joint Line had to be shut down, cutting coal shipments out of the PRB along the Joint Line by 15 percent. It took a year for repairs to be completed and PRB coal deliveries to return to their prior levels.

Meanwhile, the demand for coal to produce electricity hadn't diminished and Eastern coal took up the slack. This shift from low-sulfur PRB coal to high-sulfur Eastern coal increased demand for sulfur dioxide allowances, driving up prices by 13 percent in one month. The Wyoming train derailment is an example of the sort of unexpected event that causes the price of allowances to fluctuate. Hurricanes are another type of unexpected event that can affect allowance prices. Hurricanes Katrina and Rita hit in August and September 2005 and knocked out a number of natural gas processing plants. Coal fired power plants that might not be operated in early fall were needed in 2005 to replace lost capacity due to temporary shortfalls in natural gas.[12] Demand for Eastern high-sulfur coal rose as a result, driving allowance prices up further—they had doubled by the end of the year.

These sorts of unexpected events cause the price of allowances in a cap and trade program to jump around and create price volatility. The Acid Rain Program illustrates the potential for price volatility. Allowance prices have fluctuated anywhere from zero to $1,200 just in the five years between 2005 and 2010. Price fluctuations are not limited to the EPA's Acid Rain Program. Allowance prices in the EU's ETS fell by one-third in one week in April 2006 and a further 20 percent over the next month upon release of information that initial allowance allocations had been too generous.[13]

Price uncertainty makes planning difficult for firms that have to comply with the program. It also adds to their costs. Firms can get caught short and have to buy allowances when prices unexpectedly spike. They also have to spend more time and money managing and monitoring their allowance holdings to avoid the risk of getting caught short, adding even more to their costs of compliance. This variability in allowance prices creates uncertainty for firms and complicates their strategic planning. Utility executives, automakers, and big industry have to make billion-dollar bets on investments in the coming decades, investments that will last, in many cases, into the next century. Their planning is made a great deal easier if they know the price of carbon (and its impact on energy prices) than if they have to guess the price from a schedule of emission caps over time. In a cap and trade system, that price will be determined by market forces and there can be considerable price uncertainty. With a tax, in contrast, the tax rate is the price. The tax rate and rules for how it will change over time are set out in the legislation that establishes the tax. That removes a great deal of price uncertainty.[14]

With a cap and trade program, the price is going to vary. There's no way around that. But maybe that's an acceptable trade-off for the supposed certainty that the program provides over the actual pollution that will be allowed. "After all," cap and trade proponents might argue, "What we care about is controlling pollution, right?"

Well, not exactly. We should care about getting the right level of pollution. Whatever type of carbon price is in place—a tax or cap and trade—we want to balance the costs of reducing pollution against the benefits of the readily available, relatively inexpensive, fossil fuels around which we have built our economy. Moreover, no cap and trade system has a hard-and-fast cap on emissions; the claim that this policy provides certainty over the level of pollution is simply not correct. Political concerns about price volatility have led to various features to limit price fluctuations, many of which serve to loosen the cap. California's program is instructive.

The California program has a design feature called a *price collar* to prevent prices from falling too low or rising too high. In other words, it keeps prices within a band. The point of a price collar is to reduce the uncertainty over future allowance prices while still allowing the market for allowances to operate. A floor on allowance prices is maintained by the state setting a minimum acceptable bid for allowances in California's quarterly allowance auctions. If the minimum acceptable bid is $13, for example, then no one would buy allowances in the auction if they can buy allowances from others for less than $13. Pretty quickly, the supply of existing allowances for sale at a price below the floor price would get snapped up and used; anyone needing allowances subsequently would buy in the auction at the floor price (or higher).

At the other end of the price band, the state stands ready to sell additional allowances at a given price and so prevents the price from exceeding an upper limit.[15] The price ceiling acts as a *safety valve* to keep the price from sky-rocketing if demand unexpectedly far outstrips supply. It works in the following way. If the safety-valve price were $50, for example, then whenever demand for allowances rose enough to drive the market price of allowances above $50, anyone needing allowances could simply turn to the government and buy them at $50 apiece. If there were no limits on the number of allowances that the government would sell at that price, then the cap and trade program acts exactly like a $50 per ton carbon tax when the price ceiling is hit.

Cap and trade systems with a safety valve are often referred to as *hybrid systems*. They operate like a cap and trade system at lower prices and like a carbon tax at higher prices. Both the California and RGGI cap and trade systems have a safety valve in the form of the cost-containment price (over $50 in California's case and $10 in RGGI's case).[16]

When there is a safety valve to prevent the price from rising higher than is politically acceptable, then we don't really have a firm emissions cap. The government might limit the amount of allowances it will sell at this price by taking them from a special reserve of allowances that have been set aside just for this purpose. Or they might simply borrow allowances from future allocations to hold constant the allocation over a longer time frame.

But even in the case where the allowance allocation is held constant over a twenty-year period, for example, and the safety valve is only borrowing allowances from a future allocation, we still can't say that the emissions cap is firm. If prices rise high enough, Congress serves as the ultimate safety valve. In the face of pressure from consumers and businesses facing high energy costs because of a very strict cap, Congress can legislate to loosen the cap. Whether this would be a smart thing to do is beside the point. The supposed emissions certainty with a cap and trade system is to a large extent overstated.[17]

The second difference between the two policy instruments is in administrative complexity. The United States has a well-developed tax collection system, including systems in place to collect taxes on most fossil fuels. A cap and trade system, in contrast, requires an entirely new administrative structure to create allowances, track them, hold auctions or otherwise distribute them, and develop rules to avoid fraud and abuse. Fraud is a particularly significant problem in a system that is creating brand new assets (emission allowances) worth billions of dollars. This is not just a theoretical concern. In January 2011, the EU had to suspend trading in allowances when $9 million-worth of allowances were stolen from an account in the Czech Republic. EU commissioners noted hackers had also broken into accounts in Austria, Poland, Greece, and Estonia and as much as $40 million-worth of allowances were stolen.[18] While tax evasion is certainly a potential problem, the United States has a very strong culture of tax compliance. The risk of cybertheft from electronic registries in a cap and trade system is likely to present a greater problem than the risk of tax evasion in a carbon tax.

Here's another consideration. Allowances created in a cap and trade program are valuable assets that policymakers must decide how to distribute. The Acid Rain Program created roughly ten million allowances in the year 2000, for example. With an average spot price of just under $145 a ton, the allowances disbursed that year were worth $1.45 billion. In a cap and trade program, the government can give away the allowances or sell them. Having nearly $1.5 billion of allowances to disburse to the industry each year can be extremely helpful for easing opposition to an environmental regulation. The Acid Rain Program, for example, distributed allowances for free to owners of coal fired power plants based on their historic coal use. This certainly eased opposition to the program. Using allowances to overcome opposition was certainly behind the complex allocation process in the American Clean Energy and Security Bill (HR 2454), the cap and trade bill passed by the House of Representatives in 2009 that ultimately failed in the Senate. A free allowance allocation can help grease the political wheels and contribute to passage of cap and trade legislation. But this is very expensive grease! The Congressional Budget Office estimated that the value of the free allowances in that bill would be nearly $700 billion over a ten-year period.[19]

Giving allowances to polluting firms for free raises important distributional questions. Giving firms $700 billion in free allowances has the same effect on their bottom line as giving them cash. The result is a windfall for shareholders: profits and share prices go up. This is what happened in Europe when the EU set up its carbon dioxide cap and trade program and gave allowances to the firms that were subject to the cap.[20] Whether this is fair is a matter of debate. But the very complexity of the cap and trade approach means that the public didn't really understand the massive transfer taking place in the EU's ETS or that would have taken place had the US cap and trade legislation gone into effect.

The final difference between a carbon tax and a cap and trade system is the potential for adverse policy interactions that can work against our goal of reducing emissions. This is a big problem for cap and trade systems. Let's say a cap is set with a goal of realizing allowance prices of $40 a ton. That price target would contribute to driving innovation and the development of new carbon-free technologies that we'll need to get to a zero-carbon economy by the end of the century. Investors won't place risky bets on new energy technologies that reduce emissions unless they can be confident that there's a good chance of earning a high return on that investment. The higher the carbon price, the more confident they can be that their investment will earn a return that will pay for the risk they'll be taking. That's because a high carbon price drives up the cost of natural gas, petroleum, and coal, and can make a new zero-carbon investment competitive in the market even at a cost that is high enough to repay the investor for the risks they took in underwriting a new and unproven technology.

Let's assume the demand for allowances is such that the cap would indeed lead to a $40 per ton allowance price. So far, so good. But then, suppose policymakers decide to tighten the renewable portfolio standard and require a higher percentage of renewable electricity. This is going to reduce the demand for allowances and drive allowance prices down in the cap and trade program.

This is precisely what has happened in the major cap and trade programs. They have all struggled to set a price at a level that drives significant reductions in carbon pollution. Allowances in the EU's ETS, covering the electricity sector and energy-intensive industry, traded at around $16 a ton of carbon dioxide in mid-2018. Even this price belies the struggle to maintain prices in the double digits. Since trading began in 2013 for the current phase of the ETS (2013–2020), prices have generally ranged between $3.60 and $8 per ton and only broke through the $10 barrier in March 2018. Prices in the earlier trading period (2008–2012) were not much higher. When allowances for this commitment period were first issued, prices rose to nearly $36 a ton but quickly fell by about half and subsequently drifted down.[21]

The EU is not alone in struggling to maintain a robust carbon price through its trading system. A similar problem confronts the RGGI through which nine states committed to capping carbon emissions from the electric power sector beginning in 2009. Proceeds from the emissions allowance auctions are designated to fund energy efficiency and renewable investments in the participating states. Power plants covered under the RGGI program account for roughly one-quarter of greenhouse gas emissions in the region. Allowance prices have ranged between $1.86 and $7.50 a ton. The March 2018 auction had a clearing price of $3.79 a ton. While the program has generated over $2.7 billion since its inception for participating state governments, it is unlikely that the carbon price has contributed to a significant reduction in electricity-sector emissions that would not have occurred in the absence of the program.[22] Moving to the West coast, California's cap and trade program has tried to address the pricing problem that has plagued the EU and RGGI. They've had limited success. The settlement price for allowances in the November 2017 auction was $15.06 a ton.[23]

California has tried to address the dual problem of price volatility and low prices with its price collar. A recent study by a group of California researchers predicts that the system is likely to be at the floor almost 95 percent of the time.[24] Ironically, whenever the allowance price is at the floor or the ceiling, a cap and trade system with a price collar effectively acts as a carbon tax. Firms can emit as much as they want at the fixed price (either floor or ceiling) per ton of emissions, which is exactly what a carbon tax allows. If these researchers are right, California's cap and trade system essentially operates like a carbon tax—albeit a carbon tax with a low effective tax rate.

These programs are not unique in experiencing low allowance prices. The World Bank's 2017 annual review of carbon pricing tracks carbon pricing in roughly forty countries and twenty cities, states, and regions. The highest carbon price among the cap and trade systems surveyed in the review is about $18 a ton. In contrast, five countries have carbon tax rates of at least $50 a ton with Sweden leading the group at $140.

One reason allowance prices persist at low levels is human nature. Politicians like to *do things*. When they see a problem, they want to enact a policy to fix it. So, you see complementary policies put in place to reduce emissions. These policies include subsidies for renewable electricity generation, energy efficiency programs, and motor vehicle fuel economy standards, to name a few. These complementary policies reduce emissions and so reduce demand for allowances in a cap and trade program. That in turn depresses allowance prices. While helpful for reducing the impact on consumers, this policy interaction creates two problems. First, persistently low allowance prices undercut the private sector's incentive to innovate and bring to market low- and zero-carbon technologies. Second, the policy interaction actually undercuts the complementary policy. Consider a renewable portfolio standard implemented in Spain that requires a percentage of Spanish electricity be generated from renewable sources. Since the electricity sector is part of the EU-wide cap and trade system, any reduction in demand for coal or natural gas fired electricity in Spain simply loosens the overall EU cap on emissions and allows firms elsewhere in Europe to burn fossil fuels. This is exactly the problem discussed in chapter 4 where a policy to support the sale of electric cars simply relaxes the fuel economy constraints under CAFE and allows automakers to sell additional gas guzzling cars and trucks every time they sell an electric vehicle.[25] Complementary policies are not a problem for a carbon tax. Layering an additional policy on top of a tax does not affect the tax's price signal and incentive to reduce emissions.

Of course, if the politics are such that a carbon tax can't be enacted, then a low cap and trade price beats a carbon tax rate of zero! But in the grand scheme, if the best we can do with cap and trade systems is a carbon price less than $15 a ton, then we will be hard pressed to support the innovation we'll need to move to a zero-carbon economy in this century. If anything, a low carbon price might lull us into thinking we are "dealing" with the climate problem when at best we are tinkering at the edges.

Getting the right price signal will drive innovation, encourage energy-saving investments by millions of households and firms, and lower emissions. If we use a tax to set the price, setting a price at a high enough level to get all these benefits will also raise a lot of revenue. We need a framework for thinking about how best to return that revenue to US households and firms. That is addressed in the next chapter.

CHAPTER 6

What to Do with $200 Billion: Give It Back

L et's suppose that Congress and the president enact a national carbon tax. With a tax rate starting at $50 per ton of carbon dioxide, the federal government could take in roughly $200 billion in the first year alone. Now, $200 billion is a lot of money—about $625 per person in the United States or $2,500 for a family of four. With that much money at stake, there's an obvious question: What should we do with it?

Broadly speaking, there are two things the federal government can do with the money: spend it on new programs or give it back.[1] Giving it back could be done by cutting taxes or perhaps by writing checks to families. This chapter focuses on ways to give the money back—revenue neutral reforms—rather than on new spending programs, for a couple of reasons. First, it is important to separate the issue of a carbon tax from debates over how large the federal budget should be. Carbon taxes are politically controversial enough; it would be better not to entangle the issue with the even more fraught question of federal spending. The second reason is that tying the tax to a particular spending program is not good budgeting practice. If the spending program is worthwhile, Congress should fund it whether we have a carbon tax or not.[2]

We need a framework for considering how carbon tax revenue should be returned to families. There are two key criteria for evaluating any new tax (setting aside our goal of reducing carbon pollution). The first is *efficiency*. Taxes can be a drag on the economy by discouraging firms from hiring or investing in new equipment that boosts worker productivity. While taxes are necessary to fund important public services, different taxes are more efficient than other taxes (i.e., they discourage productive activity less than other taxes). Lowering taxes on businesses is a way to reduce that drag and increase efficiency. Maybe we can use the carbon tax revenue to lower other taxes in a way that makes our economy work better and grow faster. The second criterion is *fairness*. The carbon tax revenue could be returned to the public with more of the proceeds going to those most in need. Your reaction might be, "Great. Let's improve efficiency while enhancing fairness." Alas, these two goals generally work at cross purposes. Broadly speaking, there is a tension between using carbon tax revenue to improve the tax code's efficiency and using it to enhance its fairness. Let's explore these criteria a bit.

WHAT IS AN EFFICIENT TAX?

In general, taxes are inefficient as they lead to less employment and investment which, in turn, slows economic growth. Let's say a firm sees a business opportunity that could boost profits. To take advantage of the opportunity, it needs to hire some workers. Maybe each new worker adds $150 a day of value to the company through the increased production of the company's product. Now consider someone not currently employed. That person may be tending to children at home, volunteering at his kids' school, and doing housework. A company has to pay this person enough to make it worthwhile to add a job to his other responsibilities and, perhaps, hire help to offload some work at home. Let's imagine the person would be willing to accept $130 a day to take the job. This looks like a win-win. If the worker were paid $140 per day, the worker is better off and the company's profits would go up.

Here's where taxes create economic drag. Let's say we have a 20 percent income tax to finance necessary government spending. The worker earns $140 each day but must pay $28 in taxes, leaving him with $112. Now it's not worth it to the worker to take the job and the business growth potential goes unfulfilled. While this is a simplistic example, the problem is very real. Because an income tax is a tax on various forms of income (labor, dividend, interest, and small business income), it discourages new hiring, savings and investment, and business expansions.

Now, it is possible to design a tax that doesn't discourage workers from taking jobs or firms from investing in new business opportunities. We could levy a *head tax*. This is an equal tax on every person in the United States. A head tax doesn't depend on income. If it doesn't depend on income, it won't discourage people from taking jobs or working harder to earn more money. Nor will it discourage business investment.

But there's a problem with a head tax. We would need to collect nearly $4,500 per person to replace the individual income tax.[3] That works out to $18,000 for a family of four. While that tax would be a pretty good deal for a family earning $200,000 a year, it's an incredibly onerous tax for a family earning $20,000 a year. In fact, anyone earning the federal minimum wage ($7.25 an hour) would have to work nearly fifty hours a week just to cover the head tax for a family of four.

You could imagine designing a more equitable head tax that taxes people according to their ability. But how do you measure ability? Our income tax essentially uses income as a proxy for ability. But we already see that the income tax discourages people from working. Maybe we could use education as a proxy for ability. But that will just discourage people from getting more education. Perhaps you could mandate that everyone take an IQ test and then set the head tax based on their performance on the test. You could bet that people would, all of a sudden, show extremely low IQs on this test! Simply put, there is no good measure of ability. Income is a good proxy but taxing income discourages work effort and job seeking.

All this is to say that there is an essential tension between efficiency and fairness. The most efficient tax is a head tax. But head taxes are inherently unfair. Since fairness is clearly an important tax design consideration, it's worth understanding how fairness is measured.

DEFINING FAIRNESS IN TAXATION

Fairness is an ethical or political concept, and highly subjective. One measure of fairness focuses on the *progressivity* of a tax. Progressivity considers how the average tax rate differs across income groups. The average tax rate is the burden of the tax divided by income. If someone earns $80,000 a year and has an annual tax burden of $8,000, then her average tax rate is 10 percent. A tax is *progressive* if the burden of a tax is a higher share of income for a rich person than for a poor person. A tax is *proportional* if the average tax rate is constant across income. Finally, a tax is *regressive* if the average tax rate goes down as income rises. The argument that energy taxes are not fair since they hit the poor harder than the rich is another way of saying that the tax is regressive.

While it's hard to find anyone who will argue that regressivity is a desirable feature in taxation, there is greater disagreement on whether it is more fair for a tax to be proportional or progressive. Proponents of a proportional tax say it's fair that everyone face the same burden per dollar of income. Someone earning $100,000 will have ten times the burden of someone earning $10,000, but their average burden is the same. Supporters of a progressive tax, on the other hand, argue that progressivity helps address income inequality by shifting resources to those for whom the value of additional income is greater. Moreover, the loss of $1,000, say, to Facebook CEO Mark Zuckerberg is trivial compared to the benefit that $1,000 may provide to someone earning $9,000 a year.[4]

If one way of evaluating fairness is against income, another way to think about fairness in the context of a carbon tax is to make the tax burden proportional to one's carbon footprint—the amount of greenhouse gas emissions induced from your activities and the goods and services you consume. This is reminiscent of the *polluter pays* principle, which argues that whoever produces pollution should bear its cost.[5] A carbon tax on fossil fuel producers would be consistent with the polluter pays principle. If the tax is fully passed forward to consumers in the form of higher prices, then everyone's tax burden will be proportional to their carbon footprint. But it's possible that the tax might fall in part on workers in carbon-intensive sectors (e.g., coal mining, oil and gas production, steel and aluminum manufacture) in the form of lower wages or lost jobs. If we want the tax to fall on people based on their consumption of fossil fuels, we would need to figure out a way to compensate workers in industries disproportionately impacted by the tax. Measuring the impact, however, for purposes of compensation is not straightforward. Lots of factors affect wages, and disentangling the carbon tax's impact would be extremely difficult.[6]

Another concept of fairness might be to relate the tax burden to the benefits of reducing emissions. If homeowners in coastal communities are likely to experience more flooding and severe weather from climate change, then, based on this concept, the carbon tax would be fair if the burden falls on those coastal homeowners in proportion to the risk reduction they enjoy from the carbon tax's impact on reducing greenhouse gas emissions. On its face, this seems like a plausible metric: people pay in relation to the benefits they receive. But this metric is as thorny as any other fairness doctrine. First, one might object that polluters should be paying to reduce pollution, not those being damaged by the pollution. A second objection is that the poor are among those who stand to suffer the most from climate change. Low-income families tend to live in areas more likely to suffer damages from extreme weather, and in lower-quality housing, and so suffer more from higher-intensity storms. They are also less likely to have funds for capital investments to adapt to higher temperatures (e.g., air conditioning). It hardly seems fair to tax poor people disproportionately just because they live in harm's way.

Many other elements may play into people's concepts of fairness. Is it fair that a carbon tax is more burdensome on Midwesterners who have enjoyed low-cost coal-fired electricity for years than on Northeasterners who had limited access to coal and have relied more on natural gas and hydropower? How about residents of sparsely populated Western states versus residents of densely populated Eastern states? The former drive more and would be hit harder by a carbon tax's impact on gasoline prices. But keep the following in mind when considering if a carbon tax is fair or unfair on a geographic basis. Residents of Southern and Midwestern states have the most to gain from a carbon tax in avoided damages. One study finds that these states suffer the greatest losses from climate change, in contrast to Northern and Western states that could actually benefit from climate change.[7]

While geographic and other factors are important, policymakers place considerable emphasis on understanding and addressing the burden of a tax on families at different income levels. In fact, one of the arguments often put forward by opponents of energy taxes (like a carbon tax) is that it is regressive: low income households spend a higher fraction of their income on energy than do higher income households and so, it is argued, any tax on energy disproportionately burdens them. That turns out to be incorrect and to understand why, we need to consider how to measure the burden of a tax.

WHO BEARS THE BURDEN OF A TAX ANYWAY?

To say that someone is *burdened* by a tax is to say they can't afford to purchase things they could afford before the tax was enacted. That could be because the goods and services they previously bought are now more expensive or because their income has fallen. The latter could happen if a firm cuts wages or dividends in response to a new tax. A key point is that changes in prices or incomes determine the burden of a tax, not who collects the tax and remits it to the government. Here's a simple example to illustrate this point.

Let's imagine a carbon tax is adopted with a rate of $50 per ton of carbon dioxide. Based on the carbon content of gasoline, a $50 per ton carbon tax works out to about $0.45 per gallon. Assume that the wholesaler selling gasoline to a local service station is responsible for paying the tax to the federal government. Who bears the burden of the carbon tax on gasoline?

That depends. One possibility is that the wholesaler raises the price of a gallon of gasoline by $0.45 and the service station, in turn, raises the price at the pump by the same amount. In that case, the consumer bears the burden of the tax and has to either cut back gasoline consumption or spend less on something else to pay for the now more expensive gas.

If that is the outcome, the person who bears the burden of the tax (the driver) is not the person who is responsible for paying the tax to the government (the wholesaler). Economists use the term *tax incidence* to describe the burden of a tax. They also distinguish between the *statutory incidence* of a tax (who is responsible for remitting the tax to the government) and the *economic incidence* (who is made worse off by the tax). If the price of a good goes up by the full amount of the tax, then the customer bears the economic incidence of the tax while the wholesaler bears the statutory incidence. When talking about a tax's fairness, we need to focus on the economic incidence. And that is determined by what happens to prices.

One possible outcome is that the wholesaler and, in turn, the service station raise the price of gasoline by the full amount of the tax—forty-five cents. But that's not the only possible outcome. The station owner may be in a bind. If he raises prices too much, his sales may fall as people respond to the price increase by seeking alternatives to driving: perhaps they can take the commuter train to work; walk to local shops; or get around by bicycle. In the long run, drivers can buy an electric car and give up gas altogether. If enough people alter their behavior and cut back on their gas purchases, the owner may find he can't afford to raise his price by the amount of the tax.

If the price at the pump doesn't go up, then customers don't bear any burden of the tax. Who, then, does? You might say the service station owner. But, facing higher costs (including the tax) and flat revenue, the station owner has to make a decision: either bear the burden of the tax himself in the form of lower profits, or pass the burden on to his workers by paying them less or employing fewer of them. The burden could also be shared between the owner and the workers.

These are two extreme examples: the price goes up by the full amount of the tax or it doesn't go up at all. If drivers can easily find alternatives to getting around or trade in their gas guzzler for a more fuel-efficient car, then it will be hard for the service station owner to pass the tax on to consumers. This is an example of a situation where a small price increase leads to a big drop in demand. If, on the other hand, local public transit is lousy and there aren't many shops in easy walking distance, then it's more likely the service station can safely raise the price of gasoline without needing to fear a big drop in demand. Now the demand for gasoline is not very responsive to the price increase. It's also possible for the price to go up by less than the full tax. In general, the ability of a business to pass a tax on to its customers in the form of a price increase depends on the nature of supply and demand. The more responsive consumers are to price increases, the less the business can raise its prices and pass the tax on to its customers. Similarly, if service station workers have lots of other job opportunities, it will be difficult for the owner to pass the tax on to his employees since they can find jobs elsewhere. That makes it more likely that either the owner's profits go down or the price of gasoline goes up.[8]

A carbon tax affects more than the gas station owner. It will affect buyers and sellers of all fossil fuels, as well as the price of any goods and services that use energy to produce them—in other words, everything! Energy-intensive manufactured goods (e.g., home appliances and automobiles) will be affected more than services (e.g., legal and financial services). Tracing through the impact of a carbon tax requires understanding how incomes change as well as consumer prices. That is extremely complicated! Fortunately, models of the US economy exist that can be used to analyze the distributional and economic impacts of a carbon tax. Let's look at one of these models in more detail.

MEASURING THE DISTRIBUTIONAL IMPACT OF A CARBON TAX

In the waning hour of the Obama Administration, a relatively unknown office, the Office of Tax Analysis (OTA), within the US Department of the Treasury released a report with the rather bland title, *Methodology for Analyzing a Carbon Tax*. The OTA has one of the best collections of tax experts and researchers in all of the US government, and this is the first public report it has ever put out on a carbon tax. The report's authors noted that "[c]arbon taxes have been sufficiently widely discussed that a technical assessment of the issues involved [in estimating the revenue and distributional effects of a carbon tax] was warranted."

The study modeled a carbon tax beginning at $49 per ton in 2019 and rising to $70 a ton by 2028, and as part of its analysis, looked at how the average tax burden varied across income groups from the lowest to highest incomes. OTA drew on an incredibly rich data set of tax and information returns to calibrate the model to real-world behavior, tracking changes in wages and returns to capital arising from the carbon tax.[9] It also details how prices of carbon-intensive goods rise relative to the prices of goods that are not very carbon intensive. After accounting for changes in income resulting from the tax, the model traces through the effects of the fall in wage and capital income on income and payroll tax collections. It also accounts for how changes in the prices of consumer goods affect households at different income levels given the differences in the share of income spent on various goods and services at different incomes.[10]

The results of the OTA distributional analysis can be summed up in a few figures. Figure 6.1 shows the burden of the $49 a ton carbon tax as estimated by the study.

Let's start with the punchline. A common belief is that carbon taxes are regressive. But figure 6.1 shows that this belief is wrong. The burden falls more on those with higher incomes. In other words, even if we ignore how the carbon tax revenue is used, the tax is progressive. How does the OTA analysis come to this conclusion? Let's look more closely at the chart.

Each bar represents the average carbon-tax burden for the roughly 17 million families in a particular income group (10 percent of the roughly 170 million families in the United States). If a bar extends down (below zero), it means the carbon tax has reduced real disposable income for families in that income group. If the bar extends up (above zero), disposable income has gone up. The latter case is only relevant when we take into account how the carbon tax revenue is returned to households.

Income groups are listed on the horizontal axis, from the 10 percent of families with the lowest income on the left (labeled 0 to 10) to the highest income on the right (labeled 90 to 100). The four bars in the right part of the figure break up the top 10 percent of families into finer groupings, including breaking out the top one-tenth of one percent of families with the

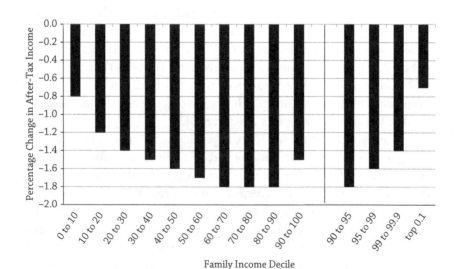

Figure 6.1. Carbon-tax burden—ignoring use of revenue
Source: US Department of the Treasury (2017)

highest incomes. The vertical axis measures the carbon-tax burden as a percentage of after-tax income, the income available for saving or consumption. The burden includes all the ways a carbon tax can affect a household's budget. It includes the tax's impact on reducing wage and capital income. And it measures the tax's impact on the various price changes for goods and services purchased by households. The burden is higher for a family with a bigger than average carbon footprint, such as a family that drives a lot, flies a lot, and has a big house with multiple TV sets, computers, and other appliances. In contrast, the burden is lower for a family with a smaller than average carbon footprint living in a small house, taking public transit or walking to local shops, and not traveling internationally.[11]

Because wealthier families consume goods and services with higher carbon inputs, the carbon tax is progressive over most of the income distribution, meaning the burden as a fraction of income goes up as income rises. The burden rises through the deciles (groups with 10 percent of families ordered by income) until the maximum burden of 1.8 percent for those in the sixtieth to ninetieth percentiles. The burden then drops to 1.5 percent for the top 10 percent of families. The bars on the right break down that top decile further and show that the burden falls as income rises within this top decile. The top one-tenth of one percent of families have an average burden of 0.7 percent. In other words, figure 6.1 shows that a carbon tax is progressive over much of the income distribution but is regressive at the very top of the distribution. This finding explodes the myth that carbon taxes are regressive.[12]

A BETTER MEASURE OF THE DISTRIBUTIONAL IMPACT OF A CARBON TAX

Figure 6.1 tells only part of the story. What are the distributional effects of recycling the tax revenue? For a tax that collects around $200 billion in the first year, it matters a great deal how that revenue is spent. The revenue can be returned by lowering other taxes or by giving the revenue back to families (perhaps through a quarterly rebate check from the government). No matter how the government uses the revenue, we should account for it in a proper reckoning of a carbon tax's distributional impact.[13]

The 2017 OTA study carried out just such an analysis and considered several ways of rebating the tax revenue. Figures 6.2 and 6.3 illustrate two of the results from their analysis.

Figure 6.2 considers a reform where the carbon tax revenue is returned to families as a fully refundable tax credit equal to $583 per person.[14] A carbon

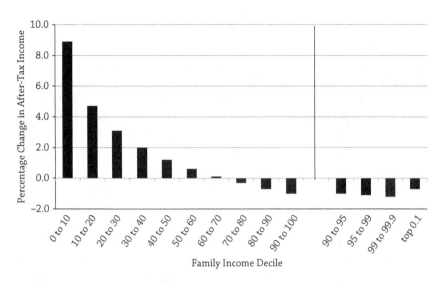

Figure 6.2. Carbon tax burden with equal per-person rebates
Source: US Department of the Treasury (2017)

tax with family rebate benefits those families in the bottom 70 percent of the income distribution. While the tax by itself is progressive—as figure 6.1 showed—so is the rebate. The tax and rebate makes the reform even more progressive than the tax by itself. People at the lower end of income distribution benefit from the refundable tax credit because on average the rebate exceeds the loss in income and higher costs of goods for families caused by the carbon tax. In other words, families in this income bracket on average get more money back from the tax credit than they pay in higher costs due to the carbon tax. The 10 percent of families with the lowest income see a nearly 9 percent increase in disposable income. The highest burden is on the top 10 percent of families for whom the burden equals one percent of after-tax income. Within that group, the biggest hit is to families in the 99–99.9 percentile with an average burden of 1.2 percent. The larger burden at higher incomes simply reflects the larger carbon footprint of these families, who live in larger homes with more energy-using appliances and cars and tend to live in the suburbs where they drive more.

The OTA also considered combining a carbon tax with a reduction in the corporate income tax rate (see fig. 6.3). Such a reform seems unlikely after the major corporate tax reduction in the 2017 Tax Cuts and Jobs Act. But imagine that Congress had decided to pay for the tax cuts rather than run up the national debt by roughly a trillion dollars over the next decade. One way they could have paid for the tax cut was with a carbon tax. If they had, what would have been the distributional impact? The OTA analysis

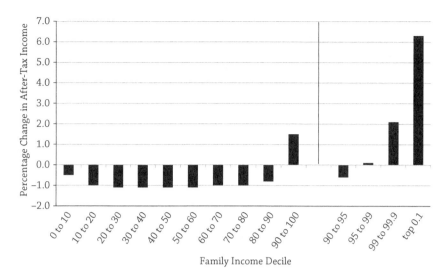

Figure 6.3. Carbon tax burden with corporate tax reduction
Source: US Department of the Treasury (2017)

shows that such a reform is distinctly regressive with 90 percent of families seeing their after-tax income falling by between one-half and one percent of after-tax income. The top 10 percent of families, in contrast, gain on the order of 1.5 percent of after-tax income with the greatest gains going to the top one-tenth of one percent of the income distribution. This group gains by over 6 percent of after-tax income. They may have a big carbon footprint, but the cut in corporate income taxes boosts the value of their shareholdings. Given the concentration of wealth among the families with the highest incomes, the gains from the tax cut far exceed the carbon tax impact on them.

The contrast in distributional impacts of the refundable tax credit and reduction in corporate income tax rates highlights a classic trade-off in tax policy. Returning the carbon tax revenue equally to all families is highly progressive. This is the approach favored by the bipartisan Climate Leadership Council (CLC). Cutting the corporate tax rate, on the other hand, sends most of the benefits to high-income families. It does encourage economic growth, since business owners get to keep more of the profits from investments in new equipment and machinery that make our economy more productive. But that benefit comes at the cost of considerable regressivity.

The OTA analysis likely overstates the regressivity of a carbon tax used to pay for reductions in the corporate income tax, since it does not account for the growth in capital investment that adds to worker productivity over time and ultimately leads to higher wages. While growth effects would reduce the regressivity, it won't eliminate it. The tension between equity and efficiency highlighted in the OTA analysis remains even after accounting for the stimulative impacts of cutting tax rates.[15]

Figures 6.2 and 6.3 also clearly illustrate why we shouldn't focus just on the distributional impact of a carbon tax. How we return the revenue to families matters. These are just two examples of how to return the revenue. The key take-away is that we can design a carbon tax reform to have *any* distributional outcome we want.

One more point bears mention. The OTA study focuses on the average impact for a group of families. Within an income group, there can be a considerable variation in the burden of a tax. Some families in the lowest 10 percent of the income distribution may live in less energy efficient homes than others, driving up the burden for them. Others may live in the Midwest which is more reliant on carbon-intensive coal for electricity generation than the Northeast. And yet again, others in this lowest income group may live in rural parts of the country with poorer access to mass transit, where they must drive long distances between work and home.[16]

Meanwhile, certain groups of workers are disproportionately impacted by carbon pricing than others. Coal miners are perhaps the most obvious group. We can address some of these disparities in a reform package. We might, for example, want to provide some economic transition assistance to communities whose local economy is heavily depending on coal mining.

But even after addressing some of the obvious disparities, the hard fact remains that any tax reform will lead to different tax impacts for families with similar incomes. A carbon tax reform is no different. Smart complementary policies may help address some of this burden. But to the extent that the variation in impacts is driven by a taste for carbon-intensive consumption, the tax reform will, by design, have differential impacts. And that's the way it should be. The whole point of the carbon tax is to use prices to nudge people to reduce their carbon footprint.

How the revenue from a carbon tax gets used is, above all, a political decision. But it is likely to be guided by principles of equity and efficiency. Having $200 billion or more each year to cut other taxes or reimburse families should help reduce the opposition to a carbon tax. But we're left with an unanswered question. If the burden of the carbon tax does not depend on who is responsible for collecting and sending in the tax revenue to the government, who *should* be obligated to collect and pay the tax? In other words, we need to consider the nuts and bolts of crafting the carbon tax.

CHAPTER 7

So You Want a Carbon Tax: How Do You Design It?

The previous chapter showed that the burden of a carbon tax does not necessarily fall on whoever it is that sends the revenue to the government. Prices will adjust depending on which sector the tax is imposed on. The final price to the consumer is the same whether a tax on gasoline, for example, is imposed on the service station, the wholesale distributer, or the refiner. If it doesn't matter where the tax is imposed, what principles should guide Congress in designing the tax?

The first and most basic principle relates to what should be taxed. Here, the 1930s bank robber Willie Sutton had a relevant insight. Asked why he robbed banks, Sutton reportedly replied, "Because that's where the money is." With over three-quarters of US greenhouse gas emissions coming from the burning of coal, natural gas, and petroleum for energy-related purposes, the obvious place to start is by taxing our use of those fuels—because that's where the carbon is.[1]

More generally, the guiding principles of carbon tax design are straightforward: the tax should be simple to administer, entail low compliance costs for whoever pays it, and ensure broad coverage of greenhouse gas emissions. In addition, the design should not get in the way of the tax providing the right price signal to reduce carbon pollution. These basic principles play out differently in different circumstances, however. It is thus important to look at how various sources of energy are used, where they come from, and how they are distributed. For example, nearly all coal emissions are from electricity generation; most petroleum emissions are from transportation;

Table 7.1. ENERGY-RELATED CARBON DIOXIDE EMISSIONS IN 2017

	Coal	Natural Gas	Petroleum	Total
Residential	0%	5%	1%	6%
Commercial	0%	3%	1%	4%
Industrial	2%	10%	7%	19%
Transportation	0%	1%	36%	37%
Electricity	24%	10%	0%	34%
Total	26%	29%	45%	100%

Source: US Energy Information Administration (2018)

and natural gas is balanced between industrial and electricity generation with lower shares in the residential and commercial sectors. Table 7.1 gives the breakdown of carbon dioxide emissions by fuel and sector.[2]

FROM WELL TO GAS TANK: TRACKING CARBON

If petroleum is predominantly used in transportation, where along the chain of production should the carbon tax related to gasoline use, for example, be imposed? To answer that question, it may help to imagine a typical transaction that occurs millions of times a day across the country: buying gasoline for the family car. My wife, Rebecca, pulls her Toyota Prius into a neighborhood gas station in a town west of Boston. As she swipes her credit card at the pump and unscrews the gas cap to start pumping gas, she notices a tanker truck pulling up to deliver gasoline to the station. While she fills her car and buys a cup of coffee for the road, the tanker truck driver unspools hoses to begin filling the underground storage tanks with regular, midrange, and premium gasoline. After setting the dials on his truck to fill the gas station's storage tanks, he too goes inside to get a cup of coffee for his return trip to the wholesale terminal rack in Chelsea, Massachusetts, a blue collar, industrial city just north of Boston. He had arrived at the terminal early that morning to fill his tanker truck just as the sun was rising. The sun reflected off the large petroleum barge rocking gently at the terminal dock on the Chelsea Creek unloading gasoline into the large storage tanks that—from an airplane on its landing approach to nearby Logan Airport—look like old-fashioned candy buttons lined up on a strip of paper.

A powerful tugboat is lashed to the barge at the dock. The tug moves the barge from point to point—either by towing with thick steel hawsers or by pushing the barge, useful in crowded or tight waterways. As the barge crew offloads nearly 50,000 barrels of gasoline, the tugboat captain pauses to watch the sunrise over the water. He then goes to his navigation station to plot the course he will take once the delivery in Chelsea is completed. At a speed of nearly 12 knots, once he clears Boston Harbor, he'll cross Cape Cod Bay and pass through the 8-mile long Cape Cod Canal and emerge into Buzzards Bay. In Long Island Sound, the tug shifts from pushing the barge to towing it and heads west along the Connecticut coast through Fisher Sound toward New York City. Pausing before Throgs Neck to switch back to pushing the barge, the tug enters the East River, turns south just past Rikers Island, and passes through Hell Gate, an area of swift currents just east of 96th Street in Manhattan. Emerging into the Upper Bay of New York Harbor, the tug noses the barge to an anchorage just off Staten Island, where it waits its turn at the Bayway Refinery along the Arthur Kill, a narrow waterway in New York Harbor between New Jersey and Staten Island. Nearby, the captain can see several tankers anchored in the harbor with crude oil from Nigerian oil fields in the Gulf of Guinea on Africa's western coast. They will eventually offload their oil at Bayway. The captain's trip ends the following day when he pushes the gasoline barge into the Kill Van Kull, a narrow passageway between Staten Island and Bayonne, and then south into the Arthur Kill, adjacent to the New Jersey Turnpike, to a fuel dock near the Bayway Refinery. As the captain shuts down the tug engines, he can just hear a train whistle from one of the many trains that ship oil by rail from the Bakken region of North Dakota to Bayway.[3]

Consider a trainload of oil coming to the Bayway Refinery from the Bakken oil fields. Where, between the oil fields of North Dakota and the gas pump in the Boston suburb, should the carbon tax be collected? A gallon of gasoline will release just under 20 pounds of carbon dioxide when it is burned in a car's engine. A $50 per ton carbon tax works out to a tax of $0.45 per gallon of gasoline no matter where we tax it—when it leaves the Bayway refinery in New Jersey, when it is pumped into the tanker truck at the Massachusetts terminal, or when it is sold by the neighborhood convenience store to my wife. The final price of gasoline at the pump—including the carbon tax—will be the same whether the tax is paid by the gas station owner, the wholesale supplier, the refiner, or even further up the supply chain at the well in North Dakota that pumps the oil out of the ground.

How much the consumer price rises is a function of supply and demand but does not depend on who is responsible for sending the taxes to the government. Regardless of who is responsible for sending in the tax revenue, the price (after subtracting out the carbon tax) received by producers or suppliers throughout the chain of production is the same.

This gives us great flexibility in designing a carbon tax. We can look at the entire chain of production of fossil fuels—from mine mouth or well head to combustion in a factory, someone's car, or wherever the fuel is burned—and pick the most convenient place to collect the tax. We can levy the tax *upstream*, meaning early on in the production chain (e.g., the wellhead or refinery for petroleum), or *downstream*, closer to the retail sale of the fuel. A downstream tax could be on the wholesale distributor or the gasoline service station.

Where is it most convenient to levy the carbon tax? That depends on the fuel in question but in general the administrative burden is lower if there are relatively few businesses having to fill out the paperwork and send in quarterly carbon tax checks to the government. It is also helpful if the business is already reporting its fossil fuel consumption to the government. That way, the business owner doesn't need to institute new reporting systems or use valuable workers to collect the information to comply with the tax. With that as background, let's consider each fossil fuel in turn.[4]

Coal

If all the coal the United States produced annually were put in one long train, it would circle the earth three times. Nearly all that coal is consumed domestically, mainly to produce electricity. In keeping the principle of ease of compliance and administration, it makes sense to tax coal at the mine. That would require tax returns from the owners of the roughly 700 mines that produced coal in 2016. The major advantage of taxing mine owners is that they are already paying a coal excise tax to assist miners afflicted with black lung disease and other coal-related ailments. The carbon tax could easily piggy-back on the existing coal tax. If taxed at the mine, a carbon tax would also need to be imposed on the nearly 8 million tons of coal imported in 2017. That tax could be collected at the port of entry.[5]

Alternatively, coal could be taxed *downstream* where it is burned in coal fired electricity generating plants or large industrial plants. As with upstream taxation, relatively few firms would need to pay the tax. In 2016, there were 369 plants burning coal to produce electricity in the United States. In addition, there are an estimated 500 factories that burn enough coal to require tracking and reporting its use to the federal government. These factories burn coal in their boilers for purposes ranging from steel production to processing sugar beet to produce sugar. Having these factories pay the carbon tax would not create new paperwork for the firms since they are already tracking and reporting coal use.[6]

Petroleum

Most of the gasoline burned in our cars, the diesel oil burned in trucks, and other refined products (e.g., jet fuel, heating oil) is refined in one of 139 operating refineries in the United States and then sold to wholesale dealers, like the one in Chelsea, Massachusetts, that then dispenses to trucks to deliver to the retail seller. Taxing crude oil at this small number of refineries would be straightforward. Simplifying things further, refineries already pay a tax on the crude oil they purchase to fund the Oil Spill Liability Trust Fund, which pays for the clean-up costs of oil spills not covered by the responsible party. Just as the carbon tax applied to coal at the mine could piggy-back on an existing coal excise tax, so too could the carbon tax paid by refiners on the crude oil they purchase.[7]

Natural Gas

Unlike coal, for which there are a relatively small number of mines, or oil, which passes through a small number of refineries, natural gas does not have an obvious point of taxation. There are roughly a half a million operating natural gas wells in the country. As a small number of well operators are responsible for a large share of natural gas production, one option would be to levy the tax on them.[8] Consider natural gas production in Pennsylvania to see how natural gas flows from the ground to where it is burned to provide energy. This will help sort out the other options for taxing natural gas.

Western Pennsylvania sits atop the Marcellus Gas Basin, a massive shale formation rich in natural gas extending from the Finger Lakes region of New York state through western Pennsylvania, parts of Ohio, Maryland, West Virginia, and into Virginia. Two technological advances have sparked a massive gas boom here (and elsewhere in the country). The first is hydraulic fracking—water is injected under high pressure into shale formations to create microscopic fractures in the shale to release the natural gas. The second is horizontal drilling—drills can make ninety degree turns thousands of feet underground and extend a well horizontally for a mile or more in various directions. Annual natural gas production in the Keystone State averaged less than 150 billion cubic feet a year in the ten years up to 2005. By 2010, annual production had risen to nearly 600 billion cubic feet, and in 2016, production exceeded 5 trillion cubic feet.

The natural gas produced in one of Pennsylvania's more than 60,000 wells feeds into a spider's web of thousands of small, gathering pipelines that deliver the raw gas to one of the many processing plants in the state, like the Houston Processing Plant in the small town of Washington 25 miles from Pittsburgh. The Houston facility is owned by MarkWest Energy Partners and can process over 500 million cubic feet of raw natural gas a day, removing water, impurities, and natural gas plant liquids such as propane (for your gas grill), butane (for inexpensive lighters), and other natural gas products (used to make plastics and other petrochemicals, among other products).

After removing water, impurities, and liquid gas products, the dry gas that remains—pure methane—is fed into various pipeline transmission networks like the Columbia Gas Transmission network, a 12,000-mile network in ten states serving electric power generating stations, natural gas utilities (known as local distribution companies or LDCs) that serve residential and commercial customers, and large industrial users.[9]

If not taxed at the wellhead, the feasible options for point of taxation are either processing plants like MarkWest's Houston plant in Pennsylvania (upstream implementation) or further downstream where natural gas is sold to the customers who burn the fuel to heat homes, produce electricity, or fire industrial boilers. Let's consider each option. There are just over 500 processing plants like the Houston plant in the United States. Imposing the tax on natural gas processers seems a plausible upstream option. However, only two-thirds of marketed natural gas in the United States has gone through a processing facility. For many wells, the gas can be minimally processed in small "skid" processing units near the well and sent directly into the pipeline network for delivery to end users. Some gas is also processed in so-called "straddle" plants, small processing plants along the pipeline that can remove water and other impurities. Taxing upstream at the processing plant leaves lots of room for natural gas to escape taxation.

A better option would be further downstream: the tax could be collected by the roughly 1,300 LDCs that primarily serve residential, commercial, and small industrial customers. These are companies like Peoples Gas serving over 800,000 Chicago residents or Black Hills Energy serving 1.2 million customers in eight Midwestern states. Typically subject to state regulation, LDCs provide both gas and local distribution services either by selling natural gas directly to customers or acting as the distributor of gas that customers directly purchase from pipelines or other owners of gas. LDCs provide nearly all the natural gas consumed by residential and commercial customers, about half the natural gas consumed by industrial users, and just over one-quarter of the natural gas consumed by electricity generators.[10] Downstream implementation of the tax, therefore, could be on LDCs for its sales; on companies that operate natural gas electric generating plants that did not purchase gas from an LDC; and on industrial users that purchase natural gas directly from suppliers other than LDCs.

Taxing Other Sources of Greenhouse Gas Emissions

In addition to taxing our energy use of coal, petroleum, and natural gas, several other sources of emissions—unrelated to energy—can be included in the carbon tax. Cement manufacturing is a good example. An intermediate stage in cement production is *clinker*, a key ingredient in cement. To produce clinker, raw ingredients such as limestone are fed into a kiln and heated to temperatures as high as 2,700 degrees Fahrenheit. As the kiln temperature rises, a chemical reaction takes place and carbon dioxide is released as the clinker forms. For every two tons of clinker produced, roughly one ton of carbon dioxide is released. This is in addition to the carbon dioxide released when coal or natural gas is burned to generate the heat. Since the carbon dioxide emissions in cement production are directly proportional to the production of clinker, the tax could be applied to clinker production at each of the roughly one hundred cement plants in the United States. This is over and above the tax paid on the fossil fuels burned to produce the high kiln temperatures.

Some greenhouse gases are hard to tax. Take methane, which accounts for just over one-tenth of US greenhouse gas emissions. Methane from livestock accounts for nearly one-third of methane emissions. Regulating livestock feed to reduce methane emissions from enteric fermentation ("cow burping") and regulating agricultural manure operations is a more sensible approach to controlling these emissions than applying a carbon tax. It is simply too difficult to measure and monitor these emissions. Another major source of methane emissions are leaks that occur in oil and natural gas drilling as well as in the gathering pipelines taking gas out of the fields and putting it into the major gas transmission pipelines. Again, it would be exceedingly difficult to tax field emissions given the challenge in tracking and measuring the many small leaks. In this case, regulation mandating improved production techniques or equipment might be a cheaper and more effective approach to reducing emissions. The Obama Administration took a step in that direction when it issued draft rules in early 2016 seeking information on methane emissions from oil and natural gas drilling operators. The Trump Administration, however, withdrew the information request in March 2017.[11]

Unlike field-related methane releases, some greenhouse gas emissions could be easily taxed. Fluorinated gases, for example, which account for about 3 percent of emissions, could be taxed directly upon manufacture.[12] Taxes have been levied on similar ozone-depleting chemicals and both the Treasury and the Internal Revenue Service (IRS) have experience in writing tax rules for these types of gases, so it would be straightforward to include these gases in a carbon tax.

Deciding which greenhouse gases should be covered by a carbon tax—beyond the carbon dioxide from fossil fuels burned for energy—is a judgment call. The advantage of including more gases is that a broader base lowers the overall cost of any given reduction in emissions. The disadvantage is that emissions for many non-combustion sources are not easily measured and writing the tax rules could be time-consuming and burdensome. Also, if the tax is linked to output (as with clinker), it eliminates the incentive to find production methods that lower emissions. In the end, Treasury would need to decide on a case-by-case basis how best to handle these sorts of emissions. Fortunately, only small amounts of emissions are involved, and it may be best not to include them at the outset but rather consider extending coverage of the tax later.

Storing Emissions

Taxing emissions based on the carbon content of the fuel assumes that all the carbon dioxide is released into the atmosphere when the fuel is burned. Technologies exist, however, to capture the carbon dioxide before it is released. If that carbon dioxide is permanently stored so that it doesn't enter the atmosphere, we should not tax the fuel associated with the stored gases. *Carbon capture and storage*, or CCS, is just as it sounds: carbon dioxide is captured from the smoke stack of a plant burning fossil fuels and stored either in underground formations that permanently trap the carbon dioxide or deep underwater where, under the pressure of thousands of feet of seawater, the carbon dioxide puddles in a liquid form in the seabed at the ocean floor.[13]

CCS is prohibitively expensive at present, and we lack the legal and regulatory structures to oversee it and deal with any potential problems in the transport and storage of gases. We also lack a network of pipelines to move carbon dioxide from where it is captured to where it will be permanently stored. But we should be sure to design the tax to provide the right incentive to capture and store carbon dioxide by not taxing those emissions. If coal is taxed at the mine mouth, we'd simply exempt from the tax any coal sold to a company that captures and stores carbon dioxide emissions in an approved facility. If taxed where the coal is burned, any facility that captures and stores its emissions would be exempt from the carbon tax. The same goes for petroleum and natural gas.[14]

BORDER ADJUSTMENTS: HOW TO HANDLE IMPORTS AND EXPORTS

During the 2016 presidential election campaign, Donald J. Trump promised that he'd bring jobs back to the United States by slapping taxes on imported products. These taxes—known as tariffs—are controversial as a tool to affect trade, and economists generally believe they drive up prices and discourage trade. But taxes on imports make sense in certain situations. One such tax that is a helpful precedent for a carbon tax is a national consumption tax, or value added tax (VAT), which targets consumption within a country. If I travel to France to do some sightseeing, I will pay a VAT on my restaurant meal in Paris's Latin Quarter and my ticket to Versailles—because I am "consuming" both in France. If, however, I buy a case of wine and ship it home, I don't have to pay the VAT since I will be consuming the wine in the United States. My French friend who orders some wine from California to be delivered to her Paris apartment will have to pay a tax when the wine is imported into France, since she will consume it there.

A border tax adjustment in a VAT taxes all imports into a country and exempts from tax all goods exported out of the country. In that case, we call it a *destination basis* VAT, meaning the tax is applied based on the place of consumption (the destination). Just as a VAT taxes consumption within the country, our carbon tax should tax greenhouse gas emissions based on the place where the consumption that led to the release of greenhouse gas emissions occurs. Taxing on a destination basis means we levy a tax on goods consumed in the United States based on the carbon dioxide emissions released in the making of the goods. Taxing emissions on this consumption basis is the theoretically correct way to deal with the *carbon leakage problem*. Leakage refers to the shifting of manufacturing activities from the United States to a foreign country to avoid the carbon tax. If the manufactured good is then imported back to the United States, the carbon tax doesn't reduce overall emissions but just shifts them from the United States to foreign countries. As with a VAT, we can discourage leakage in a carbon tax by including a *border tax adjustment* with two parts. First, imports are taxed on the basis of the emissions released in their production. Second, exports are not taxed. If a carbon tax was paid on inputs used to produce exports, those taxes are rebated. With this two-part border adjustment, we ensure that carbon intensive goods consumed in the United States are subject to the carbon tax regardless of where they are produced. This eliminates an incentive to off-shore production of these carbon intensive goods.

The border adjustment would also be applied to fossil fuels so that firms don't have an incentive to import coal or oil to avoid paying the tax on domestically produced fuels. Border adjustments are straightforward for imported and exported fossil fuels. Assuming Bayway is responsible for paying the tax on all oil that it refines, it would pay the tax equally on oil offloaded from tankers bringing oil from Nigeria as well as the railcars bringing oil from the Bakken oil fields of North Dakota. Any refined products (e.g., gasoline) that are imported would also be taxed, since these products would not have been taxed at a US refinery.[15]

The rebate of the carbon tax on exported fuels is also straightforward. If crude oil is exported, no rebate is necessary since no carbon tax was paid on the crude oil. (Remember, only crude oil that passed through a domestic refinery is subject to the tax.) A rebate of the tax would be allowed on refined products (gasoline, diesel fuel, kerosene, etc.) since these products were taxed at the refinery. Exporters could file a simple form to the IRS that indicates the amount of exported product for which they should receive a tax refund.[16]

Taxing the emissions associated with the production of imported goods (e.g., chemicals and automobiles), thereby addressing carbon leakage, is more difficult. Ideally, we would calculate the emissions associated with every import from each country. But, that is not practical for a couple of reasons. First, most imported goods are produced with very little energy and it is simply not worthwhile administratively to track and tax the trivial amounts of emissions associated with their production. We should focus instead on the few products that are very carbon intensive and for which there is a high amount of trade. This narrows our focus to a few commodities like imported steel, aluminum, chemicals, paper, and cement.[17]

Taxing these carbon-intensive, trade-exposed goods would not likely affect the trade of those few commodities, since the bulk of imports of those commodities comes from countries that have a carbon price in place (e.g., Canada, the EU). But enough imports come from countries like China that the political pressure to impose a border tax will be intense. So, let's see how we can avoid creating a cumbersome or unworkable administrative structure.

As a first step, applying the border tax on a small group of imported goods simplifies matters. But how do we measure the emissions that occurred during the production of these goods? Ideally, we'd like to tax a ton of imported steel based on the emissions involved in its production. To do this properly would require a different tax rate for every country from which we import steel, since each country's energy mix and production processes differ so that carbon dioxide emissions per ton of steel would vary across countries. To further complicate things, emissions per ton of steel could vary across regions and factories within a country.

One approach would be to assess the carbon tax on imported steel based on the average carbon emissions associated with the production of steel in the United States. Our government can calculate that number based on existing data collected by the US government's Bureau of Economic Analysis, and many academic studies demonstrate the feasibility of this approach.[18] The advantage of this approach is that the US government doesn't need to collect detailed information on production processes in different countries and set different tax rates accordingly. This approach "levels the playing field" so that a ton of imported steel faces the same cost increase due to the carbon tax as a similar ton of domestically produced steel. One disadvantage of this approach, though, is that the border tax adjustment provides no incentive to Chinese steel producers to reduce their greenhouse gas emissions in response to our carbon tax. But keep in mind that less than one-tenth of one percent of Chinese steel is exported to the United States. It is unlikely that a carbon tax applied to Chinese steel based on actual production-related emissions would have much of an impact on Chinese emissions. A final advantage of a border tax based on US carbon content is that the border adjustment is unlikely to run afoul of the complex World Trade Organization (WTO) rules on allowable tariffs.[19]

Alternatively, the tax could be linked to a measure of actual emissions involved in the production of carbon-intensive imported goods. This could be done by relying on government- or industry-developed standards for measuring greenhouse gas emissions in key sectors and mandating reporting of emissions for any goods that a firm wishes to import into the United States. Whether international standards could be developed is not clear. But the stick to motivate developing acceptable standards would be that firms could only import into the US goods from industries and exporting countries using those standards.[20]

If a border tax on imports is applied in select carbon-intensive sectors that are heavily traded, then a rebate of the tax on exports in those sectors should also be allowed. This would be in keeping with the notion of a carbon tax applied to the emissions associated with goods consumed in the United States. It would also be consistent with our treatment of exported fossil fuels that would not be subject to the carbon tax.

How do we treat the "early mover" states that already have carbon pricing schemes? This includes California's cap and trade system as well as the Northeast states' RGGI. Meanwhile, other states are considering enacting some form of carbon price that could come into effect before a federal carbon tax is passed. How, then, should a federal carbon tax interact with state-level carbon pricing programs?

One view is that having a state-level carbon tax alongside a federal tax is double taxation and should be avoided. Based on that view, state-level carbon pricing programs, whether a tax or cap and trade, should be preempted by a federal tax. There is much to be said for having a uniform carbon price nationwide. But before jumping to the conclusion that state programs must be dismantled when a federal tax is enacted, let's consider an alternative perspective.

There is ample precedence for having multiple layers of taxation in a federal system. Consider the income tax. Forty-three states tax some or all of the same income as does the federal income tax. Some states actually piggy-back on federal filing forms for simplicity. Rather than thinking of this as double taxation, it would be more accurate to say that states have the flexibility to subject income to a total tax (federal and state—and in some instances local) that can vary according to individual state views on the desired taxation of income.

Here's a second consideration. States that have moved early to enact carbon pricing rely on the revenue from those programs for various purposes. It would be unfair to ask them to give up that revenue without some form of adjustment mechanism. One possibility would be for transitional assistance whereby states are guaranteed federal funds to replace lost carbon revenue, to be phased out over a period of time, perhaps a decade. Alternatively, it could be argued that states will be getting that revenue back in whatever form carbon tax revenue is returned to US taxpayers, whether through family rebate checks or cuts to federal tax rates. If federal taxes are cut, states that give up their carbon revenue could raise state-level taxes to recoup that lost revenue.

This is all needlessly complicated when a federal carbon tax could easily coexist with state-level carbon pricing programs. One of the virtues of our federal system is that it allows states to approach problems differently. If certain states want a higher carbon price to decarbonize their economy more aggressively, why should other states stand in their way? A national carbon tax would simply put in place a carbon price floor across all states. Some states may choose a higher price. But no state may go below the floor.

There is good precedence for this approach from our neighbor to the north. Canada's Pan-Canadian Framework for Climate Change sets a floor price on carbon pollution for all provinces but allows for even higher prices if individual provinces so wish.

HOW DO WE SET THE TAX RATE?

Once we know what we're going to tax and who's going to be responsible for collecting and sending the tax revenue to the government, we need to decide what the tax rate will be. If we followed the advice of the British economist Arthur Pigou, we'd set the tax rate equal to the social cost of carbon dioxide emissions, the increase in damages to society from a ton of carbon dioxide emissions. Based on analyses done by the US EPA and other federal agencies during the Obama Administration, the tax rate in 2020 would be roughly $50 a metric ton of carbon dioxide. The difficulty with an estimate like this is that the models used to construct it make a number of heroic assumptions and modeling decisions that lead to great uncertainty over the value of incremental damages. That has led some observers to propose other approaches to estimating the social cost of carbon dioxide.[21]

Alternatively, we could set a sequence of tax rates over time to achieve a set reduction in emissions by some date. International climate negotiators have focused on a global goal of reducing emissions by 80 percent relative to 2005 by 2050. The United States set this as an aspirational goal in the promises it made in 2015 as part of the international climate negotiations that led to the Paris Agreement. Most economic analyses suggest that given the current state of technological progress, an 80 percent reduction by 2050 would be extremely costly. Whether policymakers settle on an 80 percent reduction by 2050 or some other target, a carbon tax will likely be designed with some emissions reduction target in mind.

Let's assume that's the case. A second question then arises. How do you ensure you hit the target given our use of a carbon tax? One simple way to do that is to enact a carbon tax with a "policy thermostat" that adjusts the tax rate in a known and predictable way between now and some future date. Here's how the thermostat would work. The carbon tax might be enacted with a starting tax rate of $40 a ton. The legislation could also mandate that the tax rate grow at a "standard" annual increase of 5 percent per year. The law would also include emission reduction benchmarks between now and 2035. If emissions fall so that the benchmark reductions are met, the tax rate continues to increase each year by 5 percent. If, however, the emissions are not falling as rapidly as desired so that the benchmarks are missed, the tax rate would increase each year by some higher amount (say, 10 percent per year). While the difference in the tax rates from year to year would be relatively modest, the cumulative impact of several years of the tax rate rising by 10 percent per year would be a powerful pricing incentive to reduce emissions and get the economy back on track to hit the benchmarks. When that happens, the tax rate reverts to increasing each year by 5 percent. This sort of mechanism would provide greater assurance that the United States would reach desired emission reduction targets while still providing the price predictability that the business community needs.[22]

THINGS TO AVOID IN DESIGNING A CARBON TAX

Finally, there are some possible pitfalls that policymakers should avoid when designing a carbon tax. The first is exempting certain sectors from the tax. It is especially tempting to consider exempting certain carbon-intensive sectors that face international competition. But keep in mind our principle that we should not dilute the carbon price signal. We want to encourage firms to reduce carbon pollution, so, exempting carbon-intensive sectors makes no sense. If the purpose of a proposed exemption is to reduce the tax burden on certain sectors, then there are alternative approaches that maintain the price signal while providing some tax relief. One is taxing emissions above a floor.[23] As an example, a firm might be able to exempt from taxation emissions equal to 10 percent of its historic emissions (maybe an average of its past five years of emissions). All emissions above that level are taxed, and so the firm faces the correct price signal as it considers expanding or reducing production. But, while better than exempting the sector entirely from taxation, exemptions like this erode the tax base and eat into revenues.

A second pitfall concerns small emitters. It is similarly tempting to exempt them, since any single emitter is not a major source of emissions, and the costs of compliance and oversight may exceed the benefits of including small emitters in the tax base. This problem can often be more readily addressed by levying the tax at a different point of production. Gasoline is a good example. There are millions of gas stations in the United States, and no single station sells enough gasoline to be considered a major emitter. Having gas station owners file paperwork and pay the carbon tax would be administratively cumbersome and burdensome. But all gas stations have to get their gasoline somewhere, and ultimately that gasoline originates at a refinery. Having refiners pay the tax on the gasoline they sell (along with importers of gasoline refined in other countries) would simplify recordkeeping and avoid placing the administrative burden on small businesses.

The last pitfall is setting different tax rates on carbon pollution based on how the products are used. You can imagine a policymaker calling for a lower carbon tax on gasoline sold for personal use to help families living in the suburbs who don't have access to good public transportation. Avoid this temptation! Most European VAT systems have fallen into this trap, with different commodities taxed at different rates. There are two problems here. First, having multiple tax rates drives up compliance costs. It would require, for example, developing elaborate systems to make sure the lower-taxed gasoline is not being purchased by businesses that should be paying the higher tax rate.[24] Second, there are much better ways to provide relief to tax-squeezed families than lower rates. After all, while the family that earns $30,000 a year and drives a six-year-old car would appreciate the lower tax rate, so too will the multimillionaire with four cars in his garage. To provide tax relief, use some carbon tax revenue to lower income tax rates, increase the generosity of the earned income tax credit, or use some other approach to return tax revenue to households that isn't tied to their consumption of fossil fuels.

It's one thing to design a carbon tax that is simple, easy to comply with, and not overly burdensome on taxpayers. But readers may still have concerns that a carbon tax is a good idea. After all, lots of objections have been raised about a carbon tax by many opponents. I'll tackle those objections head on in the next chapter.

CHAPTER 8

Objections to a Carbon Tax

Climate change is costly, but the benefits of enacting a carbon tax far exceed the costs. The tax is a cost-effective way to cut emissions, is straightforward to administer and comply with, and will drive innovation in the marketplace. It will also allow us to eliminate a number of costly energy subsidies and cumbersome regulations. Despite all this, many have concerns about a carbon tax and raise various objections. Let's consider those objections now.

ISN'T THE SCIENCE TOO UNCERTAIN FOR US TO ENACT COSTLY POLICIES?

This first objection is a common one and, perhaps, the easiest to address. Opponents of carbon policy argue that quantifying the damages from climate change is difficult and that damage estimates range widely depending on model assumptions. Indeed they do. But to leap to the conclusion that we should do nothing because we are unsure of the exact magnitude of the damages is a very big leap indeed. The British economist Arthur Pigou devised a cost-effective solution to pollution over a century ago: set the tax rate on emissions equal to the additional social damages from one more ton of pollution. While economists may not be able to measure those damages precisely, it is clear that zero—no carbon tax—is not the right value. Waiting to enact a carbon tax until we know with "certainty" the correct rate is an example of the perfect being the enemy of the good. We don't need—and can't afford—to wait: we can design policy to account for the inherent uncertainties in the science of climate change. Studies that do this still conclude that moving forward with a carbon tax would be good for society.[1]

WON'T IT HURT THE ECONOMY?

Opponents of carbon taxes often invoke a more general argument against taxes: that they are a drag on the economy. A carbon tax, specifically, is not likely to promote economic growth. That should come as no surprise. To focus only on the cost of cleaning up pollution while ignoring the costs of climate damages on the economy is short-sighted. It would be like my neighbor complaining about the cost of his having to take his trash to the dump when he's been accustomed to simply throwing it over the fence into my yard.

That reducing our carbon pollution will have a cost has been the subject of over twenty-five years of academic research focused on an environmental *double dividend*, or the idea that there are two benefits from taxing pollution. The first is an improvement in the environment—less pollution—and the second is an improvement in economic efficiency from using the pollution tax revenue to reduce other taxes that discourage work and investment. That led some analysts to posit that an environmental tax reform—using a carbon tax to lower personal or corporate income taxes—would actually lead to higher output and welfare. This notion, known as the *strong double dividend*, is unpersuasive. We're not going to get a cleaner environment for free. However, there is a bigger boost to the economy by using pollution tax revenue to lower an especially distortionary tax, like the corporate income tax, rather than simply giving the money back to households in a household rebate.[2]

But the fact is that a carbon tax will not jeopardize our future standard of living and create real risks for our economy. Let's briefly ignore the benefits from reducing emissions and consider just how costly it is to tax carbon emissions. One potential cost of any tax is the prospect of slower economic growth. Slower growth means lower income in the future relative to the economy with higher growth. That reduction in future income is a real cost. How much would a carbon tax hurt economic growth? Not very much. A study by economists at RFF shows four ways of rebating revenue from a $30 per ton carbon tax and their impact on economic growth. Three of the four rebate approaches show GDP falling between 0.5 and 3.5 percent by 2035. Only the revenue-neutral option, when the carbon tax is used to cut taxes on capital income, yields growth in GDP (one percent by 2035).[3] A cut in GDP of 3.5 percent looks very large. After all, per capita GDP generally grows each year around 2 percent. But the reduction in GDP is not relative to GDP today or even to GDP growth in any given year. Rather, it is a reduction in GDP "relative to baseline" GDP. That is, assuming no carbon tax in place (the baseline), per capita GDP in 2035 might be $83,000. If there is a carbon tax, and the revenue was returned to households proportional to the number of members in each, then per capita GDP might be $80,000, or 3.5 percent lower than the baseline.

But keep in mind that per capita GDP in 2035 will be much higher than today, even after accounting for population growth and inflation. The RFF researchers estimate in their model that real GDP per capita will be over 40 percent higher than today.[4] Figure 8.1 illustrates how the economy grows under the baseline (solid line) and assuming a carbon tax is imposed that cuts real per capita GDP by 3.5 percent by 2035 (dashed line). Another way to think about the impact of the carbon tax on the economy is illustrated in the figure. Consider the date when the economy grows to the point where real GDP per person equals $80,000. A carbon tax delays hitting that milestone by about eighteen months. Hardly a devastating blow to the US economy.

Note that baseline GDP growth doesn't account for damages from climate change. To the extent a carbon tax helps reduce the damages from climate change, then the real GDP per capita could be even higher than 40 percent by 2035. It is extremely difficult to measure how rising

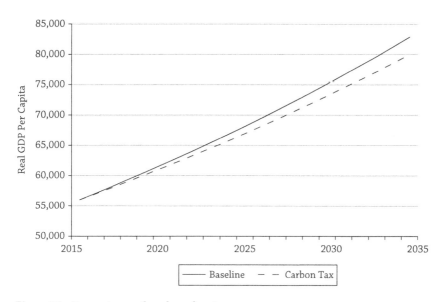

Figure 8.1. Economic growth and a carbon tax
Source: Author's calculations based on Carbone et al. (2013)

temperatures will affect economic growth rates. One study finds that a one degree Celsius increase in global temperatures is associated with a decline in GDP growth on the order of one to two percentage points in poor countries. Developed countries appear less vulnerable to declines in growth from climate change.[5] Even if US growth rates are unaffected by climate change, we'll still face higher costs from damages and the cost of adaptation that climate change forces on us.

The fact that families in the future will be richer brings up another objection raised by opponents to a carbon tax. Why should people today pay to increase incomes of future generations who will be richer even if we don't act to reduce carbon pollution? Setting aside the moral argument that people should clean up their own messes, there is a simple economic response: the cost of reducing emissions is less than the cost of anticipated damages from climate change. Estimating the damages of climate change is challenging. As the Intergovernmental Panel on Climate Change (2014) warns, "Estimates . . . are partial and affected by important conceptual and empirical limitations" (p. 79). With that caution in mind, one recent study suggests global incomes could be reduced by over 20 percent by the end of the century if we take no action.[6] The estimates of the cost of action, in contrast, range from 3 to 11 percent with a mid-range estimate below 5 percent.

Any estimate of costs and damages occurring at the end of this century needs to be treated with great caution. Much can happen between now and then that will affect costs and benefits. But given what we know now, the benefits of cutting carbon pollution outweigh the costs. Focusing on average damages also ignores the fact that the damages are disproportionately concentrated on residents of the world's poorest countries and, more generally, low-income people in all affected countries.

WHAT ABOUT COAL MINERS?

Donald Trump campaigned for the presidency in part on a pledge to save coal mining jobs in the United States, rhetoric he has continued to use in office. "We are going to put our coal miners back to work," Trump promised a packed rally in Freedom Hall in Louisville, Kentucky, a major coal producing state in March 2017. The following week, at the EPA in Washington, DC, Trump, surrounded by coal miners, signed an executive order to roll back a number of Obama Administration energy and climate policies including the Clean Power Plan (CPP). The CPP was the first-ever federal initiative to reduce carbon pollution in the electricity sector and would have forced the existing fleet of power plants to reduce emissions by 32 percent below 2005 levels by 2030. Trump claimed that "perhaps no single regulation threatens our miners, energy workers, and companies more than this crushing attack on American industry." EPA Administrator Scott Pruitt made good on Trump's promise in October 2017 when he travelled to Kentucky to announce that the EPA was formally repealing the CPP. "The war on coal is over," Pruitt proclaimed.[7]

Are Trump and Pruitt right? Did federal policies under President Obama represent a "crushing attack" on the coal sector? Coal mining jobs certainly have been disappearing at a rapid rate over the past six or so years. Since the 2016 election, coal mining jobs have hovered at about 50,000, down from roughly 91,000 in 2011. About half of those jobs are in mines with the rest in transport, engineering, clerical, or other positions.[8] To understand what caused the sharp drop in jobs, we need to consider the economics of coal and natural gas.

Coal is mined predominantly in Appalachia (mainly in West Virginia, Pennsylvania, Eastern Kentucky, and Ohio), the Illinois Basin (Illinois, Indiana, and Western Kentucky), and the PRB (Wyoming and, to some extent, Montana). There's quite a disconnect between production and jobs— in other words, the mines with the most workers are not producing the most coal. In 2015, three-quarters of the jobs were in Appalachia and the Illinois Basin. The PRB, in contrast, accounted for 10 percent of all jobs in the sector. However, nearly 45 percent of the coal mined in 2015 came from the PRB, while Appalachia and the Illinois Basin together accounted for less than 40 percent. Put differently, PRB mines produced nearly thirty tons of coal per hour of a coal miner's work day while a coal mine in West Virginia produced less than three tons per hour.

This contrast helps explain what is killing coal jobs in the United States. Digging coal in the PRB just doesn't require very many workers. Coal seams in this region are incredibly thick and near the earth's surface, making it very easy to extract with giant power shovels and other mechanized equipment. The Powder River Coal Company, for example, operates four mines in the region with coal seams that are anywhere from sixty-five to over a hundred feet thick. Giant earth moving machines called draglines remove the topsoil and expose the thick coal seams underneath. Forty-foot haul trucks with eleven-foot-diameter tires cart the coal off the face of the mine to fill mile-long trains transporting the coal throughout the country. A 320-ton haul truck is three stories high and carries enough coal to power a US home for forty years.[9]

The economics of coal have changed dramatically over time. In 1983, Kentucky and West Virginia produced more than two tons of coal for each ton mined in Wyoming. By 2015 this relation was turned on its head, and Wyoming was producing nearly two and a half tons of coal for every ton from Kentucky and West Virginia.

The lower cost of Western coal is one factor driving down coal employment. In addition, the passage in 1990 of President George H. W. Bush's Acid Rain Program to reduce sulfur dioxide emissions from the nation's electricity plants raised demand for Western low-sulfur coal. Western low-sulfur coal could be burned without the need for expensive sulfur-dioxide-capturing scrubbers. Adding to the rise in demand for Western coal was the deregulation of the railroads triggered by the Staggers Rail Act of 1980, which lowered transport costs and made it more economical to ship Western coal to the East rather than burn Eastern coal.[10]

The shift to Western low-sulfur coal was aided in the late 1990s by the shift in some states from a regulated electricity sector to an increasingly deregulated sector. Traditionally, electricity rates were set by state public utility commissioners on a cost-of-service basis. Under cost-of-service regulation, electric utilities are allowed to set rates to cover their costs plus earn a profit. The profit is determined as a negotiated percentage of the value of their capital infrastructure in service. The negotiated rate was the outcome of protracted and often contentious state-level regulatory proceedings. When utilities had to decide how to reduce their sulfur dioxide emissions, cost-of-service regulation was a thumb on the scale favoring installing scrubbers and continuing to burn Eastern high-sulfur coal. A multi-million-dollar scrubber adds to the capital infrastructure, increasing profits for the utility shareholders. In contrast, it might be cheaper to buy low-sulfur Western coal, but those costs are recovered in rates and do nothing to increase profitability. Utilities in states that deregulated reduced costs by, among other things, shifting to Western low-sulfur coal.[11] Electricity deregulation only exacerbated the loss of coal mining jobs.

The final factor killing coal jobs is natural gas. At the beginning of 2008, coal accounted for over half of the electricity generated in the United States. By the first quarter of 2017, its share had fallen to about 30 percent. Meanwhile, the share of natural gas has risen from 20 percent to between 30 and 35 percent. The fracking revolution in the United States has led to a massive increase in the production of natural gas, with the result that its price has fallen by between 60 and 70 percent relative to coal since 2008. That's why over one hundred coal fired power plants were shut down in 2015 and why another ninety or so are expected to retire by 2020.[12] In September 2017, plans fell through for construction of an 895-megawatt expansion to a coal fired power plant in Holcomb, Kansas. With the Holcomb expansion dead for now and two other plants facing delays or legal challenges, there is only one domestic coal plant under construction as of mid-2018—a tiny seventeen-megawatt plant at the University of Alaska in Fairbanks.[13]

Coal jobs are being lost to automation and cheap natural gas. That is going to happen whether or not there is a carbon tax. But we should acknowledge that a carbon tax will further kill coal jobs and help coal mining communities transition to a more hopeful future. Coal has roughly twice the carbon content per BTU of energy as natural gas. In the short run, a carbon price will bring about modest reductions in coal use as the electricity system operators shuffle existing facilities to use natural gas plants more and coal plants less. But over time, more coal plants will be retired and new natural gas, wind, and other renewable power plants will be built. And the demand for coal will drop even more dramatically.[14] A decision to enact a carbon tax needs to be realistic about the job impacts in coal mining and other carbon-intensive sectors. To be clear, we're not talking about many jobs, but it is reasonable to consider policies to help communities that are heavily dependent on coal mining to adjust to a new economy that does not depend on coal.

We should also recognize that lots of new jobs will be created by the transition to a zero-carbon economy. In fact, we've already created many more green jobs than the number of jobs that would be lost if coal mining stopped completely right now. The Department of Energy reports that solar technology employs nearly 374,000 workers, or five workers for every worker in coal mining. Wind technology adds another hundred thousand jobs. For utility-scale renewable power, like large-scale solar farms providing electricity directly to the grid, wages are comparable for fossil fuel power generation and solar or wind. Residential solar installers require roofers, home remodelers, and plumbing and electrical contractors. Wages in these sectors ranged from $45,000 to $60,000 in 2016 depending on the skill level. This is considerably less than coal sector wages ($82,000 for surface miners and $84,000 for underground miners) but many more job opportunities exist in these new areas and in many more locations throughout the country.[15] Moreover, the jobs are safer. Mining accidents are at a record low, but epidemiologists are finding large, new clusters of advanced black lung disease outbreaks in central Appalachia. Black lung disease is caused by inhaling coal and silica dust in mines. In its most advanced form, black lung makes breathing so difficult that the patient is essentially suffocating. The only cure is a lung transplant.[16]

Moving to a zero-carbon economy is not going to lead to a net loss of jobs. But we will have to confront the fact that jobs in certain sectors are going to go away. Government policy should not be to resist that economic force but to help ease the transition to the new economy.

WHAT ABOUT CHINA? THE TRADE QUESTION

Trade and jobs are a hot button issue. One of the most vivid images of the 1992 presidential campaign was independent candidate Ross Perot's characterization of the North American Free Trade Agreement (NAFTA) as "the giant sucking sound [of jobs leaving the United States and] going south." Perot's contempt for this trade agreement between the United States, Canada, and Mexico drove his third party presidential bid and arguably led to George H. W. Bush's loss in his re-election bid against the upstart Bill Clinton.

Fast forward twenty-five years to Donald Trump's announcement on June 1, 2017, that he would pull out of the Paris Agreement. "The Paris Climate Accord is simply the latest example of Washington entering into an agreement that disadvantages the United States to the exclusive benefit of other countries," Trump asserted, "leaving American workers—who I love—and taxpayers to absorb the cost in terms of lost jobs, lower wages, shuttered factories, and vastly diminished economic production."

Trump complained that the agreement would block the development of coal in the United States while other countries faced no such restrictions. "China will be allowed to build hundreds of additional coal plants. So we can't build the plants, but they can, according to this agreement. India will be allowed to double its coal production by 2020." Trump then summed up what in his view was a bad deal: "In short, the agreement doesn't eliminate coal jobs, it just transfers those jobs out of America and the United States, and ships them to foreign countries."[17]

Trump mischaracterized the terms of the Paris Agreement—nothing in it prohibited US firms from building coal plants—but his view neatly sums up the issues of carbon leakage and trade competitiveness. Carbon leakage is the concern that when the US enacts a policy to reduce carbon pollution (whether it's a carbon tax or cap and trade), firms may respond by moving their factories overseas to avoid the higher cost of fossil fuels that results from carbon pricing. They can then simply import and sell the finished products to US consumers. The result: no net reduction in global carbon pollution but jobs have been lost in the United States. And, so the argument goes, it could be worse! If the factories in China—or wherever the jobs go—are less efficient than US factories, the carbon pollution could be worse for the same products that would have been produced in the

United States. Now we've lost jobs and contributed to even more carbon emissions.

Is leakage a real problem? Certainly, millions of manufacturing jobs in the United States have disappeared. US manufacturing jobs peaked at just under twenty million in 1979, fell to between seventeen and eighteen million through the 1990s, but then dropped dramatically starting in 2001. Between the short recession of 2001 and the Great Recession of 2007 to 2009, they dropped to a low of about eleven and a half million and have only slowly recovered. In late 2017, manufacturing employment stands at just under twelve and a half million workers. Just as surface mining in the PRB has reduced employment through automation, gains in worker productivity have allowed US manufacturers to produce more with fewer workers. Between 1992 and 2007, worker productivity was growing at an average rate of 4.6 percent per year. That may not seem like a big deal but that growth means that in 2007 the same amount of manufactured goods could be produced with half as many workers as in 1992. And while manufacturing jobs may be declining, manufacturing itself is not. Manufacturing output has grown by 70 percent between 1992 and 2017.

Global trade does lead to some job loss but not nearly as many jobs as are lost to automation. Would a carbon tax make matters worse? Jobs are lost if US manufacturing costs are driven up, putting domestic firms at a competitive disadvantage. Carbon pricing would have a trivial impact on costs for most manufacturing sectors. A $40-per-ton carbon dioxide raises the costs of manufacturing output in the United States by, on average, just over a penny for every dollar of goods produced. US manufacturing simply is not very carbon intensive. Roughly 95 percent of all US manufactured goods (in dollar terms) are produced in sectors where a $40-per-ton carbon tax would raise costs by five cents or less per dollar of output.[18]

A few sectors have a higher proportion of carbon emissions per dollar of output. About 2 percent of manufactured goods come from sectors where a $40 carbon tax would raise costs by 10 percent or greater, such as nitrogen fertilizer, cement, and aluminum, which account for just over one-fifth of the emissions from manufacturing. Other high emission sectors include iron and steel, organic chemicals, paper, and plastics. A carbon tax would raise costs for these sectors by between one cent (plastics) and four cents (paper). Together, all these carbon-intensive sectors account for nearly two-thirds of manufacturing emissions.

The main takeaway here is that there are just a few carbon-intensive sectors that could see their costs increase significantly if a carbon tax is imposed. Not all of these sectors face foreign competition (electricity generation, for example) but some do. If we are going to address competitiveness concerns, we need only focus on the few products that are very energy intensive and for which there is also a high amount of trade. This narrows our focus to a few commodities, which account for roughly 750,000 jobs nationwide. That represents about 5 percent of all manufacturing jobs or less than 1 percent of overall employment.[19]

But it's not even clear that there's any real need to address competitive concerns. That's because most of our major trading partners are already putting climate policies in place to raise the cost of fossil fuels. Some of those policies are explicit carbon pricing policies and others are regulatory restrictions that will also raise the price of burning coal or other fossil fuels in factories. Take steel, for example. The EU and Canada, two political systems with strong carbon policies, account for nearly 40 percent of the steel imported into the United States. Korea, which has a cap and trade system, adds another 10 percent. A similar story holds for the other major imported carbon-intensive goods. Of the top five countries from whom the United States imports the most carbon-intensive and heavily traded goods, all the developed countries have a strong commitment to reducing carbon pollution. The remaining developing countries all have some form of carbon pricing. China, for example, is moving forward with what will be the largest carbon cap and trade program in the world. Once fully operational, it will be nearly double the size of the EU's ETS.[20]

To the extent leakage is a concern, we can address it with a border carbon adjustment. A border carbon adjustment applies the tax to carbon-intensive imports at the border based on their carbon content and rebates the tax on domestically produced goods that are exported. This adjustment means that carbon-intensive goods consumed in the United States are subject to the carbon tax whether they are produced domestically or abroad. Meanwhile, any goods that are exported are not subject to the tax. The border carbon adjustment levels the playing field between domestic and imported goods. Border carbon adjustments would be feasible and not overly burdensome for the federal government to administer given the small number of sectors of manufactured goods that are carbon intensive and subject to international competition.[21]

There's a second and more subtle reason why the competitiveness argument is flawed. A US carbon tax provides incentives for domestic firms to innovate and find new ways to cut emissions. This new knowledge can benefit firms in other countries. When a US firm enhances the efficiency of a coal fired boiler, for example, other firms in the US and around the world will adopt that practice. This sort of innovation creates positive spillovers that make us all better off. A US carbon tax increases the profitability of zero-carbon technologies—just the sort of incentive we should be giving

US entrepreneurs. One study finds that even a modest carbon tax could increase green innovation by as much as 50 percent. An added benefit is that the increased innovation lowers the cost of zero-carbon energy and means a lower tax rate is needed to reach any given environmental goal. But the certainty of the carbon price is key to driving that innovation.[22]

WILL IT MAKE ANY DIFFERENCE?

Another argument that opponents raise is that US policy won't make any difference in global emissions. After all, they argue, what good will it do for the United States to reduce its emissions when it accounts for only one-sixth of global carbon dioxide emissions? Moreover, developed country emissions have been relatively flat over the past twenty-five years while developing country emissions have doubled and now exceed emissions from developed countries.[23] So, a strong carbon tax in the United States will do little by itself to dent global emissions.

Strictly speaking, that's true. But it is difficult to imagine that developing countries struggling to move their citizens out of poverty will take the lead in reducing emissions if the world's wealthiest country is not taking strong climate action itself. It is true that major emitting countries and blocs like the EU and China have reiterated their commitment to the promises they made in the Paris Agreement despite the Trump Administration's retreat from the US commitments. But it is doubtful parties to the Paris Agreement will strengthen those commitments to the extent needed to address the climate problem in a meaningful way without US engagement.

If the United States enacted a carbon tax and showed leadership in moving to a zero-carbon economy, it would strengthen the hand of leaders in major developing countries like China, India, and Brazil who want to reduce emissions. A US carbon tax will not guarantee that developing countries will dramatically ramp up their efforts to reduce carbon pollution. Our acting to reduce emissions significantly is a necessary condition for more ambitious global engagement on what is, after all, a global problem.

HOW CAN WE BE SURE EMISSIONS WILL FALL?

Supporters of strong policies to reduce emissions have raised concerns that a carbon tax won't guarantee we make the major reductions in emissions we need to make to deal with the problem of climate change. That's one reason many environmental groups have gotten behind cap and trade programs such as the EU's ETS or California's allowance trading program. How do we ensure we'll get the emissions reductions we need with a carbon tax? The simplistic answer is that Congress can adjust the rates as needed to hit any desired target ten, twenty, or more years out. But a carbon tax will be a heavy political lift and we can't expect Congress can revisit this issue every few years and tweak the tax rate as needed. One solution to this problem is to set the tax rate to grow annually for ten or fifteen years and then stream-line the process for resetting the tax rate for the next ten or fifteen years. The process might include the following steps: A report by a blue-ribbon commission of experts that assesses the state of climate science and tech-nology and makes a recommendation of a tax rate schedule for the next period of time would lead to Congressional legislation, with a streamlined process requiring consideration within a fixed time period, limits on amendments, and a final up or down vote that could not be filibustered. Precedents for this streamlined process exist in the Congressional Review Act and in the 1974 Trade Act that sets out a process for reviewing trade deals.[24]

Another approach that reduces policy uncertainty even more is to in-clude in the initial carbon tax legislation the "policy thermostat" discussed in the previous chapter. The Emissions Assurance Mechanism (EAM) would automatically adjust the annual change in the tax rate in a gradual manner to keep emissions on track with a benchmark emissions trajectory set out in the initial legislation. While the difference in the tax rates from year to year would be relatively modest, the cumulative impact of several years of the tax rate rising at the upper limit of the thermostat setting would be a powerful pricing incentive to reduce emissions and get the economy back on track to hit the benchmarks. When that happens, the tax rate reverts to increasing each year at a so-called "standard" rate of increase. With an EAM, then, prices for goods would be predictable, even as the tax changed, while the United States would be more likely to reduce emissions suffi-ciently to meet targets.[25]

CAN WE DEPEND ON THE REVENUE?

Carbon tax revenue can be used to achieve one or more budgetary goals: to improve the progressivity of the US tax code, pay for tax rate reductions, pay down the federal deficit, or compensate households through carbon dividend checks. But critics say that if the point of a carbon tax is to achieve a zero-carbon economy, then we can't depend on the carbon tax revenue in the budget—if there's no carbon, there will be nothing left to tax.[26] That's certainly true in the long run. But that's the long run. We will be able to depend on carbon tax revenue over the next thirty years while simultaneously making large emissions reductions. The reduction in the tax base as less and less carbon is burned will be offset by increases in the tax rate. A recent study I did with MIT researchers found that a carbon tax starting at $40 a ton and growing 4 percent per year in real terms would result in growing revenue between now and 2050 even as emissions fall.[27]

Our study showed that even with higher carbon taxes designed to hit a very ambitious target—80 percent reduction by 2050—the carbon tax revenue would not peak until around 2040 (depending on the assumptions about the availability and cost of zero-carbon electricity sources) and then would slowly decline. In short, losing the carbon tax revenue decades from now—because we have eliminated what is arguably the world's greatest threat—is not a good reason to stand idle now.

None of the objections to a carbon tax is very compelling. So what stands in the way of action? That's a political question and the subject of the next chapter.

CHAPTER 9

Enacting a Carbon Tax: How Do We Get There?

No one doubts that enacting a carbon tax in the United States will be difficult. Energy taxes, in general, raise an almost visceral opposition among the public. Opposition to climate policy appears deep, although polling suggests it may not be as deep as it seems at first blush but rather is concentrated among small but powerful special interests. If we are to enact a carbon tax, it will require strong citizen support and a powerful campaign to overcome the vested interests that oppose the tax.

This final chapter is about how to move forward in the face of that opposition. To that end, let me lay out a framework for designing a winning carbon tax reform. A framework is more useful than a specific reform because any reform that could actually get through Congress will require compromise and will likely build on unexpected and unpredictable alliances.

A framework can help us keep our eyes on the important elements of any reform that can get lost in the hustle and bustle of political dealmaking. Knowing what is important and what should be part of any carbon tax solution is essential and the framework can help us with that. The framework should be sensitive both to the good design principles that economists focus on when thinking about taxes as well as to what is politically feasible.

Lest you think we're on a fool's errand, consider where the public stands on climate policy today. The monthly Quinnipiac University Poll is a useful indicator of public opinion on topical issues and has been tracking opinions on climate change for some time, with pretty consistent results. Nearly half of respondents in the March 2018 survey are very concerned about climate change and another quarter somewhat concerned. Nearly two-thirds feel that the United States needs to do more to address climate change. The aggregate numbers do mask some important partisan differences. While 92 percent of Democrats and 64 percent of independent voters feel more should be done, only 27 percent of Republicans feel that way. A similar split exists for other climate-related questions, pointing at the political hurdles that are blocking a bipartisan path forward.[1]

Researchers at Yale and George Mason universities have been polling registered voters on climate change for years. In the May 2017 poll, two-thirds of respondents felt the United States should reduce its emissions no matter what other countries do. While Democrats and independents were more likely to take that position, just over half of Republicans also agreed that the United States should act. Asked whether fossil fuel companies should pay a carbon tax, 70 percent strongly or somewhat supported that position. Again, Democrats and independents were more likely to take this view, but, nearly one-half of Republicans supported this position.

Despite Donald Trump's claims that climate change is a hoax, half of the voters who supported him in the 2016 presidential election agreed that global warming is happening while another 20 percent are uncertain and are not prepared to dismiss the problem. Even more interesting, over 60 percent of Trump voters supported taxing or regulating carbon pollution as a way to reduce it.[2]

A FRAMEWORK FOR REFORM

Notwithstanding the polling data, a carbon tax won't be an easy sell. Here is where a framework for the proposal can help. By focusing our attention on important elements of the carbon tax as part of any fiscal reform, a framework can impose discipline that can help overcome some of the hurdles to the reform's passage in Congress. Ronald Reagan's call for a massive tax reform in 1984 provides just such a model framework.

On January 25, 1984, Ronald Reagan stood before a joint session of Congress to give his last State of the Union Address before facing re-election later that year. With Speaker of the House Tip O'Neill (D-MA) and Vice President George H. W. Bush sitting behind him, Reagan called for "an historic [tax] reform for fairness, simplicity, and incentives for growth." He called for a plan that would raise no additional revenue but "make the tax base broader, so personal tax rates could come down, not go up." With those few lines, the president launched perhaps the most significant reform of the tax code since the introduction of the modern income tax in 1913.[3]

In this speech, Reagan established a framework for what would become the Tax Reform Act of 1986. The framework had just two principles: It had to be revenue neutral and it had to lower tax rates. This meant that Congress would have to eliminate many tax shelters to broaden the tax base. This simple framework masked devilish complexity that needed to be overcome before the reform was completed, but it imposed an important discipline that helped keep lawmakers on track.

Here's my framework: A US carbon tax should be revenue neutral, contribute to fairness, streamline national climate policy, and lead to significant emission reductions over time.

REVENUE NEUTRALITY

Republicans and Democrats have argued for years over the size of the federal government. Republicans traditionally favor a smaller role and blame Democrats for enlarging government's presence in our daily lives.[4] It is a contentious debate and one that should not ensnare climate policy. Revenue neutrality means that all carbon tax revenue should be returned to US residents either through tax cuts, direct payments, or some combination of the two. It should not be spent on new "green investment" programs, subsidies for renewable energy, or otherwise earmarked for new spending. I'm not arguing against investing in some of these areas—indeed, I think we should and I'll say more about this in a bit—but we should not link carbon tax revenue to green spending programs. If those programs are worthwhile, they are worthwhile regardless of where the money comes from.[5]

Revenue neutrality is likely to be an important element of any bipartisan effort to enact a carbon tax. A few examples from across the political spectrum support this. The CLC's Republican-led effort for a carbon tax makes the return of revenue to the American people through carbon dividends a centerpiece of their proposal. Prior to the passage of the tax-cut bill in late 2017, the conservative American Action Forum released a "20/20 proposal" for a carbon tax starting at $20 a ton to help reduce the corporate tax rate to 20 percent. Revenue neutrality is also a key element in the national carbon "fee and dividend" proposed by the grassroot advocacy group Citizens' Climate Lobby (CCL). I would, however, make one small accommodation in spending, and that is for transitional fairness.

FAIRNESS

Fairness is often raised as an obstacle to a carbon tax. Because energy makes up a more significant share of the budget of low-income families than higher-income families, many worry about a carbon tax's impact on poorer households. Tax reform packages can be designed to offset any regressive impact on lower income households. One could take the approach of the CLC's tax and dividend approach and rebate all of the revenue to US families. This would have bipartisan appeal. Climatologist Jim Hansen, former director of the NASA Goddard Institute of Space Studies and perhaps best known for his 1988 Congressional testimony on global warming that helped raise public awareness of climate change, also has called for a tax and dividend approach.

But a carbon tax plan can achieve fairness without necessarily giving *all* the revenue back through a dividend scheme. A portion of the revenue could go to low- and moderate-income households to offset higher energy bills while the remainder could be used to lower income tax rates. Lowering tax rates would disproportionately benefit higher-income households and so ensure benefits across the entire income distribution. Using revenue to lower tax rates also increases the efficiency of our economy by reducing disincentives to work or save.

There is another aspect to fairness. How should we treat workers in industries that are disproportionately affected by the shift to a zero-carbon economy? Nearly one-quarter of all US coal miners work in West Virginia. Kentucky has another 15 percent of all coal mining jobs. No other state comes close to the number of coal miners in these two states. If we focus on a state's dependence on coal rather than on the absolute number of jobs, West Virginia and Wyoming stand out. They have the highest share of employees working in coal mining and diversifying each state's economy to become less dependent on coal would benefit the economies of these states.

Programs like the Solar Holler program in West Virginia are helping people like Ethan Spaulding, age 26, prepare for life after coal. Spaulding had hoped to work in a coal mine after graduating from high school in Crum, West Virginia, (estimated population, 175), but no jobs were available. Spaulding enrolled in the two-year Solar Holler apprenticeship program that trains solar installation technicians. While the wage is less than he might have earned in a coal mine, the work is steady and safe. Solar Holler, a nonprofit, partners with community development groups like Coalfield Development to bring solar power to homes and businesses. Their training program is part of a local economic development project to diversify the state's economy and prepare for a post-coal era. Solar Holler's motto "Mine the Sun" sums up its home-grown approach to powering Appalachia while providing jobs with a future in the region.[6]

People in coal mining communities, and in the oil and gas boom towns of North Dakota or western Pennsylvania, will need jobs as we move away from a fossil-fuel-based economy—and the federal government should partner with state and local governments to develop plans to help these communities transition. Pretending that change is not inevitable or that we can go back to the heyday of coal mining is neither realistic nor helpful to these communities.

STREAMLINED CLIMATE POLICY

US climate and energy policy is a hodgepodge of tax breaks and subsidies mixed with regulatory oversight. There's a rule of thumb in economics that you need at least as many policy instruments as policy goals you hope to achieve.[7] Whether you need more instruments than goals is debatable, but it's pretty clear that we have too many instruments in our basket of energy and climate policies.

We could start by eliminating some costly energy-related tax breaks. Whether we enact a carbon tax or not, we should get rid of tax breaks for oil and gas production in the United States. These are a waste of about $4 billion a year, don't do anything to enhance national security or help us reach any other reasonable goal, and run counter to good environmental and climate policy.[8] Next, we can remove various investment and production tax credits for renewable energy projects. These tax breaks, discussed in chapter 4, only make sense as a way of supporting renewable energy investment and production if we can't tax carbon pollution. The existing tax breaks are a way to level the playing field between carbon-polluting fuels and carbon-free fuels. If we can't raise the cost of the polluting fuel, then the next best thing is to lower the cost of the nonpolluting fuel. But if we enact a carbon tax, a reasonable bargain is to cut those tax breaks. That's another $3 billion a year.

While I've argued that we should not use carbon tax revenue to expand government spending, there's a good argument for diverting the roughly $7 billion a year from tax breaks for fossil and renewable energy to basic and applied energy R&D. Doing so would double federal spending on energy R&D.[9] R&D is a textbook example of the private market falling short in providing the socially optimal amount of private spending. The private sector will invest in R&D based on the return earned from any new discoveries. Typically, the societal benefits from new discoveries are far greater than the returns the inventors can actually earn. And an invention in one sector may trigger innovations in other sectors in ways that the original inventor can't benefit from. Patent protection is intended to make sure inventors get some of the gains from their creativity, but it is an imperfect tool and falls short. Moreover, even if we could somehow restrict the spillovers of an idea to other areas to prevent others from freeriding on the creativity of some R&D lab, why would we want to do that? After all, if clever innovations have lots of useful applications in society, we should not restrict their spread. But we should recognize that if the private sector can't reap all the gains from innovations, markets will underprovide R&D. In other words, just as there is a role for government to enact policies that reduce pollution, there is a role for government to enact policies to encourage R&D. One of those tools is federal funding for R&D, especially for basic science.

The revolution in battery storage is a good example of the potential societal payoff to R&D that exceeds the private return. With transportation responsible for 34 percent of energy-related carbon dioxide emissions, low-cost batteries will be key to moving transportation off of fossil fuels if electric vehicles are to play a major role in the transition. Companies like Tesla are pushing hard to bring those costs down. And they have come down. The price of battery storage has fallen from nearly $600 a kWh in 2013 to under $300 in 2016. To bring costs and battery weight down even further will likely require new advances in technology that move us away from the lithium ion battery. That is why ARPA-E, the Department of Energy (DOE) funding agency that focuses on high-potential, high-risk energy R&D funding, initiated the Batteries for Electrical Energy Storage in Transportation (BEEST) program. The BEEST program set a high goal for battery advances. For projects to be considered, the innovative technology had to have the promise of allowing electric vehicles to travel 300 to 500 miles on a single charge for less than $10 per charge.[10] Batteries that cost less, are lightweight and compact, and recharge at faster rates can transform the transportation sector. But they will, no doubt, help transform other sectors, including electricity generation, by allowing for electricity storage to eliminate the need for costly and polluting peaking power plants (diesel and gas power plants that are used for only a few hours a year when electricity demand is especially high). While battery innovators will capture many of the economic gains from selling these new technologies, the social gains will far exceed what shareholders in battery companies gain in dividends and earnings. In short, given the need for new technologies to bring us zero-carbon energy at affordable prices, it makes good sense to ramp up energy-related R&D. Doubling federal spending by diverting money saved by closing energy-related tax breaks would do just that.

Now we get to the hard question. What do we do about the requirement under the Clean Air Act that the EPA regulate and reduce greenhouse gas emissions? Here's what the CLC's plan calls for. In return for an initial carbon tax high enough to achieve greater emission reductions than would be achieved under current regulations, EPA's regulatory authority over carbon dioxide would be phased out.[11] While the idea of replacing an inefficient regulatory approach with an efficient pricing mechanism is appealing, it is worth noting that the Clean Air Act has been a powerful tool for improving environmental quality in this country over the past half-century. Simply giving up Clean Air Act oversight of carbon pollution is asking quite a bit given the potential for Congress to pass a carbon tax today only to have a future Congress repeal the tax. The challenge is to construct a carbon tax that provides the assurances that we will meet environmental goals over the course of this century.

One way forward is to preserve EPA regulatory authority over greenhouse gas emissions but suspend any regulatory action for emissions covered by a carbon tax so long as demonstrable progress in reducing emissions is being made. That, of course, requires that we define "progress." Progress could be measured as a target reduction in emissions relative to a given base year (e.g., 2005 emissions) at various milestone years between now and 2050. Failure to hit the targeted emission reductions would automatically trigger resumption of the EPA regulatory process under the Clean Air Act. An independent commission or advisory group established under law could oversee progress toward the emission reductions. In addition, the carbon tax could be designed so that the tax rate automatically adjusts over time to keep the United States on target to reach long-run emission reduction goals.[12]

This is not to argue that *all* greenhouse gas regulations should be put on hold. It is not realistic to subject all greenhouse gas emissions to a carbon tax. Some emissions are simply too hard to measure. A good example is methane emissions associated with fossil fuel extraction. Methane is a potent greenhouse gas with an impact on the environment some thirty times that of carbon dioxide and a source of the expression "canary in a coal mine." As recently as 1986 in the UK, canaries were taken down into coal mines to detect poisonous gases such as methane. The idea was that the sensitive birds would die before concentrations of the gases rose to levels lethal to miners.[13] When underground coal mining was the dominant source of coal in the United States, coalbed methane was a major source of greenhouse gas emissions. Now with the shift to surface coal, methane emissions are more associated with oil and natural gas fracking. These emissions are hard to measure and are found at nearly every drill site to some extent. Rather than try to measure and tax these emissions, it makes more sense to put strong regulations in place that require state-of-the-art drilling and extraction techniques and equipment be used to minimize methane leaks. That would be coupled with strong monitoring and enforcement. Similarly, agricultural and land use emissions are difficult to tax and so more suitable to regulation.

In summary, we need to avoid a "bait and switch" where regulatory oversight over greenhouse gases is traded for a carbon tax only to find Congress does not have the will to set a sufficiently high tax to make a significant dent in emissions. Many environmentalists are already mistrustful of a carbon tax, and it will be important to bring them on board in order to get Congress to act. This leads to my last framework principle. The policy must significantly cut emissions.

SIGNIFICANT EMISSION REDUCTIONS

As the richest country in the world, the United States has an obligation to lead. By enacting a carbon tax aggressive enough to drive emissions down dramatically, we can demonstrate that leadership. It will not do to set a carbon tax at $25 a ton, let it rise at the rate of inflation, and call it a day. A modest carbon tax will, at best, make a modest dent in emissions. We need to do more. It is impossible to say exactly what tax rate is required to achieve a particular emissions target. Much depends on technological advancement and consumer behavior. For example, widespread adoption of battery-powered motor vehicles would shift transportation from oil to electricity and so open up opportunities for renewably generated electricity that powers our transport fleet. Whether we see that widespread adoption will depend on costs, advances in battery life, and other factors.

However technology advances, it is likely we'll need a robust carbon price. A 2014 exercise by top energy modelers, organized by researchers at Stanford University, found that a 50 percent reduction in US emissions by 2050 would require a carbon price between $10 and $60 per ton of carbon dioxide in 2020 (looking across the bulk of models and technology assumptions) and between $100 and $300 in 2050. While the international climate negotiations have focused on a target of an 80 percent emissions reduction by 2050 from 2005 levels, most research suggests that this will be extremely expensive. The Stanford modeling study corroborates that. The participating modelers estimate that the

2050 price on carbon dioxide required to hit that target would be somewhere in the range of $200 to over $500 a ton, depending on model assumptions.

What carbon price will be needed to reach any future emissions target will depend in large measure on the pace of clean energy technological development. A substantial price on carbon dioxide emissions will help spur that development. Given the very high (and probably politically unacceptable) cost of an 80 percent emissions reduction, a more modest but still aggressive goal of emission reductions between now and 2050 may be advisable. One approach would be to set a target for 2035 combined with an assessment beginning in 2030 to set a subsequent target for 2050. A 2035 target of a 45 percent reduction in carbon dioxide emissions (relative to 2005 levels), for example, would be ambitious but within reach. A subsequent target could be set for 2050, perhaps somewhere in the 60 to 80 percent range of emissions reduction by 2050, with the precise target set as new information emerges over the first fifteen years about the damages from greenhouse gas emissions as well as clean energy technology costs.[14]

Any target set out in carbon tax legislation could be conditioned on OECD countries also committing to that goal within a short time frame and the major non-OECD emitting countries committing to that goal within, say, a decade. This could be combined with the "climate club" idea that Yale economist William Nordhaus has proposed. Developed countries (or any group of major countries, for that matter) could band together and impose trade sanctions on countries that do not take effective action to reduce emissions.[15]

Once the goal is set, the carbon tax should contain a mechanism for adjustment to ensure the target is met. One simple way to do that is to enact a carbon tax with an initial tax rate (say $40 a ton of carbon dioxide emissions). The legislation would also include a clear and transparent rule for adjusting the tax rate over time to hit emission reduction benchmarks, also set out in the legislation. This would provide greater assurance that the United States would hit desired emission reduction targets while still providing price predictability.[16]

The tax should also be designed so that there is the political will to sustain high tax rates on emissions. Ted Halstead, CEO of the CLC, has argued that the rebate in its tax and dividend plan will build political support for high tax rates since rebates would rise along with tax rates. Halstead may or may not be right but he is focusing on the right question: how to build political will for the changes to our energy system necessary to move to a zero-emissions economy.

A carbon tax is a heavy lift, no doubt. But the need for action is so compelling that we should not be daunted by the hard work that will be required. There are some hopeful signs out there. It's no surprise that a number of Democrats have come out in favor of a carbon tax. Senators Sheldon Whitehouse (D-RI) and Brian Schatz (D-HI) rolled out their American Opportunity Carbon Fee Act at an event hosted by the conservative American Enterprise Institute in June 2015. Their current bill (S. 2368) calls for a carbon tax rate of $50 a ton in 2019 to rise each year at the inflation rate plus 2 percent until emissions fall to 80 percent below 2005 levels. Revenue is returned to US residents through a combination of tax credits and increases to Social Security payments. In addition, money is sent to the states to assist low-income and rural households and provide job training for workers in fossil-fuel related industries.

Perhaps more significant, Senator Lindsey Graham (R-SC) announced at the National Clean Energy Week conference in Washington, DC, in September 2017 his interest in a carbon fee to replenish the national Highway Trust Fund and to support financially struggling nuclear power plants.[17] He is the first sitting Republican senator to come out in favor of a carbon tax.

Outside Congress, the CLC has a star-studded roster of Republicans supporting a carbon tax, including former chairmen of the Council of Economic Advisers Martin Feldstein and N. Gregory Mankiw along with former US Treasury secretaries George Schultz, James Baker, and Henry Paulson. Their plan calls for the carbon tax to start at $40 a ton and increase steadily. Other Republican heavyweights who support a carbon tax include former Director of the Congressional Budget Office Douglas Holtz-Eakin whose think-tank, the American Action Forum, proposed a tax reform plan including a carbon tax to help finance corporate tax cuts in the run-up to the 2017 tax reform.[18] Other prominent Republican supporters include former South Carolina Congressman Bob Inglis, who heads up the group republicEn, a group of conservatives who "believe that with a truly level playing field, free enterprise can deliver the innovation to solve climate change." For Inglis, leveling the playing field includes a price on carbon pollution. Finally, Donald Trump's chairman of the Council of Economic Advisers is American Enterprise Institute economist Kevin Hassett, a long-time proponent of a carbon tax.[19] And in Congress, the bipartisan House Climate Solutions Caucus has seventy-eight members (as of mid-2018). The Caucus was formed to "educate members on economically viable options to reduce climate risk" and accepts members only in bipartisan pairs: one Democrat and one Republican.

CONCLUSION

A sea change has begun in Washington. Despite the Trump Administration's retreat on climate policy, more and more leading Republicans see a carbon tax as a common-sense solution—the simplest way to reduce carbon pollution at the lowest cost to the US economy. But real change won't happen unless citizens speak up and demand action. And we're beginning to see action by citizen groups at the local level across the nation. Whether it's the local chapters of the national CCL organizing for a national fee and dividend plan or state-level groups like the Massachusetts ClimateXChange working for a state-level carbon fee, more and more citizens are rallying to the idea of a carbon price. While political leadership is important, so is citizen leadership; after all, politicians like nothing better than a movement to get in front of.

The stakes are high. We're talking about our planet's future. I'm enough of an optimist to believe that our nation, along with other major carbon polluters, will eventually take strong action. But the pessimist in me believes that we won't act or, if we do, we'll act in an especially inefficient and costly way unless people rally behind a better approach. That better approach is a carbon tax. The clock is ticking. Atmospheric concentrations of carbon dioxide at the Mauna Loa Observatory crept up another two parts per million in the past year while I wrote this book. Let's get to work.

What Next?

LEARN MORE

Here are a few resources where you can learn more about climate policy in general and carbon taxes in particular.

Carbon Tax Center (www.carbontax.org): The Carbon Tax Center supports a national carbon tax. Its website has a great deal of up-to-date information on carbon taxation and carbon tax campaigns at the national, state, and local level.

Niskanen Center (niskanencenter.org): The Niskanen Center is a libertarian think tank that supports a national carbon tax. With strong roots in conservative circles, the center demonstrates that support for a carbon tax can cut across political lines. They have a section on climate issues on their policy webpage.

Resources for the Future (rff.org): Resources for the Future (RFF) is an independent and nonpartisan think tank focused on environmental, energy, and natural resource issues. Its top-notch economists and other experts publish timely research with a strong and pragmatic policy focus. When Capitol Hill staffers want to understand the impact of a new environmental law or regulation, their first call is often to an RFF expert.

National Bureau of Economic Research (nber.org): The National Bureau of Economic Research (NBER) is a private, nonpartisan organization made up of many of the top academic economists at leading US colleges and universities. Among other resources, the NBER publishes a working paper series that contains cutting-edge research on all matters of interest to economists. Working papers from the hundred or so members of the NBER's Environment and Energy Program present the most up-to-date climate change research. A word of warning: these papers can be pretty technical and wonky. But if your tastes run that way, you'll find some interesting reading there.

TAKE ACTION

Where do your two senators and your representative in Congress stand on climate policy and a carbon tax? Take the time to find out. Don't know who represents you in Washington? Many websites can help you find your senators and representative. Your search engine can help here. Or go to the League of Women Voters website (www.lwv.org). Their home page has a link to find your elected officials from the local to the national level.

If your senators and representative support strong action on climate policy or, better yet, a carbon tax, take the time to write and thank them for their support. If they haven't taken a stand or oppose taking action, politely write and explain why you think they should reconsider. Be sure to let them know that you vote (you *do* vote, right?). Maybe you could even tell them about this book. The goal is to engage with them in civil discourse. After all, the whole point is to mobilize support and get our political leaders to act.

NOTES

PREFACE

1. Maya Angelou attributed the adage about easy reading to Hawthorne in, among other places, a 1990 interview in the *Paris Review*, available at https://www. theparisreview.org/interviews/2279/maya-angelou-the-art-of-fiction-no-119- maya-angelou, accessed Oct. 11, 2017. The self-styled "Quote Investigator" Garson O'Toole finds the earliest use of the adage in 1837 by the English essayist Thomas Hood in a letter to the editor of *The Athenaeum*, https:// quoteinvestigator.com/2014/11/05/hard-writing/, accessed Oct. 11, 2017.

INTRODUCTION

1. The Weather Channel summarizes the damage at https://weather.com/storms/ hurricane/news/tropical-storm-harvey-forecast-texas-louisiana-arkansas, accessed Apr. 2, 2018.
2. The update on Puerto Rico's recovery from Hurricane Maria comes from Houser and Marsters (2018).
3. Forest fire statistics are from the National Interagency Fire Center (www.nifc. gov), accessed Apr. 20, 2018. Ten million acres burned in 2017, just one hundred thousand acres fewer than in the record-setting year of 2015. Syrian drought and conflict are discussed in Fountain (2015) and Stokes (2016).
4. Tyson quote from Gupta (2014). See US Department of State (2015) for emissions-reduction commitment. It is not quite clear what President Trump intends with respect to the Paris Agreement. In his speech in the Rose Garden on June 1, 2017, Trump said that "we're getting out [of the Agreement]. But we will start to negotiate, and we will see if we can make a deal that's fair. And if we can, that's great." The EU has made clear that there is nothing to negotiate around the Paris Agreement and neither Trump nor the State Department have clarified his remarks. See statement at https://www.whitehouse.gov/the-press-office/2017/06/01/statement-president-trump-paris-climate-accord, accessed Nov. 15, 2017.
5. The EPA announcement was published in the Federal Register on Friday, April 13, 2018, in Volume 83, No. 72, pp. 16077–16087.
6. Information about the US Climate Alliance taken from its website, https://www. usclimatealliance.org/, accessed Feb. 20, 2018.
7. ExxonMobil, Shell, and BP are corporate founding members of the Climate Leadership Council that advocates for a national carbon tax.

8. The OECD data come from OECD.Stat, available at http://stats.oecd.org/Index. aspx?DataSetCode=ENV_ENVPOLICY, accessed Oct. 5, 2017.

CHAPTER 1

1. NH woman and crop-loss statistic: "Scenes from New England's Drought: Dry Wells, Dead Fish, and Ailing Farms," *New York Times*, Sept. 26, 2016. Roxy Moore quotes from video posted on the *New York Times* website at https://www. nytimes.com/2016/09/27/us/scenes-from-new-englands-drought-dry-wells-dead-fish-and-ailing-farms.html, accessed Mar. 3, 2017. Cranberry farm and Gates-Allen description of dried up cranberry bog: "Drought Makes Cranberry Harvest Extra Hard Work," *Boston Globe*, Oct. 10, 2016.
2. Data from http://droughtmonitor.unl.edu/Data.aspx, accessed Aug. 20, 2018.
3. http://climatechange.cornell.edu/drought-takes-its-toll/, accessed Feb. 6, 2017.
4. *Crop Progress & Condition: New England*, US Department of Agriculture National Agricultural Statistics Service, Oct. 17, 2016.
5. "Drought Costs California Farmers $600 Million, But Impact Eases," *Sacramento Bee*, Aug. 15, 2016, http://www.sacbee.com/news/state/california/water-and-drought/article95771347.html, accessed Feb. 6, 2017.
6. http://floodlist.com/america/usa/houston-floods-president-declares-major-disaster, accessed Feb. 6, 2017.
7. http://floodlist.com/america/usa/texas-floods-deaths-houston-state-of-disaster, accessed Feb. 6, 2017.
8. This assumes each of the 319 million people in the United States has a fifty-gallon bathtub.
9. Water records from Fritz and Samenow (2017).
10. Lund quotation and flooding facts from Fuller (2017).
11. Climate scientist quoted in Miller (2017). The article also describes California's aquifer collapse.
12. Data on temperature patterns taken from NOAA National Centers for Environmental Information, Climate at a Glance: US Time Series, Average Temperature, published January 2018, http://www.ncdc.noaa.gov/cag/, accessed Jan. 16, 2018. Summer is defined as June through August.
13. Topsoil loss information from Vance Johnson, *Heaven's Tableland* (1947) quoted in Hansen and Libecap (2004). Economics losses are taken from an analysis by Hornbeck (2012).
14. Quotation from Elizabeth Kolbert, "A Song of Ice," *New Yorker*, Oct. 24, 2016.
15. Flood estimates reported by Copeland et al. (2012).
16. Patel (2017) and Kahn (2017a).
17. 100-year GWP with feedbacks. See Table 1-3, 2016 US Greenhouse Gas Inventory, pp. 1–10.
18. Intergovernmental Panel on Climate Change (2014) *Technical Summary* of Working Group I's contribution to the Fifth Assessment Report, p. 37.
19. Hughes et al. (2017) document the most recent pan-tropical episode of mass bleaching.
20. Cave and Gillis (2017)
21. "Russia Stakes New Claim to Expanse in the Arctic," *New York Times*, Aug. 4, 2015, http://nyti.ms/1OOLin4, accessed on Oct. 27, 2016. See also follow up article, "Russia Presents Revised Claim of Arctic Territory to the United Nations," *New York Times*, Feb. 9, 2016 at http://nyti.ms/1o1rlCF, accessed Feb. 6, 2018.

22. Mattis quote recounted by Watson (2017).
23. Historic sea level rise: p. 1150 and Table 13.5 in Church et al. (2013). Melting glaciers directly contribute to sea level rise. The other significant contributor to sea-level rise is thermal expansion of water as it heats up.
24. See Moser et al. (2014)
25. Kahn (2017b)
26. See "Wildland Fire Roundup for Sunday, May 31st." Alaska Wildland Fire Information, https://akfireinfo.com/2015/05/, accessed Jan. 15, 2018.
27. Richtel and Santos (2016).
28. Fire statistics from the National Interagency Fire Center (www.nifc.gov) and its daily Incident Management Situation Report published on October 20, 2017. Also see Loria (2017) and Daniels (2017). California insurance claims reported in a press release available at https://www.insurance.ca.gov/0400-news/0100-press-releases/2017/release135-17.cfm, accessed Jan. 16, 2018.
29. US Department of Agriculture press release, "Forest Service Wildland Fire Suppression Costs Exceed $2 billion," available at https://www.usda.gov/media/press-releases/2017/09/14/forest-service-wildland-fire-suppression-costs-exceed-2-billion, accessed Jan. 17, 2018. Also, see Thompson and Elliott (2017).
30. Dale (2010).
31. Study by Abatzoglou and Williams (2016).
32. This material comes from the Harris (2010) as well as Gillis (2010).
33. Ralph Keeling quote from Gillis (2010).
34. Roth quote from Bill McKibben "A Special Moment in History," in *Globalization and the Challenges of a New Century: A Reader*, Howard D. Mehlinger, p. 396, https://books.google.com/books?id=VLwlnhq01RIC&pg=PA396&lpg=PA396&dq=%22the+earth+is+breathing%22+keeling&source=bl&ots=BGtLPOLFWX&sig=mzPQzvDiGhdd7V7FBbxqhGjGCs0&hl=en&sa=X&ved=0ahUKEwjpyozDibjRAhXrDsAKHeZLB4cQ6AEIIjAC#v=onepage&q=%22the%20earth%20is%20breathing%22%20keeling&f=false, accessed May 9, 2017.
35. Petit et al. (1999).

CHAPTER 2

1. Information about New York City gas station closures from Hu (2012). Aerts et al. (2014), Lin et al. (2012). Current risk from Table S3 and increase in risk from Figure S4, both from Aerts et al. (2014).
2. This example draws on the NJ–NY Connect (S2) strategy described in Aerts et al. (2014). As an illustration of the costs of inaction, I have taken modest liberties with the specific estimates in their study to simplify the exposition. None of the conclusions I draw about net benefits run counter to the conclusions in their study.
3. A website search easily locates free on-line calculators that will compute the present discounted value of some future amount for a given interest rate.
4. Given the numbers for the example, the benefits of the project in the form of reduced damages is $24.5 billion in today's dollars. This is one and a half times the costs of the project so the project would more than pay for itself through reduced damages. The project passes a basic benefit-cost test: the benefits less costs (or net benefits) are positive. Whether it is a good idea to move ahead with this project or not depends on whether some alternative approach has a higher net benefit. The premise of this book is that a carbon tax has a high net benefit in contrast to business as usual.

5. Insurance companies couldn't survive if the premiums didn't exceed their average expected loss. That difference covers the administrative costs of offering insurance as well as profits to the owners of the company. It also allows them to hold reserves to protect themselves against a run of insurance payouts from a string of bad outcomes.

6. Another reason the $1 billion number is too low is that damage estimates only focus on those costs of recovery that can be measured. This includes insurance payouts to rebuild homes and the cost to cities and towns to repair roads and other infrastructure. What it does not include is the cost in people's time and inconvenience as the rebuilding process unfolds or the cost of any lives lost or injuries incurred. Factoring those in drives the cost of our climate inaction up even higher.

7. The project was a massive one. Consider the six-story Tremont House that covered an acre of land at Lake and Dearborn Streets. It was inched up a full six feet by 500 men tending 5,000 jackscrews over a two-week period. The hotel continued to operate during this process. The Chicago Magazine published an amusing illustrated history of this project in August 2010 available at http:// www.chicagomag.com/Chicago-Magazine/August-2010/Raising-Chicago-An-Illustrated-History/index.php?cparticle=3&siarticle=2#artanc. Excerpts from the Chicago Daily Tribune from February 1861 that document the raising of the Tremont House are available at http://www.jonathanriley.net/csc.html, accessed Mar. 13, 2018.

8. The risk to Miami Beach from rising sea levels is documented by Kolbert (2015).

9. The role of air conditioning in driving down death rates on high temperature days in the United States is documented in Barreca et al. (2016).

10. Department of Energy estimates reported at https://energy.gov/energysaver/ air-conditioning, accessed on May 10, 2017.

11. Estimates of household air conditioning penetration from International Energy Agency (2018).

12. Just over one billion people still lacked access to electricity in 2014 according to data reported by the international nongovernmental organization Sustainable Energy For All (http://www.se4all.org). Half of those live in rural Sub-Saharan Africa where electrification rates are very slow. Data taken from report on electrification available at http://www.se4all.org/heatmaps, accessed Feb. 11, 2018.

13. Bolstead (2017) documents the housing anecdote in Miami. Economists have studied the phenomenon of environmental gentrification. Banzhaf and Walsh (2008), for example, document the differential impacts of possible exposure to chemicals in communities and finds that increasing exposure leads to exit of higher income families and a higher concentration of poorer families remaining in those communities.

14. The survey is described in Doran and Zimmerman (2009) who report other studies showing even higher agreement among scientific experts. The American Geophysical Union survey has been criticized by some, and a good assessment of the study is provided by Kessler (2013).

15. More precisely, the Worst Outcome criterion is known as the Max-Min criterion. This discussion of Pascal's Wager, its relevance for climate change, and the role of climate skeptics is based on research by Rezai and van der Ploeg (2017).

16. Popper (1963) developed the concept of "falsification," the idea that scientists can definitively disprove theories but never actually prove them. Falsification is the bedrock of modern empirical scientific inquiry.
17. Arrow and Fisher (1974) first pointed out the role that environmental irreversibilities play in project evaluation—irreversible action has a cost that is ignored in a standard cost-benefit calculation. Pindyck (2002) explores this idea for the specific case of irreversible greenhouse gas emissions.
18. In the literature on risk, this is known as the Min-Max Regret Criterion. See Rezai and van der Ploeg (2017).

CHAPTER 3

1. Coase's 1960 paper, "The Problem of Social Cost," has over 30,000 citations on Google Scholar, more than double the citations of the top-ranked papers by other Nobel laureates such as Joseph Stiglitz, Paul Krugman, and Paul Samuelson. Douglas Allen has a precis of the case at www.sfu.ca/~allen/Sturges v Bridgman.doc, accessed May 9, 2017.
2. Coase recounts his life story in the autobiography he provided to the Nobel Committee after receiving the 1991 Nobel Prize in Economics, http://www.nobelprize.org/nobel_prizes/economic-sciences/laureates/1991/coase-bio.html, accessed May 11, 2017.
3. Burning fossil fuels also creates local pollutants such as ozone and particulate matter that have damaging health effects. Those are ignored here. But any policy to reduce carbon pollution would have the additional benefit of reducing local pollutants.
4. The statement that something is not optimal suggests there is something we are trying to optimize. In this example it is the joint profits of the confectioner and doctor. But this statement holds regardless of what we are trying to optimize, whether it is the sum of profits in society, consumer well-being, or some other societal goal.
5. This is an example of *marginal analysis* which looks at the effects on joint profits of an increase or decrease of one unit of production (a marginal change).
6. This anecdote is recounted in Coase's obituary written by Lyons (2013).
7. Power plant statistics for 2015 from the US Energy Information Administration (EIA)'s *Electric Power Annual*, Table 4.1, https://www.eia.gov/electricity/annual/. Vehicle statistics from the Bureau of Transportation Statistics publication *National Transportation Statistics*, Table 1.11, https://www.rita.dot.gov/bts/sites/rita.dot.gov.bts/files/publications/national_transportation_statistics/index.html, both accessed May 13, 2017.
8. But the cost could be lower. Bridgman might, for example, invest in new sound and vibration proofing along his back wall and install quieter machinery to grind his ingredients and so avoid having to pay a tax at all. In that case, he could continue to profitably operate ten hours a day. Let's assume the cost of the investments (converted to a daily cost) is £10. Then the cost of addressing this noise pollution is £10 rather than £31 loss in profits.
9. Mancur Olson developed this idea in his famous book *The Logic of Collective Action*. It explains how it can be difficult to enact policies with diffuse benefits and concentrated costs. Since benefits are diffuse, those benefiting from the policy have little incentive to engage in the political process to support the policy while those who incur the costs have a large incentive to defeat the policy. This

speaks to the importance of addressing the costs to sectors such as coal mining if a carbon tax is to be politically successful.

10. The revenue estimate is taken from the US Department of the Treasury (Treasury) working paper written by Horowitz et al. (2017).

11. Books that do a good job of that include, among many others, Slemrod and Bakija (2017) and Gale (2018).

12. The double dividend literature is reviewed by Goulder (1995), Fullerton and Metcalf (1998), and Bovenberg (1999), among others.

13. Historic corporate income tax rates are reported at https://taxfoundation.org/federal-corporate-income-tax-rates-income-years-1909-2012/, accessed May 13, 2017.

14. Existing and planned carbon tax regimes are summarized in World Bank Group (2016).

15. A metric ton is 1,000 kilograms or roughly 2,200 pounds. Tax rates from Swedish Ministry of Environment, "Twenty Years of Carbon Pricing in Sweden" and presentation by Ulrika Raab, Senior Advisor of the Swedish Energy Agency at the PMR Technical Workshop on Carbon Tax: Design and Implementation in Practice on March 22, 2017. Swedish krona converted to US dollars using an exchange rate (SK 1 = USD 0.11) as of May 2018.

16. The Heritage Report written by Dayaaratna et al. (2016).

17. GDP growth data from the World Bank DataBank, http://data.worldbank.org/indicator/NY.GDP.MKTP.KD.ZG, accessed May 8, 2018.

18. The idea that pollution initially increases with a country's income but then peaks and begins to decline is known as the Environmental Kuznets Curve and was first posited by Grossman and Krueger (1995).

19. All currency conversions to US dollars (CD1 = USD 0.78) use exchange rates as of late May 2018. Information about the tax rate taken from https://www2.gov.bc.ca/gov/content/environment/climate-change/planning-and-action/carbon-tax, accessed May 23, 2018.

20. Metcalf (2016) carries out a statistical analysis of the tax's effect on economic growth in the province. Yamazaki (2017) shows that while energy-intensive sectors shed workers, employment overall grew given the more-than-offsetting growth in sectors not so reliant on energy.

21. See the studies by Elgie and McClay (2013), Elgie (2014), and Rivers and Schaufele (2015). Rivers and Schaufele argue that the drop in fossil fuel consumption is greater than one would expect given the typical response of energy demand to changes in fuel prices and conclude that the salience of the tax is affecting behavior. Tax salience has been shown to have significant effects in studies of other taxes as well. Murray and Rivers (2015) argue that the tax has cut BC emissions by between 5 and 15 percent. A recent study by Ahmadi (2016), however, finds no statistical support for the tax having reduced emissions. His is a stringent and conservative test that is biased towards finding no evidence of an impact on emissions.

22. As detailed in a technical document published by Environment and Climate Change Canada (2017), the levy would be paid by fuel distributors and natural gas retailers. The levy on industry is on emissions above a floor based on a sector-specific emissions standard (tons of carbon dioxide equivalent per unit of production) times a firm's output. This is to provide some competitiveness protection to firms while maintaining the incentive at the margin to reduce emissions.

23. Complexity and fairness were the top issues identified by taxpayers in a survey by the Pew Research Center (2017).
24. Churchill speech in the House of Commons on Nov. 11, 1947, http://hansard.millbanksystems.com/commons/1947/nov/11/parliament-bill#S5CV0444P0_19471111_HOC_312, accessed May 13, 2017.

CHAPTER 4

1. Nixon's 1970 State of the Union Message is available at http://www.presidency.ucsb.edu/ws/?pid=2921, accessed June 3, 2017.
2. Revesz and Lienke (2016) detail the politics that led to the passage of the 1970 Clean Air Act. Their book makes a powerful case for the high cost of the decision to focus on pollution at *new* polluting power plants only while exempting (or "grandfathering" as it is known) existing power plants from the new stringent controls.
3. In the jargon of the Clean Air Act, these air quality standards are known as *National Ambient Air Quality Standards* or NAAQS. Counties that meet the NAAQS are *in attainment* while counties that do not meet the standards are *non-attainment* counties. States meet these standards by developing *state implementation plans* or SIPs.
4. Clean Air Act Sec. 111(a)(1). A major theme in the excellent and highly readable book by Revesz and Lienke (2016) is that requiring performance standards only for new sources and not for existing sources (grandfathering) was a "tragic flaw" (p. 3) that in the authors' words "ended up favoring old, obsolete, and very dirty generators" (p. 4) even now nearly a half-century after the passage of the Clean Air Act.
5. The 1977 provision is detailed in Ackerman and Hassler (1981) as recounted in Portney (1990) and Swift (2001). The 1990 Amendments to the Clean Air Act removed this provision as part of the wholesale change in the regulation of sulfur dioxide emissions from power plants. Scrubber costs for 2015 from Table 9.4 of EIA's *Electric Power Annual*, https://www.eia.gov/electricity/annual/html/epa_09_04.html, accessed June 5, 2017. Sulfur content for various types of coal from chapter 12 of *Assumptions to Annual Energy Outlook 2016*.
6. Not only does it cut overall costs but a deal can be struck that lower the costs for each firm. Imagine that Edison pays Insull $250,000 to cut its emissions by an additional 4,000 tons and have that count towards Edison Power's required 10 percent cut. Edison just avoided $400,000 in pollution abatement costs ($1000×4,000) at a cost of $250,000. Meanwhile, Insull incurs an additional $160,000 in costs ($40×4,000) but receives $250,000 from Edison. Both firms are better off. This is Coase all over again. But, while Coasian bargaining looks straightforward for two firms, it is impossibly complicated for thousands of firms.
7. Carlson et al. (2000) found that when a price-based approach is used to control pollution, the costs of controlling sulfur dioxide are cut in half relative to the costs of regulatory mandates.
8. Average fuel efficiency for US light duty vehicles from 1980 through 2015 published by the US Department of Transportation's Bureau of Transportation Statistics *National Transportation Statistics*, Table 4–23, https://www.rita.dot.gov/bts/sites/rita.dot.gov.bts/files/publications/national_transportation_statistics/index.html, accessed June 5, 2017.

9. McCarthy (2007) describes the politics behind the lower light-truck fuel economy standard in CAFE. See also Stuart (1978) on the jobs threat and concerns about black unemployment.

10. McCarthy (2007) tells the story of the growth in popularity of SUVs as the baby-boom generation came of age. Suzuki executive quotation from Holusha (1986).

11. Data on auto and light truck sales from the St. Louis Federal Reserve Bank's Economic Data at https://fred.stlouisfed.org, accessed on Aug. 21, 2018.

12. By installing a separate meter for my electric charger, I can get a lower time-of-use rate that makes the car cheaper to drive for gasoline prices above $1.27.

13. This is an example of what economists call *revealed preference*. Assuming no one forces me to drive more, my decision to drive additional miles must have made me better off since I could have chosen not to drove those extra miles.

14. The result that fuel economy standards can perversely lead to greater use and longer lives for more polluting and fuel consuming vehicles was first identified by Gruenspecht (1982). The fuel economy loss from delayed scrapping of vehicles is documented by Jacobsen and van Benthem (2015).

15. The RFF study is by Krupnick et al. (2010). Automakers have some limited ability to trade fuel-economy obligations so that low-cost firms can increase fuel economy more to allow for lower average fuel economy by a higher cost firm. Klier and Linn (2011) report that credit trading can reduce the cost of CAFE by 7 to 16 percent. The Krupnick et al. estimates for CAFE are similar to more recent estimates by Leard and McConnell (2017) that take credit trading into account.

16. Jacobsen (2013) shows that the impact of fuel economy standards drives up the cost of used cars and so places a disproportionate burden on lower income households who are more likely to buy and drive used cars.

17. http://programs.dsireusa.org/system/program/detail/479, accessed June 3, 2017.

18. This rate-financed subsidy is like a renewable subsidy known as a *feed-in tariff*. Feed-in tariffs are found in a number of European countries and oblige the company purchasing wholesale electricity to pay a given rate for the electricity that is above the market rate. These are coupled with market access guarantees to renewable generators to ensure their electricity will be purchased even if more expensive than alternative sources. Like RPS programs, feed-in tariffs are subsidized by rate payers rather than the government.

19. Reguant (2018) carried out the study comparing RPS and carbon taxes in the electricity sector. Fischer (2010) has shown that RPS programs can actually reduce electricity prices since the price of wind or solar at the margin is zero in contrast to natural gas which, while cleaner than coal, still has a cost at the margin.

20. Congress likes to subsidize all kinds of energy activities, not just clean energy. Since the inception of the tax code there have been large tax breaks for domestic oil and gas drilling. Metcalf (2018b) shows that these incentives have had modest impacts on domestic oil and gas production but are costly to the US Treasury.

21. Almost. The taxpayer must have a tax bill at least as large as the credit to use the credit. If your tax credits exceed the amount of taxes you owe, you can carry the credit forward and use it in future years. But the value of the credit next year is less than its value today because of the time value of money.

22. This assumes the owner of the Marshall Wind Energy project is paying enough in taxes to be able to take the credit. If the business can't take the credit in a

current year, it can carry it forward into future years when it is paying taxes and can use the credit. It can also engage in tax equity deals where it sells the rights to the production tax credits in return for up-front cash. Tax equity deals are common in the wind industry. See https://www.awea.org/financing, accessed June 5, 2017.

23. It's not just Texas where you can see negative electricity prices. Wald (2012) reports that the Chicago area experienced negative pricing 3 percent of the time in 2010.

24. This may be too conservative. Consider energy-efficient windows. Let's say a homeowner spends $2,000 to replace some older windows with energy-efficient windows. A tax credit worth $200 was available for those windows—it expired at the end of 2016. Assuming a (generous) price elasticity of –1.0—meaning demand rises by 1 percent for each 1 percent reduction in price—this credit would induce just over 10 percent in new sales. In other words, nine sales out of ten would have occurred in the absence of the subsidy. So, for the one sale of $2,000 in energy-efficient windows that was generated by the tax credit, the government paid out $2,000 in tax credits for windows. This is consistent with the findings in Houde and Aldy (2017) that 70 percent of consumers claiming rebates for an energy efficient appliance would have bought them anyway and another 15–20 percent simply delayed their purchase by a couple of weeks to become eligible for the rebate. Other research showing a high fraction of purchases that benefit from but are not influenced by a subsidy include studies by Chandra et al. (2010) and Boomhower and Davis (2014).

25. This study was done by Borenstein and Davis (2016). Some tax credits are more regressive than others. The researchers document that 90 percent of the credits for electric vehicles go to households in the top 20 percent of the income distribution.

26. It's actually better than that for General Motors. For greenhouse gas emissions fleet limits, EPA treats each 2017 plug-in hybrid sold as if it were 1.7 cars. Electric cars are treated as two cars. And they have a low emission factor (zero for electric) even if the electricity that charges the batteries comes from coal fired power plants. For fuel economy, the National Highway Transportation Safety Administration, the agency in charge of overseeing fuel economy standards, doesn't apply a multiplier but does ramp up the fuel economy by dividing the car's estimated fuel economy by 0.15. So, an electric car that is rated at 45 mpg gets treated as if it gets 45/0.15 = 300 mpg. For more information, see https://www.c2es.org/federal/executive/vehicle-standards, accessed June 10, 2017.

27. Allcott and Rogers (2014) study the persistence and cost effectiveness of information programs. Costa and Kahn (2013) study the relation between energy saving and political ideology. These information programs are examples of "nudges." A nudge is an intervention that doesn't mandate a change in behavior but takes advantage of our psychological quirks to bring about desired results. A popular nudge to increase household savings is for employee benefit programs to make participation in a voluntary saving program the default option for new employees. Opting out just requires ticking a box when new hires fill out their benefits paperwork. Despite the low cost of opting out, studies have shown that employees are more apt to participate in the program if opting in is the default option rather than requiring an active choice to participate.

This and other nudges are described in the entertaining book by Thaler and Sunstein (2008)

28. AEP discussed in the *Economist* (2013). DiCaprio quoted in Gelles (2015).

29. Estimate of emissions from the World Land Trust carbon calculator at http://www.carbonbalanced.org/calculator/flights.asp, accessed June 23, 2017. The World Land Trust sells offsets in the UK for £15 per ton, or $20 at current (March 2018) exchange rates.

30. See http://www.carbonify.com/carbon-calculator.htm, accessed June 23, 2017.

31. Offsets are an example of a *payment for environmental services* (PES). Ideally the PES should be directed to farmers who have the lowest cost of tree planting and who are most likely to care for the trees to ensure they survive. Jack (2013) has a clever field experiment in Malawi where she demonstrates how auctioning contracts for tree planting to poor farmers leads to lower costs and a higher survival rate for trees. Her paper is an example of the growing literature on the interconnections between environmental and development economics surveyed by Greenstone and Jack (2015).

32. This discussion draws on an excellent assessment of offsets published by the Natural Resources Defense Council at https://www.nrdc.org/stories/should-you-buy-carbon-offsets, accessed June 23, 2017.

33. Estimates are from the Global Carbon Project (Le Quéré et al. 2016). Land use changes added another five billion metric tons of emissions. Offset aggregates come from Hamrick and Goldstein (2016).

34. Prices from Clearview Energy, a source of green electricity, http://www.clearviewenergy.com/, accessed June 23, 2017.

35. Research activities are also a form of a positive externality meaning that the benefits of research generally flow to many people. Just as competitive markets tend to oversupply goods with negative externalities (e.g., pollution), they tend to undersupply goods with positive externalities (e.g., research). Economists are generally in agreement that the government plays a crucial role in providing spending on R&D, especially in the early stage of research to develop new technologies.

36. Pyper (2017) describes the Perry Senate confirmation hearing. The Trump budget is described in Office of Management and Budget (2017).

37. Jaruzelski and Dehoff (2007), Stepp et al. (2011).

38. Federal R&D spending from Gallagher and Anadon (2017). Comparison to chip sales from American Energy Innovation Council (2015).

CHAPTER 5

1. Damage to the Jefferson Memorial and to other Washington DC monuments is described in Notrup (2012).

2. The penalty for exceeding a plant's cap and not having the allowances to cover excess emissions was $2,000 per ton, far in excess of the expected price of an allowance on the open market. The Acid Rain Program is described and assessed by Schmalensee and Stavins (2013).

3. For the Acid Rain Program, allowances were given to generators based on their historic fuel consumption prior to the program's start date. Specifically, allowances for use starting in 2000 were allocated to owners of units equal in amount to average unit fuel consumption between 1985 and 1988 (measured in BTUs of heat input) times 1.2 pounds of sulfur dioxide per million BTUs. Joskow and Schmalensee (1998) note that special provisions modified the basic

allocation scheme in many instances. For example, section 405(b)(3) of the bill provided additional allowances for large lignite units with emission rates above 1.2 pounds of sulfur dioxide per million BTUs in a state with no nonattainment areas. This provision applied to five units in the state of North Dakota, a state represented by Senator Quentin Burdick, chairman of the Committee on Environment and Public Works which oversaw the drafting of the legislation in the Senate.

4. See the 1997 *New York Times* op-ed by Michael Sandel objecting to pollution rights trading and several responses printed in the paper and reprinted in a collection of readings by Stavins (2012).

5. The Acid Rain Program is carefully assessed by Ellerman et al. (2000). The cost savings from cap and trade relative to regulation is studied in Carlson et al. (2000).

6. The recollections by Dales's son are recounted in Fialka (2011). That Dales's book had no immediate impact is clear from the review of the book published in the American Economic Association's flagship *Journal of Economic Literature*. The author of the review writes that "Professor Dales' analysis of the economics of the problem of pollution breaks no new grounds . . ." and concludes that "Professor Dales should be commended for showing the implications of the fact that the costs of pollution are social costs. However, his relatively simplistic faith in a market solution (for in essence that's what it reduces to) is unrealistic." (Wolozin, 1970, pp. 103, 104).

7. The major cap and trade systems in the United States are documented and assessed by Schmalensee and Stavins (2017). A recent survey of cap and trade systems internationally is provided in World Bank Group (2017). Narassimhan et al. (2017) survey and assess various carbon pricing programs.

8. Convery and Redmond (2007) review the EU institutional structure and the decision to move forward with a cap and trade system rather than a carbon tax. Ellerman and Buchner (2007) discuss the US role in promoting trading and the EU resistance to the idea.

9. Originally there were ten states in the compact, but New Jersey withdrew in 2011. The remaining states are Connecticut, Delaware, Maine, Maryland, Massachusetts, New Hampshire, New York, Rhode Island, and Vermont.

10. RGGI adjusted the 2014 cap downward by 45 percent after a 2012 program review showing that the cap was too high to provide a meaningful carbon price (Dance 2013). RGGI announced in August 2017 that it would cut emissions by a further 30 percent relative to 2020 by 2030.

11. The 2006 legislation mandated programs through 2020. In July 2017, the California legislature passed, and the governor signed, legislation to extend the law through 2030. The program is described at https://www.arb.ca.gov/cc/scopingplan/scopingplan.htm, accessed on May 1, 2018 and assessed by Schmalensee and Stavins (2017).

12. The US Department of Energy (2007) carried out a study of the 2005 derailments on the Joint Line. John McPhee's 2005 two-part article on coal trains in the *New Yorker* is highly entertaining and informative. See US Department of Energy (2005) for Katrina's impacts on natural gas delivery.

13. The price decline is discussed in Metcalf (2009b).

14. Economists have debated for many years the relative benefits of targeting emissions through a cap and trade program versus targeting price through a tax. A famous 1974 paper by Harvard economist Marty Weitzman sets out

the conditions to rank the two approaches in terms of expected net benefits when the target—whether it be price or quantity—has to be set before all uncertainty over actual costs of controlling pollution as well as damages are known. Subsequent research that extends the Weitzman analysis specifically to greenhouse gas emissions finds that a tax generally is preferred to cap and trade on the basis of economic efficiency. Weitzman's analysis assumes policy is set once and for all and can't be reconsidered regardless of what new information arises. To the extent that policies are updated as new information becomes available, cap and trade and taxes fare equally well using an expected net benefit measure to rank policy instruments.

15. California maintains an allowance reserve which it can draw on to prevent allowance prices from exceeding the price ceiling. Allowances in the reserve are divided into three equal batches (or tiers) and are sold at different prices. There were 120 million allowances in the reserve available for sale in 2017 at the prices of $50.69, $57.04, and $63.37. Given auction clearing prices of under $14 a ton in 2017, there is no interest in purchasing from the reserve.

16. Both systems also limit the amount of allowances that can be sold into the market if the price ceiling is hit. With strong enough demand, the additional allowances would be sold at the set trigger price and then—assuming demand has still not been fully satisfied—prices would continue to rise until the demand for allowances equaled the supply.

17. If you still believe, despite my arguments, that the certainty of an emissions cap is both desirable and possible, let me note that a carbon tax can be designed to self-adjust to hit a desired future emissions target. I discuss this in more detail in chapter 7. See also Metcalf (2009a) and Hafstead et al. (2017).

18. The cyber-theft story is reported by Chaffin (2011) and Lehane (2011), among others.

19. Congressional Budget Office Cost Estimate of H.R. 2454, June 5, 2009, https://www.cbo.gov/publication/41189, accessed Sept. 9, 2017.

20. Smale et al. (2006) examine five energy-intensive sectors in the UK and conclude that profits in most of the sectors rise following the imposition of a cap and trade system with free allowance allocation.

21. Allowance prices for the 2013 period forward are taken from the European Energy Exchange website, https://www.eex.com/en/market-data/environmental-markets/spot-market/european-emission-allowances#!/2017/08/02, accessed Aug. 2, 2017. Prices from the 2008–2012 period are from Koch et al. (2014).

22. A 2017 study by two economists, Joseph Cullen and Erin Mansur, shows that a carbon price of $20 a ton would be needed to effect a 5 percent reduction in electricity emissions. With an average clearing price of $3 a ton, RGGI might have reduced emissions by 1 percent or so, which works out to, at most, a roughly one-million-ton reduction in carbon dioxide per year—about 0.3 percent of total annual carbon dioxide emissions from participating states.

23. Prices for EU's ETS are available at www.eex.com. RGGI's prices are posted at http://rggi.org. California's auction results are posted at https://www.arb.ca.gov/cc/capandtrade/auction/auction.htm#proceeds. All prices are as of March 2018. The March 2018 exchange rate for euros is $1.20 per euro.

24. Borenstein et al. (2015).

25. This issue is analyzed by Levinson (2012) and Metcalf (2012).

CHAPTER 6

1. It can also be used to pay down the federal deficit. Deficits lead to more borrowing, which must be repaid in the future. So, using the money to lower the deficit today simply leads to lower taxes or more spending in the future since there will be less debt that has to be repaid.

2. We should not be naive, however. Legislators make deals trading support for a tax in return for a favorite spending program. Horse trading is sure to be an element of any coalition-building to enact a carbon tax. But there is a big difference between allocating $40 million for a legislator's pet program and earmarking $200 billion for new government programs!

3. The US Internal Revenue Service (IRS) reports that $1.435 trillion in individual income taxes was paid in 2015; the total population that year was 321.8 million. If we limit ourselves to the civilian, noninstitutional population (all persons sixteen years or older who are not inmates of institutions or on active military duty), we'd need a head tax of $5,700.

4. Economists use the concept of *utility* to measure individual well-being. This argument for progressivity is that the incremental (or marginal) utility from an additional dollar of income is smaller for someone with high income than for someone with low income. In economics-speak, this is the principle of diminishing marginal utility of income. A society that wished to maximize the sum of all utility among its members would redistribute income from high- to low-income members until the marginal utility of income was equalized across all members. This is an illustration of a *utilitarian* social welfare construct, famously proposed by the nineteenth-century philosopher Jeremy Bentham. While known to economists and philosophers for his theory of utilitarianism, he is also known to generations of London university students for another reason. Upon his death, Bentham asked that his body be dissected for scientific research, then stuffed and put on display. University College London (UCL) now displays Bentham clad in a suit and perched in a reading chair. The story goes that his head became the periodic target of theft by student pranksters until UCL officials locked it away for safe keeping. His body and a wax head replica remain on public display. See http://www.ucl.ac.uk/bentham-project/who/autoicon, accessed on Mar. 3, 2018 for more information.

5. A Pigouvian tax reflects the polluter pays principle. The polluter pays principle has a long history in environmental law and is one of the principles of the Rio Declaration agreed to by over 170 countries following the 1992 Earth Summit in Rio de Janeiro. The Earth Summit gave birth to the UN Framework Convention on Climate Change (UNFCCC) that oversees the international climate negotiations and under which the Kyoto Protocol and the Paris Agreement were negotiated.

6. This is a case where an argument can be made for transitional assistance to workers disproportionately impacted by the carbon tax (e.g., coal miners). But be careful. It may be that coal miners are losing jobs not because of the carbon tax but because of low-priced natural gas or automation in coal mining. A Department of Energy (2017b) study commissioned by Secretary of Energy Rick Perry concluded, among other things, that "the biggest contributor to coal and nuclear plant retirements has been the advantaged economics of natural gas-fired generation." In other words, it is cheap natural gas due to the abundant supply of fracked gas that is squeezing coal.

7. Regional damage estimates are from Hsiang et al. (2017). Another metric of fairness is political affiliation. Brill and Ganz (2018) carry out an analysis at the county level that finds Democrat- and Republican-leaning counties are similarly impacted by a carbon tax.

8. Whether a business can pass a tax on to its customers depends on the relative price elasticities of supply and demand. The price elasticity of demand (supply) measures the percentage change in demand (supply) for a 1 percent increase in price. The price elasticity of demand is generally negative (or zero) and the price elasticity of supply positive (or zero). Economists focus on the magnitude of the price elasticity of demand and ignore the minus sign. The more elastic demand is relative to supply, the less the business can raise its prices to pass a tax on to its customers. If the price elasticity of demand is very high, a store owner cannot raise prices because doing so will lead customers to stop buying from that store. For less extreme cases in competitive markets, the burden can be shared between buyers and sellers (e.g., workers or store owners). If the elasticities are equal, for example, then exactly one-half of the tax is passed on to consumers. In that case, a $0.45 carbon tax on gasoline would lead to a price increase of $0.22.

9. Taxes affect people either by raising the price of things they purchase or by lowering their income (or a combination of the two). If a carbon tax were passed forward, it would raise overall prices (e.g., contribute to a one-time uptick in inflation). As part of its methodology for analyzing any tax, OTA holds the overall price level constant in its revenue and distribution analyses. The policy is rooted in a long history at the Treasury but can be justified by arguing that whether prices go up depends in large measure on what action the Federal Reserve takes when the tax is put in place.

10. The carbon content of all the goods and services we consume can be tracked using the Department of Commerce's Input-Output data that track the use of commodities to make commodities. For example, it tracks how coal is used to make electricity which in turn is used to make other commodities including coal (e.g., the electricity to keep the lights on and fans running in underground coal mines). Metcalf (1999) was the first to use input-output accounts to trace the impact of a carbon tax through to commodity prices.

11. The OTA analysis assumes the family does not alter its spending in response to the carbon tax. More sophisticated analyses using computable general equilibrium models that trace through how a carbon tax affects demand and alters prices come to similar conclusions as this approach. Rausch et al. (2011a) is one such analysis focused on the United States. Beck et al. (2015) show that the BC carbon tax is progressive before considering how the revenue is used. Factoring in how the revenue is used, the tax is even more progressive. The authors show that the progressivity is primarily driven by changes in wages, dividends, and other capital returns.

12. OTA's analysis is conservative in the sense of erring against finding the tax to be progressive. Sorting families by annual income can distort the picture in that some families have low income only temporarily and other families may have low cash income while having considerable assets to draw on. If we could measure each family's income over its lifetime, we'd find that carbon taxes are even more progressive than the OTA analysis indicates. See the studies by Poterba (1989, 1991), Bull et al. (1994), Metcalf (1999), Hassett et al. (2009), Mathur and Morris (2014), and Cronin et al. (2017), among others. Their research builds on the path-breaking work by Milton Friedman (1957) on the consumption

function, which contributed to his winning the Nobel Prize in Economics in 1976.

13. Beginning in Metcalf (1999), I have stressed the distinction between the distributional impact of a carbon tax and a carbon tax reform. The former ignores the use of the carbon tax revenue while the latter accounts for the distributional impact of the tax *and* the use of revenue. The latter is clearly the more sensible approach.

14. Usually, a tax credit can only be used to offset an existing tax liability. A refundable tax credit means that the credit is paid whether the taxpayer owes taxes or not. A family of four with income sufficiently low that they owe no federal income tax would file a simple form and receive 4×$583=$2,332 from the federal government. This approach is similar in spirit to a proposal by the Climate Leadership Council (CLC), a bipartisan group that includes a number of Republican elder statesmen, to enact a carbon tax and have funds returned to Americans through an equal per person rebate paid in quarterly installments. Baker et al. (2017) lay out the CLC arguments for this approach.

15. Studies that account for the effect of tax cuts on economic growth include Rausch et al. (2011) and Jorgenson et al. (2015), among others.

16. Cronin et al. (2017) measure the degree of variation of impacts within income groups for various carbon tax and rebate scenarios and finds the per capita rebate has the least amount of variation within income groups. Their study is not able to explain what is driving the variation within groups, however.

CHAPTER 7

1. Sutton denied the quotation in his autobiography and claims a reporter made it up. But it has lived on in various forms including *Sutton's Law* in medical training, used to admonish first-year medical students to focus on the obvious diagnosis rather than exotic alternatives when working up a case. The share of energy-related carbon dioxide in total US greenhouse gases is for the year 2016 and comes from US Environmental Protection Agency (2018).

2. Energy consumption data from the EIA's March 2018 *Monthly Energy Review* (Table 1.3), http://www.eia.gov/totalenergy/data/monthly.

3. The Bayway Refinery in Linden, New Jersey, can handle as much as 238,000 barrels of crude oil each day. In 2014, it opened up a rail facility to handle as much as 75,000 barrels of crude oil delivered on trains, thereby giving it access to increased domestic oil production spurred by the fracking revolution. See http://www.phillips66.com/EN/about/our-businesses/refining/Pages/Bayway-Refinery.aspx . Crowley is a major provider of barge and tanker service in the United States, http://www.crowley.com/What-We-Do/Petroleum-and-Chemical-Transportation/Vessel/650-Class-Articulated-Tug-Barges-ATBs. Margonelli (2007) is an entertaining and informative survey of the various stages of oil production from the well to the gas pump.

4. Much of the following is based on the analysis of Metcalf and Weisbach (2009) and Metcalf (2017).

5. Data from EIA Form 7A and the US Mine Safety and Health Administration, http://www.eia.gov/coal/data.php#coalplants, accessed Apr. 20, 2018. Multiple mines are often owned by the same individual thereby decreasing the number of tax returns that would need to be filed. Black lung disease is the common name given to diseases associated with inhaling coal dust. Known more formally as coal workers' pneumoconiosis, it can trigger chronic bronchitis and chronic

obstructive pulmonary disease (COPD). The coal excise tax does not apply to sales of lignite or imported coal. The tax guidance on covered coal could easily be extended to these currently non-covered types of coal. Note that the tax would vary depending on the type of coal.

6. Electric generating plant data from EIA Form-860, https://www.eia.gov/electricity/data/eia860/. All coke plants and any other company that burns more than 1,000 tons of coal annually are required to report their coal use to the EIA, https://www.eia.gov/survey/form/eia_3/faqs.cfm.

7. In addition to taxing crude at refineries, we would need to tax imported refined products. Motor gasoline, for example, was imported at thirty-two ports in the United States in June 2017, according to EIA data collected on Form EIA-814.

8. Ernst and Young Global (2015) report that the top fifty companies produced just under half of the natural gas extracted in the United States in 2015.

9. Houston plant information at http://www.markwest.com/operations/marcellus/. Columbia Gas Transmission information at https://www.transcanada.com/en/operations/natural-gas/columbia-gas-transmission/.

10. The shares are for 2015 and were calculated from data at the American Gas Association website, https://www.aga.org/annual-statistics/energy-consumption, accessed Jan. 18, 2017.

11. See Hess (2017).

12. Recycled fluorinated gases should not be subject to taxation. That would constitute double taxation and discourage recycling.

13. While there appears to be enough space to store hundreds of years' worth of captured carbon dioxide throughout the world, there are numerous unresolved questions about monitoring and ensuring carbon dioxide does not leak, the need for pipelines to transport liquefied carbon dioxide from place of combustion to place of storage, and—perhaps most important—whether CCS can be done at a politically acceptable cost. The MIT study, *The Future of Coal*, (Deutch and Moniz 2007) has an excellent, albeit slightly dated, discussion about CCS. The 2012 *North American Carbon Storage Atlas* discusses possible storage sites in Canada, the United States, and Mexico.

14. The carbon tax should also not apply to fossil fuels used in the production of petrochemicals, plastics, lubricants such as motor oil, road asphalt, and other products where the carbon is permanently trapped in the products. Fossil fuels used in production rather than burned for combustion are referred to as *feedstocks*. Fuels used as feedstocks could be treated like fuels whose emissions are captured in CCS processes.

15. The tax rate could vary based on the carbon content of the oil. On a lifecycle basis (from extraction all the way to its use), the emissions from Canadian tar sands oil is about 20 percent higher than refined products from conventional domestic crude oil according to Cai et al. (2015).

16. The tax would also be rebated on the nearly ninety-seven million tons of coal exported in 2017, since the carbon tax should only be applied to fossil fuels consumed in the United States.

17. This list is based on an analysis done by Kortum and Weisbach (2017).

18. These studies use the input-output accounts data from the US Department of Commerce Bureau of Economic Analysis, which track the inputs in production in the US economy. See, for example, Metcalf (1999), and Hassett et al. (2009) for a description of how carbon emissions can be traced through to finished products.

19. Data on Chinese steel production and trade from International Trade Administration, *Global Steel Trade Monitor*, March 2018. Kortum and Weisbach (2017) provide an excellent overview of competitiveness and leakage issues. How the WTO would treat border taxes under a carbon tax is uncertain and the literature on the topic is vast. See Trachtman (2017) for a detailed analysis of the intricacies of the WTO. In general WTO rules prohibit border taxes that are based on a country's production processes, as would be the case if the US applied the carbon tax based on some measure of actual carbon emissions in Chinese steel.

20. The World Business Council for Sustainable Development and the World Resources Institute convened the Greenhouse Gas Protocol in 1998 to work with governments and industry to develop standards for reporting greenhouse gas emissions in various industry sectors. Flannery et al. (2018) have developed a proposal for a US carbon tax border adjustment based on this approach.

21. The $50 figure is based on the US Interagency Working Group on the Social Cost of Carbon (2016) estimate for 2020, which is equal to $42 in 2007 dollars. I've converted the estimate to 2020 dollars using the Consumer Price Index (CPI) deflator. This is not precisely the right estimate given the methodology used by the Interagency Working Group, but it is close enough given the uncertainties discussed in the text. Pindyck (2017) is a prominent critic of using the Interagency Working Group's methodology to set the tax rate on carbon dioxide. He suggests convening an expert panel to recommend values rather than rely solely on computer modeling of damages.

22. I proposed this rate adjustment mechanism in Metcalf (2018a) where it is called an Emissions Assurance Mechanism.

23. Canada's backstop carbon levy has this feature as it taxes industry on emissions above a level that depends on each firm's output times an industry-wide emissions standard (emissions per unit of output). It goes a step further by allowing a credit for emissions that fall short of that industry-wide standard times the firm's level of output.

24. Off-road diesel (used, for example, in farm tractors) is not subject to the federal motor vehicles fuel tax. To detect illegal sales of off-road diesel to non-exempt drivers (e.g., trucks on the road), off-road diesel is dyed red so it can be easily identified. Blue dye is added to diesel sold to the government for its on-road use.

CHAPTER 8

1. Even MIT economist Robert Pindyck, who has called the models used to estimate climate damages and the social cost of carbon "close to useless," argues forcefully for a carbon tax despite our not knowing precisely the optimal tax rate. He would set the tax rate equal to an estimate of the social cost of carbon obtained through expert elicitation (Pindyck, 2017).

2. This is an example of a *weak double dividend*. Stanford economist Larry Goulder (1995) analyzes the various forms a double dividend can take in a useful reader's guide. Some have interpreted the weak double dividend to mean that using pollution tax revenues to lower a distorting tax is always preferable to simply rebating the revenue to households. Babiker et al. (2003) show that this is incorrect, though it is true that there exists some reduction in distortionary taxes that is efficiency enhancing relative to simple rebates.

3. The RFF study cited here is by Carbone et al. (2013).

4. The RFF study assumed a 3 percent real growth rate for GDP in the baseline and a 1 percent population growth rate.
5. The literature on the interaction between climate change and economic growth is surveyed in Dell et al. (2014).
6. Burke et al. (2015).
7. Kentucky rally reported by Landler (2017). Trump's executive order signed among coal miners reported by Korte (2017) and Helman (2017). Pruitt's announcement reported by Friedman and Plumer (2017).
8. Data from Bureau of Labor Statistics, *Employment, Hours, and Earnings.*
9. Information on the Powder River Coal Company from http://web.ccsd.k12. wy.us/mines/pr/Pr.html, accessed Sept. 13, 2017. See also Braasch (2013) and a YouTube video put out by the Black Thunder coal mine, https://youtu.be/ 2LQwxTm94Ps, accessed Oct. 10, 2017.
10. West Virginia Congressman Harley O. Staggers championed railroad deregulation and so created opportunities for Western coal to compete with West Virginia coal.
11. Utilities underwent a wave of deregulation in many states starting in the 1990s. See Joskow (2006) for a description and assessment of this deregulatory wave. Cicala (2015) shows that utilities in deregulated states reduced their coal costs by 12 percent and documents the shift to Western coal in place of investing in expensive scrubbers to comply with sulfur dioxide regulations.
12. Data on coal retirements from Energy Information Administration's *Annual Electric Generator Report*, https://www.eia.gov/electricity/data.php#gencapacity, accessed Apr. 16, 2018.
13. Kansas coal plant announcement reported in Storrow (2017).
14. Cullen and Mansur (2017) provide a short-run estimate of the reduction in coal fired electricity generation due to a carbon tax. Cullen and Reynolds (2016) argue that "even a modest price on carbon can have a dramatic effect on emissions through reinvestment in capacity." In other words, a carbon price would speed the retirement of coal plants and their replacement by low- and zero-carbon generating capacity.
15. The jobs report was written by US Department of Energy (2017a). Average annual wages in 2016 taken from the Bureau of Labor Statistics, *Quarterly Census of Employment and Wages*. The job skills required for residential solar installations are detailed in Friedman et al. (2011).
16. Coal mining accidents and fatalities are reported by the Mine Safety and Health Administration, https://www.msha.gov/data-reports/statistics, accessed on Oct. 10, 2017. The black lung outbreak is documented in Blackley et al. (2018). The cases were first reported on National Public Radio by Berkes (2016).
17. Transcript of the 1992 presidential debate at http://www.nytimes.com/1992/ 10/16/us/the-1992-campaign-transcript-of-2d-tv-debate-between-bush-clinton-and-perot.html. Trump's speech is posted on the White House website at https://www.whitehouse.gov/the-press-office/2017/06/01/statement-president-trump-paris-climate-accord, both accessed on Oct. 10, 2018.
18. Carbon intensity estimates based on research by Gray and Metcalf (2017).
19. This discussion draws on a large body of research including Aldy (2017a), Gray and Metcalf (2017), Kortum and Weisbach (2017), and Trachtman (2017).
20. The data on imports come from Kortum and Weisbach (2017). Feng (2017) describes the state of China's cap-and-trade system as of late 2017.

21. It is often argued that the border adjustment is a boon to exports. This ignores foreign exchange considerations. The border adjustment discourages imports and so reduces our demand for foreign currency (if you want to buy goods from Japan, you have to pay in yen, not dollars). This will boost the value of the US dollar relative to other currencies and, in turn, make our exports more expensive. McKibbin et al. (2017) argue that the border adjustment would cause exports to fall.
22. The innovation study is by Fried (2018).
23. Caldeira and Davis (2011) note that how one accounts for emissions depends on whether you count emissions based on where emissions occurred or where the goods responsible for those emissions were consumed. Either way, emissions from developing countries have passed those of developed countries.
24. This approach is proposed by Aldy (2017a).
25. The EAM is described in detail in Metcalf (2018).
26. Cass (2015), for example, likens a carbon tax to a Ponzi scheme. "The further emissions fall," Cass asserts, "the higher rates must go. And because the revenue is equal to the base multiplied by the rate, as the base declines toward zero the rate must increase toward infinity to hold revenue constant" (p. 175).
27. Yuan et al. (2018).

CHAPTER 9

1. Quinnipiac poll released March 22, 2018, https://poll.qu.edu/national/release-detail?ReleaseID=2530, accessed on May 2, 2018.
2. See Leiserowitz et al. (2017a).
3. Reagan's speech is available at the University of California Santa Barbara's American Presidency Project, http://www.presidency.ucsb.edu/index.php. Birnbaum and Murray (1988) have an entertaining history of the law's rocky road to passage.
4. The 2016 Republican platform called for balancing the budget through measures that would make new spending difficult and new taxes even more difficult. As the platform puts it, "[i]s a particular expenditure within the constitutional scope of the federal government? If not, stop it. Has it been effective in the past and is it still absolutely necessary? If not, end it. Is it so important as to justify borrowing, especially foreign borrowing, to fund it? If not, kill it" (Republican National Committee, 2016, p. 23). The enormous increase in the deficit that will result from the 2017 tax cut makes clear that Republicans are more concerned with government spending than with deficits. Liberals often push back that conservative Republicans don't really support small government when it comes to military spending and social issues. See Meadors (2016) for example. Regardless of the merits of either side, this debate should have nothing to do with climate policy.
5. Polling evidence analyzed by Kotchen et al. (2017), however, suggests that public support for a carbon tax may be higher when the revenue is used to invest in clean energy and infrastructure. The challenge will be to find worthwhile clean energy projects to spend upwards of $100 billion a year on. It may be that political support for a carbon tax can be enhanced by including *some* spending on clean energy.
6. Spaulding's story is told in Cardwell (2017). More information about Solar Holler is available at http://www.solarholler.com/, accessed on Apr. 20, 2018.

7. Economists know this as the Tinbergen Rule named for the Dutch economist and 1969 Nobel Prize winner Jan Tinbergen. The rule derives from Tinbergen's work showing that a government targeting unemployment and inflation would need at least two policy instruments. Adjusting the money supply alone would not be sufficient to achieve both employment and inflation goals. Some interpret Tinbergen's Rule to mean that you need one and only one policy instrument for each policy target.
8. My analysis of this tax break is published in Metcalf (2018b).
9. Anadon et al. (2017) provide a breakdown of spending by the Department of Energy (DOE) on R&D. Roughly one-third of the $6.4 billion enacted in the 2017 fiscal year was for basic energy research and the remaining two-thirds for applied research. Trump's budget proposal for the 2017 fiscal year proposed cutting R&D spending by nearly 60 percent.
10. The decline in battery costs is documented in Randall (2017). ARPA-E's BEEST program is described on its website, https://arpa-e.energy.gov/?q=arpa-e-programs/beest.
11. Baker et al. (2017), p. 1.
12. Hafstead et al. (2017) and Metcalf (2018a) lay out the idea of a self-adjusting carbon tax to hit emission targets. The independent commission idea is a variation of a proposal by Aldy (2017a) for an independent commission to set carbon tax rates to achieve emission targets.
13. The story of canaries as mine workers is told by Eschner (2016). Canaries were used in the United States as well. A Department of Labor photograph shows a miner in 1911 holding up a small bird cage containing a canary in the Cross Mountain Mine No. 1 in Briceville, Tennesee, https://arlweb.msha.gov/CENTURY/CANARY/PAGE4.asp, accessed Oct. 4, 2017.
14. The Stanford Energy Modeling Forum exercise (EMF 24) is described in Clarke et al. (2014). Metcalf (2018a) discusses the use of sequential targets for a carbon tax and proposes a 45 percent reduction by 2035 that would be consistent with a 60 percent reduction target by 2050. If clean energy technology costs fall more rapidly than expected, the 2050 target could be strengthened when set in the mid-2030s.
15. Nordhaus argues that non-participating countries could be punished with carbon tariffs or a uniform tariff on all imported goods to club members. He finds that a modest uniform tariff is more effective at promoting club membership than a carbon tariff. How Nordhaus's club idea would dovetail with the existing international trade order overseen by the WTO is unclear.
16. This rate adjustment mechanism is set out in a proposal in Metcalf (2018a) where it is called an EAM. This proposal builds on work by Hafstead et al. (2017). Other approaches to ensuring greater certainty of given emissions reduction targets are proposed by Aldy (2017a) and Murray et al. (2017)
17. Graham's speech reported by Northey (2017).
18. The American Action Forum (AAF) proposed a carbon tax starting at $20 a ton and rising annually at the rate of inflation plus 5 percent with proceeds used to cut the corporate income tax rate to 20 percent. Their analysis showed this reform would be revenue neutral over a ten-year budget window. The actual tax bill passed in late 2017, in contrast, raised deficits by over one trillion dollars over the coming decade.

19. The CLC's website https://www.clcouncil.org/ has a number of op-eds making the case for their plan. The AAF's 20/20 plan is detailed at https://www.americanactionforum.org/research/tax-reform-initiative-group-briefing-book/. Bob Inglis's group is detailed at http://www.republicen.org. Hassett has written a number of papers on carbon taxation including several with me.

REFERENCES

Abatzoglou, John T. and Williams, A. Park (2016), "Impact of Anthropogenic Climate Change on Wildlife Across Western U.S. Forests," *PNAS*, 113 (42), 11770–75.

Ackerman, Bruce and Hassler, William (1981), *Clean Coal/Dirty Air*; New Haven, CT: Yale University Press.

Aerts, Jeroen C. J. H., et al. (2014), "Evaluating Flood Resilience Strategies for Coastal Megacities," *Science*, 344 (6183), 473–75.

Ahmadi, Younes (2016), "How Effective Are Carbon Taxes in Reducing Emissions? Evidence from the Revenue Neutral Carbon Tax in British Columbia," (Department of Economics, University of Calgary).

Aldy, Joseph E. (2017a), "Designing and Updating a U.S. Carbon Tax in an Uncertain World," *Harvard Environmental Law Review*, 41, 28–40.

——— (2017b), "Frameworks for Evaluating Policy Approaches to Address the Competitiveness Concerns of Mitigating Greenhouse Gas Emissions," *National Tax Journal*, 70 (2), 395–420.

Allcott, Hunt and Rogers, Todd (2014), "The Short-Run and Long-Run Effects of Behavioral Interventions: Experimental Evidence from Energy Conservation," *American Economic Review*, 104 (10), 3003–37.

American Energy Innovation Council (2015), "Restoring American Energy Innovation Leadership: Report Card, Challenges, and Opportunities," (Washington, DC: Bipartisan Policy Center)

Anadon, Laura D., Gallagher, Kelly Sims, and Holdren, John P. (2017), "Rescue US Energy Innovation," *Nature Energy*, September 25.

Arrhenius, Svante (1908), *Worlds in the Making; The Evolution of the Universe*; New York: Harper.

Arrow, Kenneth J. and Fisher, Anthony C. (1974), "Environmental Preservation, Uncertainty, and Irreversibility," *Quarterly Journal of Economics*, 88 (2), 312–19.

Babiker, Mustafa, Metcalf, Gilbert E., and Reilly, John (2003), "Tax Distortions and Global Climate Policy," *Journal of Environmental Economics and Management*, 46, 269–87.

Baker, James A., III, et al. (2017), "The Conservative Case for Carbon Dividends," (Washington, DC: Climate Leadership Council).

Banzhaf, H. Spencer and Walsh, Randall P. (2008), "Do People Vote with Their Feet? An Empirical Test of Tiebout's Mechanism," *American Economic Review*, 98 (3), 843–63.

Barreca, Alan, et al. (2016), "Adapting to Climate Change: The Remarkable Decline in the U.S. Temperature–Mortality Relationship Over the 20th Century," *Journal of Political Economy*, 124 (1), 105–59.

Beck, Marisa, et al. (2015), "Carbon Tax and Revenue Recycling: Impacts on Households in British Columbia," *Resource and Energy Economics*, 41, 40–69.

Berkes, Howard (2016), "Advanced Black Lung Cases Surge in Appalachia," *All Things Considered*, https://www.npr.org/2016/12/15/505577680/advanced-black-lung-cases-surge-in-appalachia, accessed October 1, 2017.

Birnbaum, Jeffrey H. and Murray, Alan S. (1988), *Showdown at Gucci Gulch: Lawmakers, Lobbyists, and the Unlikely Triumph of Tax Reform*; New York: Vintage Books.

Blackley, David J., et al. (2018), "Progressive Massive Fibrosis in Coal Miners from 3 Clinics in Virginia," *JAMA*, 319 (5), 500–501.

Bolstead, Erika (2017), "Gentrification Fears Grow as High Ground Becomes Hot Property," *Climatewire*, May 1.

Boomhower, Judson and Davis, Lucas W. (2014), "A Credible Approach for Measuring Inframarginal Participation in Energy Efficiency Programs," *Journal of Public Economics*, 113, 67–79.

Borenstein, Severin and Davis, Lucas W. (2016), "The Distributional Effects of U.S. Clean Energy Tax Credits," in Jeffrey Brown (ed.), *Tax Policy and the Economy* (Chicago: University of Chicago Press), 30.

Borenstein, Severin, et al. (2015), "Expecting the Unexpected: Emissions Uncertainty and Environmental Market Design," (Cambridge MA: NBER).

Bovenberg, A. Lans (1999), "Green Tax Reforms and the Double Dividend: an Updated Reader's Guide," *International Tax and Public Finance*, 6 (3), 421–43.

Braasch, Gary (2013), "Powder River Basin Coal On the Move," *Daily Climate*.

Brill, Alex and Ganz, Scott (2018), "The Political Economy of a Carbon Tax: A County-by-County Investigation," (Washington, DC: American Enterprise Institute).

Bull, Nicholas, Hassett, Kevin A., and Metcalf, Gilbert E. (1994), "Who Pays Broad-Based Energy Taxes? Computing Lifetime and Regional Incidence," *Energy Journal*, 15 (3), 145–64.

Burke, Marshall, Hsiang, Solomon M., and Miguel, Edward (2015), "Global Non-Linear Effect of Temperature on Economic Production," *Nature*, 527, 235–39.

Cai, Hao, et al. (2015), "Well-to-Wheels Greenhouse Gas Emissions of Canadian Oil Sands Products: Implications for U.S. Petroleum Fuels," *Environmental Science & Technology*, 49 (13), 8219–27.

Caldeira, Ken and Davis, Steven J. (2011), "Accounting for Carbon Dioxide Emissions: A Matter of Time," *PNAS*, 108 (21), 8533–34.

Carbone, Jared C., et al. (2013), "Deficit Reduction and Carbon Taxes: Budgetary, Economic, and Distributional Impacts," (Washington, DC: Resources For the Future).

Cardwell, Diane (2017), "What's Up in Coal Country: Alternative-Energy Jobs," *New York Times*, September 30.

Carlson, Curtis, et al. (2000), "Sulfur Dioxide Control by Electric Utilities: What Are the Gains From Trade?" *Journal of Political Economy*, 108 (6), 1292–1326.

Cass, Oren (2015), "The Carbon-Tax Shell Game," *National Affairs*, (Summer), 163–80.

Cave, Damien and Gillis, Justin (2017), "Large Sections of Australia's Great Reef Are Now Dead, Scientists Find," *New York Times*, March 15.

Chaffin, Joshua (2011), "Cyber-Theft Halts EU Emissions Trading," *Financial Times*, January 19.

Chandra, Ambarish, Gulati, Sumeet, and Kandlikar, Milind (2010), "Green Drivers or Free Riders? An Analysis of Tax Rebates for Hybrid Vehicles," *Journal of Environmental Economics and Management*, 60, 78–93.

Church, J. A., Clark, P. U., Cazenave, A., Gregory, J. M., Jevrejeva, S., Levermann, A., Merrifield, M. A., Milne, G. A., Nerem, R. S., Nunn, P. D., Payne, A. J., Pfeffer, W. T., Stammer, D., and Unnikrishnan, A. S. (2013), "Sea Level Change," in T. F. Stocker, D. Qin, G. -K. Plattner, M. Tignor, S. K. Allen, J. Boschung, A. Nauels, Y. Xia, V. Bex, and P. M. Midgley (eds.), *Climate Change 2013: The Physical Science Basis. Contribution of Working Group I to the Fifth Assessment Report of the Intergovernmental Panel on Climate Change* (Cambridge, UK and New York, NY: Cambridge University Press), 1137–216.

Cicala, Steve (2015), "When Does Regulation Distort Costs? Lessons from Fuel Procurement in US Electricity Generation," *American Economic Review*, 105 (1), 411–44.

Clarke, Leon E., et al. (2014), "Technology and U.S. Emissions Reductions Goals: Results of the EMF 24 Modeling Exercise," *The Energy Journal*, 35 (S11), 9–31.

Coase, Ronald (1960), "The Problem of Social Cost," *Journal of Law and Economics*, 3, 1–44.

Collard, David (2004), "Pigou, Arthur Cecil (1877–1959)," *Oxford Dictionary of National Biography*, http://www.oxforddnb.com/view/article/35529, accessed February 13, 2017.

Convery, Frank and Redmond, Luke (2007), "Market and Price Developments in the European Union Emissions Trading Scheme," *Review of Environmental Economics and Policy*, 1 (1), 88–111.

Copeland, Baden, Josh Keller, and Bill Marsh (2012), "What Could Disappear," *New York Times*, online at https://archive.nytimes.com/www.nytimes.com/interactive/2012/11/24/opinion/sunday/what-could-disappear.html, accessed May 2, 2018.

Costa, Dora L. and Kahn, Matthew E. (2013), "Energy Conservation 'Nudges' and Environmental Ideology: Evidence from a Randomized Residential Field Experiment," *Journal of the European Economic Association*, 11 (3), 680–702.

Cronin, Julie-Anne, Fullerton, Don, and Sexton, Steven E. (2017), "Vertical and Horizontal Redistributions from a Carbon Tax and Rebate," (Cambridge, MA: National Bureau of Economic Research).

Cullen, Joseph A. and Mansur, Erin T. (2017), "Inferring Carbon Abatement Costs in Electricity Markets: A Revealed Preference Approach Using the Shale Revolution," *American Economic Journal: Economic Policy*, 9 (3), 106–33.

Cullen, Joseph A. and Reynolds, Stanley S. (2016), "The Long Run Impact of Environmental Policies on Wholesale Electricity Markets: A Dynamic Competitive Analysis," Washington University Olin School of Business Working Paper St. Louis, April.

Dale, Lisa (2010), "The True Cost of Wildfire in the Western U.S.," (Lakewood, CO: Western Forestry Leadership Coalition).

Dales, J. H. (1968), *Pollution, Property, and Prices*; Toronto: University of Toronto Press.

Dance, Scott (2013), "Tighter Greenhouse Gas Limits Adopted for Md., Northeast," *Baltimore Sun*, February 7.

Daniels, Jeff (2017), "Death Toll in California Wildfires Grows to 42, PG&E Sued by Couple Who Lost Home," https://www.cnbc.com/2017/10/18/

death-toll-in-california-wildfires-grows-to-42-pge-hit-with-lawsuit.html, accessed October 20, 2017.

Davis, Lucas W. and Metcalf, Gilbert E. (2015), "Does Better Information Lead to Better Choices? Evidence from Energy-Efficiency Labels," *Journal of the Association of Environmental and Resource Economists*, 3 (3), 589–625.

Dayaaratna, Kevin, Loris, Nicolas, and Kreutzer, David (2016), "Consequences of Paris Protocol: Devastating Economic Costs, Essentially Zero Environmental Benefits," The Heritage Foundation, Washington, DC.

Dell, Melissa, Jones, Benjamin F., and Olken, Benjamin A. (2014), "What Do We Learn from the Weather? The New Climate-Economy Literature," *Journal of Economic Literature*, 52 (3), 740–98.

Deutch, John and Moniz, Ernest (2007), "The Future of Coal," (Cambridge, MA: MIT).

Doran, Peter T. and Zimmerman, Maggie Kendall (2009), "Examining the Scientific Consensus on Climate Change," *Eos*, 90 (3), 22–23.

Elgie, Stewart (2014), "British Columbia's Carbon Tax Shift: An Environmental and Economic Success," http://blogs.worldbank.org/climatechange/british-columbia-s-carbon-tax-shift-environmental-and-economic-success, accessed September 10, 2014.

Elgie, Stewart and McClay, Jessica (2013), "BC's Carbon Tax Shift After Five Years: Results," (Ottawa: Sustainable Prosperity).

Ellerman, A. Denny and Buchner, Barbara K. (2007), "The European Union Emissions Trading Scheme: Origins, Allocation, and Early Results," *Review of Environmental Economics and Policy*, 1 (1), 66–87.

Ellerman, A. Denny, et al. (2000), *Markets for Clean Air: The U.S. Acid Rain Program*; Cambridge: Cambridge University Press.

Environment and Climate Change Canada (2017), "Technical Paper on the Federal Carbon Pricing Backstop," (Gatineau: ECCC).

Ernst and Young Global (2015), "U.S. Oil and Gas Reserves Study 2015."

Eschner, Kat (2016), "The Story of the Real Canary in the Coal Mine," *Smithsonian SmartNews*, December 30.

Feng, Emily (2017), "China Moves Towards Launch of Carbon Trading Scheme," *Financial Times*, December 19.

Fialka, John (2011), "Cap and Trade—the Meandering Path of an Idea to Curb Pollution," *ClimateWire*, November 16.

Fischer, Carolyn (2010), "Renewable Portfolio Standards: When Do They Reduce Price?" *The Energy Journal*, 31 (1), 101–19.

Flannery, Brian, et al. (2018), "Framework Proposal for a US Upstream Greenhouse Gas Tax with WTO-Compliant Border Adjustments," (Washington DC: Resources For the Future).

Fountain, Henry (2015), "Researchers Link Syrian Conflict to a Drought Made Worse by Climate Change," *New York Times*, March 2.

Fried, Stephie (2018), "Climate Policy and Innovation: A Quantitative Macroeconomic Analysis," *American Economic Journal: Macroeconomics*, 10 (1), 90–118.

Friedman, Barry, Jordan, Philip, and Carrese, John (2011), "Solar Installation Labor Market Analysis," (Golden, CO: NREL).

Friedman, Lisa and Plumer, Brad (2017), "E.P.A. Announces Repeal of Major Obama-Era Carbon Emissions Rule," *New York Times*, October 9.

Friedman, Milton (1957), *A Theory of the Consumption Function*; Princeton, NJ: Princeton University Press.

Fritz, Angela and Samenow, Jason (2017), "Harvey Unloaded 33 Trillion Gallons of Water in the U.S.," *Washington Post*, September 2.

Fuller, Thomas (2017), "California, Parched for 5 Years, Is Now Battered by Water," *New York Times*, Februrary 19.

Fullerton, Don (1996), "Why Have Separate Environmental Taxes?," in James M Poterba (ed.), *Tax Policy and the Economy* (Volume 10. Cambridge: MIT Press for the National Bureau of Economic Research), 33–70.

Fullerton, Don and Metcalf, Gilbert E. (1998), "Environmental Taxes and the Double Dividend Hypothesis: Did You Really Expect Something for Nothing?" *Chicago-Kent Law Review*, 73 (1), 221–56.

Gale, William G. (2018), *Fiscal Therapy: Balancing Today's Needs with Tomorrow's Obligations*; New York: Oxford University Press.

Gallagher, Kelly Sims and Anadon, Laura D. (2017), "DOE Budget Authority for Energy Research, Development, and Demonstration Database," (Fletcher School of Law and Diplomacy, Tufts University; Department of Politics and International Studies, University of Cambridge; Belfer Center for Science and International Affairs, Harvard Kennedy School).

Gelles, David (2015), "Microsoft Leads Movement to Offset Emissions with Internal Carbon Tax," *New York Times*, September 27.

Gillis, Justin (2010), "A Scientist, His Work and a Climate Reckoning," *New York Times*, December 22.

Goulder, Lawrence H. (1995), "Environmental Taxation and the 'Double Dividend': A Reader's Guide," *International Tax and Public Finance*, 2, 157–83.

Gray, Wayne and Metcalf, Gilbert E. (2017), "Carbon Tax Competitiveness Concerns: Assessing a Best Practices Income Tax Credit," *National Tax Journal*, 70 (2), 447–68.

Greenstone, Michael and Jack, Kelsey (2015), "Envirodevonomics: A Research Agenda for an Emerging Field," *Journal of Economic Literature*, 53 (1), 5–42.

Grossman, Gene and Krueger, Alan (1995), "Economic Growth and the Environment," *Quarterly Journal of Economics*, 110, 353–77.

Gruenspecht, Howard K. (1982), "Differentiated Regulation: The Case of Auto Emissions Standards," *American Economic Review*, 72 (2), 328–31.

Gupta, Prachi (2014), "Neil deGrasse Tyson: Science is True 'Whether or Not You Believe in It'," *Salon*, March 11, https://www.salon.com/2014/03/11/neil_degrasse_tyson_science_is_true_whether_or_not_you_believe_in_it/, accessed on August 20, 2018.

Hafstead, Marc, Metcalf, Gilbert E., and Williams, Roberton C., III (2017), "Adding Quantity Certainty to a Carbon Tax: The Role of a Tax Adjustment Mechanism for Policy Pre-Commitment," *Harvard Environmental Law Review*, 41, 41–57.

Hamrick, Kelley and Goldstein, Allie (2016), *Raising Ambition: State of the Voluntary Carbon Markets 2016*; Washington, DC: Forest Trends.

Hansen, Zeynep K. and Libecap, Gary D. (2004), "Small Farms, Externalities, and the Dust Bowl of the 1930s," *Journal of Political Economy*, 112 (3), 665–94.

Harris, Daniel C. (2010), "Charles David Keeling and the Story of Atmospheric CO_2 Measurements," *Analytical Chemistry*, 82, 7865–70.

Harrison, Kathryn (2013), "The Political Economy of British Columbia's Carbon Tax," Organization for Economic Co-Operation and Development Environment Working Paper, Paris, October 8.

Hassett, Kevin A., Mathur, Aparna, and Metcalf, Gilbert E. (2009), "The Incidence of a U.S. Carbon Tax: A Lifetime and Regional Analysis," *Energy Journal*, 30 (2), 157–79.

Helman, Christopher (2017), "Trump, In the Name of American Energy Independence, Moves to Scrap Obama's Climate Plans," *Forbes*, March 28.

Hess, Hannah (2017), "Obama's Air Chief Sees 'First Concrete Steps' of Retreat by Pruitt," *Greenwire*, March 3.

Holusha, John (1986), "For Drivers, the Fun Is Back: 4-Wheel Drive Lifting Sales Luring More Buyers," *New York Times*, p. D1. June 16.

Hornbeck, Richard (2012), "The Enduring Impact of the American Dust Bowl: Short- and Long-Run Adjustments to Environmental Catastrophe," *American Economic Review*, 102 (4), 1477–507.

Horowitz, John, et al. (2017), "Methodology for Analyzing a Carbon Tax," (Washington, DC: U.S. Department of the Treasury).

Houde, Sebastien and Aldy, Joseph E. (2017), "'Consumers' Response to State Energy Efficient Appliance Rebate Programs," *American Economic Journal: Economic Policy*, 9 (4), 227–55.

Houser, Trevor and Marsters, Peter (2018), "The World's Second Largest Blackout," (New York: Rhodium Group).

Hsiang, Solomon, et al. (2017), "Estimating Economic Damage from Climate Change in the United States," *Science*, 356 (6345), 1362–69.

Hu, Winnie (2012), "Mayor Mandates Rationing of Gas to Ease Shortage," *New York Times*, November 8, online at https://nyti.ms/VKb5F9, accessed February 11, 2018.

Hughes, Terry P., et al. (2017), "Global Warming and Recurrent Mass Bleaching of Corals," *Nature*, 543 (7645), 373–77.

Intergovernmental Panel on Climate Change (2014), "Climate Change 2014: Synthesis Report. Contribution of Working Groups I, II and III to the Fifth Assessment Report of the Intergovernmental Panel on Climate Change," (Geneva IPCC).

International Energy Agency (2018), "The Future of Cooling," (Paris: IEA).

International Trade Administration (2018), *Global Steel Trade Monitor*, March.

Jack, Kelsey (2013), "Private Information and the Allocation of Land Use Subsidies in Malawi," *American Economic Journal: Applied*, 5 (3), 113–35.

Jacobsen, Mark R. (2013), "Evaluating U.S. Fuel Economy Standards in a Model with Producer and Household Heterogeneity," *American Economic Journal: Economic Policy*, 5 (2), 148–87.

Jacobsen, Mark R. and van Benthem, Arthur A. (2015), "Vehicle Scrappage and Gasoline Policy," *American Economic Review*, 105 (3), 1312–38.

Jaruzelski, Barry and Dehoff, Kevin (2007), "The Customer Connection: The Global Innovation 1000," (New York: Booz Allen Hamilton).

Jorgenson, Dale W. et al. (2015), "Carbon Taxes and Fiscal Reform in the United States," *National Tax Journal*, 68 (1), 121–38.

Joskow, Paul L. (2006), "Markets for Power in the United States: An Interim Assessment," *Energy Journal*, 27 (1), 1–36.

Joskow, Paul L. and Schmalensee, Richard (1998), "The Political Economy of Market-Based Environmental Policy: The U.S. Acid Rain Program," *Journal of Law and Economics*, 41, 47–83.

Kahn, Brian (2017a), "The Larsen C Iceberg Finally Broke Away. Now There's a Trillion-Ton Iceberg Adrift," http://www.climatecentral.org/news/larsen-c-trillion-ton-iceberg-break-21610, accessed October 19.

Kahn, Matthew E. (2017b), "Protecting Urban Places and Populations from Rising Climate Risk," (Washington, DC: The Hamilton Project).

Kessler, Glenn (2013), "Cherry-Picking One Survey to Discredit a Survey of Scientists on Climate Change," https://www.washingtonpost.com/blogs/fact-checker/post/cherry-picking-one-survey-to-discredit-a-survey-of-scientists-on-climate-change/2013/05/07/e69607d2-b77b-11e2-92f3-f291801936b8_blog.html?utm_term=.b2f24ea6cd3d, accessed January 4, 2017.

Klier, Thomas and Linn, Joshua (2011), "Corporate Average Fuel Economy Standards and the Market for New Vehicles," *Annual Review of Resource Economics*, 3, 445–62.

Koch, Nicolas, et al. (2014), "Causes of the EU ETS Price Drop: Recession, CDM, Renewable Policies or a Bit of Everything? New Evidence," *Energy Policy*, 73, 676–85.

Kolbert, Elizabeth (2015), "The Siege of Miami," *New Yorker*, December 21 and 28.

——— (2016), "A Song of Ice," *New Yorker*, October 24.

Korte, Gregory (2017), "Energy Independence, Not Climate Change, Becomes Priority Under Trump Order," *USA Today*, March 28.

Kortum, Sam and Weisbach, David (2017), "The Design of Border Adjustment for Carbon Prices," *National Tax Journal*, 70 (2), 421–46.

Kotchen, Matthew J., Turk, Zachary M., and Leiserowitz, Anthony A. (2017), "Public Willingness to Pay for a US Carbon Tax and Preferences for Spending the Revenue," *Environmental Research Letters*, 12 (9), 094012.

Krupnick, Alan J., et al. (2010), "Toward a New National Energy Policy: Assessing the Options," (Washington, DC: RFF).

Landler, Mark (2017), "Embattled in Washington, President Recharges among Friendly Crowd in Kentucky," *New York Times*, March 21.

Le Quéré, C. et al. (2016), "Global Carbon Budget 2016," *Earth Systems Science Data*, 8, 605–49.

Leard, Benjamin and McConnell, Virginia (2017), "New Markets for Credit Trading Under US Automobile Greenhouse Gas and Fuel Economy Standards," (Washington, DC: RFF).

Lehane, Bill (2011), "Hackers Steal Carbon Credits," *Prague Post*, January 26.

Leiserowitz, Anthony, et al. (2017a), "Trump Voters & Global Warming," (New Haven CT: Yale University and George Mason University).

Leiserowitz, Anthony, et al. (2017b), "Politics & Global Warming," (New Haven, CT: Yale University and George Mason University).

Levinson, Arik (2012), "Belts and Suspenders: Interactions Among Climate Policy Regulations," in Don Fullerton and Catherine Wolfram (eds.), *The Design and Implementation of U.S. Climate Policy* (Chicago: University of Chicago Press), 127–40.

Lin, Ning, et al. (2012), "Physically Based Assessment of Hurricane Surge Threat Under Climate Change," *Nature Climate Change*, 2, 462–67.

Loria, Kevin (2017), "Nearly 2 Million Acres of Land are Burning Across the US in One of the Worst Fire Seasons We've Ever Seen," http://www.businessinsider.com/wildfire-season-western-us-2017-9, accessed October 20, 2017.

Lyons, Patrick J. (2013), "Ronald H. Coase, 'Accidental' Economist Who Won a Nobel Prize, Dies at 102," *New York Times*, September 4.

Margonelli, Lisa (2007), *Oil on the Brain: Adventures from the Pump to the Pipeline*; New York: Nan A. Talese.

Mathur, Aparna and Morris, Adele C. (2014), "Distributional Effects of a Carbon Tax in Broader U.S. Fiscal Reform," *Energy Policy*, 66 (March), 326–34.

McCarthy, Tom (2007), *Auto Mania*; New Haven: Yale University Press.

McKibbin, Warwick J., et al. (2017), "The Role of Border Adjustments in a Carbon Tax," Climate and Energy Economics Discussion Paper (Washington, DC: The Brookings Institution).

McPhee, John (2005), "Coal Train-I and II," *New Yorker*, October 3 and 10, 72–83, 62–71.

Meadors, Marvin (2016), "Republicans Believe in Small Government Right? Think Again!" http://www.huffingtonpost.com/marvin-meadors/republicans-believe-in-sm_b_9647486.html, accessed October 3, 2017.

Metcalf, Gilbert E. (1999), "A Distributional Analysis of Green Tax Reforms," *National Tax Journal*, 52 (4), 655–81.

——— (2009a), "Cost Containment in Climate Change Policy: Alternative Approaches to Mitigating Price Volatility," *Virginia Tax Review*, 29, 381–405.

——— (2009b), "Market-based Policy Options to Control U.S. Greenhouse Gas Emissions," *Journal of Economic Perspectives*, 23 (2), 5–27.

——— (2012), "Comment on Belts and Suspenders: Interactions among Climate Policy Regulations," in Don Fullerton and Catherine Wolfram (eds.), *The Design and Implementation of U.S. Climate Policy* (Chicago: University of Chicago Press), 140–44.

——— (2016), "A Conceptual Framework for Measuring the Effectiveness of Green Fiscal Reforms," *International Journal on Green Growth and Development*, 2 (2), 87–126.

——— (2017), "Implementing a Carbon Tax," (Washington, DC: Resources For the Future).

——— (2018a), "An Emissions Assurance Mechanism: Adding Environmental Certainty to a Carbon Tax," (Washington, DC: Resources For the Future).

——— (2018b), "The Tax Treatment of Oil and Gas Production in the United States: Assessing the Options," *Journal of the Association of Environmental and Resource Economists*, 5 (1), 1–37.

Metcalf, Gilbert E. and Weisbach, David (2009), "The Design of a Carbon Tax," *Harvard Environmental Law Review*, 33 (2), 499–556.

Miller, Jeremy (2017), "California's Drought May Be Over, But Its Water Troubles Aren't," *New Yorker*, March 21.

Moser, Susanne C., et al. (2014), "Coastal Zone Development and Ecosystems," in Jerry Melillo, Terese Richmond, and Gary W. Yohe (eds.), *Climate Change Impacts in the United States: The Third National Climate Assessment Report* (Washington, DC: U.S. Global Change Research Program), 579–618.

Murray, Brian and Rivers, Nicholas (2015), "British Columbia's Revenue-Neutral Carbon Tax: A Review of the Latest 'Grand Experiment' in Environmental Policy," *Energy Policy*, 86, 674–83.

Murray, Brian, Pizer, William A., and Reichert, Christina (2017), "Increasing Emissions Certainty Under a Carbon Tax," *Harvard Environmental Law Review*, 41, 14–27.

Narassimhan, Easwaran, et al. (2017), "Carbon Pricing in Practice: A Review of the Evidence," (Medford, MA: CIERP, Tufts University).

Nordhaus, William D. (2015), "Climate Clubs: Overcoming Free-Riding in International Climate Policy," *American Economic Review*, 105 (4), 1339–70.

North American Carbon Atlas Partnership (2012). *North American Carbon Storage Atlas*. Joint publication of Natural Resources Canada, Mexico Secretaria de Energia, and U.S. Department of Energy. Available at https://www.netl.doe.

gov/File%20Library/Research/Carbon-Storage/NACSA2012.pdf, accessed
September 3, 2018.

Northey, Hannah (2017), "Graham Talks Up Carbon Tax Cash as Lure for GOP,"
Environment and Energy Daily, September 27.

Notrup, Megan (2012), "Acid Rain's Slow Dissolve," https://www.nps.gov/nama/
blogs/acid-rains-slow-dissolve.htm, accessed May 22 2017.

Office of Management and Budget (2017), "America First: A Budget Blueprint to
Make America Great Again," (Washington, DC: OMB).

Olson, Mancur (1965), *The Logic of Collective Action*; Cambridge, MA: Harvard
University Press.

Patel, Jugal (2017), "A Crack in an Antarctic Ice Shelf Grew 17 Miles in the Last Two
Months," *New York Times,* February 7.

Petit J. R., Jouzel J., Raynaud D., Barkov N. I., et al. (1999), "Climate and Atmospheric
History of the Past 420,000 Years from the Vostok Ice Core, Antarctica,"
Nature, 399, 429–36.

Pew Research Center (2017), "Top Frustrations with Tax System: Sense That
Companies, Wealthy Don't Pay Fair Share," (Pew Research Center).

Pindyck, Robert S. (2002), "Optimal Timing Problems in Environmental Economics,"
Journal of Economic Dynamics & Control, 26, 1677–97.

——— (2013), "Climate Change Policy: What Do the Models Tell Us?" *Journal of
Economic Literature*, 51 (3), 860–72.

——— (2017), "Coase Lecture—Taxes, Targets and the Social Cost of Carbon,"
Economica, 84, 345–64.

Popper, Karl (1963), *Conjectures and Refutations: The Growth of Scientific Knowledge*;
New York: Harper & Row.

Portney, Paul R. (1990), "Policy Watch: Economics and the Clean Air Act," *Journal of
Economic Perspectives*, 4 (4), 173–81.

Poterba, James (1989), "Lifetime Incidence and the Distributional Burden of Excise
Taxes," *American Economic Review*, 79 (2), 325–30.

——— (1991), "Is the Gasoline Tax Regressive?" *Tax Policy and the Economy*, 5, 145–64.

Pyper, Julia (2017), "Rick Perry Pledges Support for DOE Research, Renewables
as Trump Plans Drastic Agency Cuts," *Greentech Media*, https://www.
greentechmedia.com/articles/read/doe-nominee-rick-perry-vows-to-support-
research-and-renewables-as-trump-pla, accessed June 5, 2017.

Randall, Tom (2017), "Tesla's Battery Revolution Just Reached Critical Mass,"
Bloomberg Technology, January 30.

Rausch, Sebastian, Metcalf, Gilbert E., and Reilly, John M. (2011a), "Distributional
Impacts of Carbon Pricing: A General Equilibrium Approach with Micro-Data
for Households," *Energy Economics*, 33, S20-S33.

Rausch, Sebastian et al. (2011b), "Distributional Impacts of a U.S. Greenhouse Gas
Policy: A General Equilibrium Analysis of Carbon Pricing," in Gilbert E. Metcalf
(ed.), *U.S. Energy Tax Policy* (Cambridge: Cambridge University Press), 52–107.

Reguant, Mar (2018), "The Efficiency and Sectoral Distributional Implications of
Large-Scale Renewable Policies," (Cambridge: National Bureau of Economic
Research).

Republican National Committee (2016), "Republican Platform 2016," online at https://
www.gop.com/the-2016-republican-party-platform/, accessed August 21, 2018.

Revesz, Richard L. and Lienke, Jack (2016), *Struggling For Air: Power Plants and the
"War on Coal"*; New York: Oxford University Press.

Rezai, Armon and van der Ploeg, Frederick (2017), "Climate Policies Under Climate Model Uncertainty: Max-Min and Min-Max Regret," OxCarre Research (Oxford: Oxford Centre for the Analysis of Resource Rich Economies).

Richtel, Matt and Santos, Fernanda (2016), "Wildfires, Once Confined to a Season, Burn Earlier and Longer," *New York Times*, April 12.

Rivers, Nicholas and Schaufele, Brandon (2015), "Salience of Carbon Taxes in the Gasoline Market," *Journal of Environmental Economics and Management*, 74, 23–36.

Schmalensee, Richard and Stavins, Robert N. (2013), "The SO_2 Allowance Trading System: The Ironic History of a Grand Policy Experiment," *Journal of Economic Perspectives*, 27 (1), 103–22.

Schmalensee, Richard and Stavins, Robert (2017), "Lessons Learned from Three Decades of Experience with Cap-and-Trade," *Review of Environmental Economics and Policy*, 11 (1), 59–79.

Slemrod, Joel and Bakija, Jon (2017), *Taxing Ourselves: A Citizen's Guide to the Great Debate Over Tax Reform*; fifth edn., Cambridge, MA: MIT Press.

Smale, Robin, et al. (2006), "The Impact of CO_2 Emissions Trading on Firm Profits and Market Prices," *Climate Policy*, 6 (1), 31–48.

Stavins, Robert (ed.), (2012), *Economics of the Environment*; sixth edn., New York: W.W. Norton.

Stepp, Matthew, Trembath, Alex, and Goldfarb, Daniel (2011), "All About the Fundamentals: Three Misconceptions of the Heritage Foundation's Deficit/ Energy Proposal," (Washington, DC: ITIF).

Stokes, Elaisha (2016), "The Drought That Preceded Syria's Civil War Was Likely the Worst in 900 Years," *Vice News*, March 3.

Storrow, Benjamin (2017), "Hope Fades for a Rarity: A New Coal Plant," *Climatewire*, September 15.

Stuart, Reginald (1978), "Compromise Hinted on Proposed Truck Fuel Rules," *New York Times*, Jan. 18.

Swift, Byron (2001), "How Environmental Laws Work: An Analysis of the Utility Sector's Response to Regulation of Nitrogen Oxides and Sulfur Dioxide Under the Clean Air Act," *Tulane Environmental Law Journal*, 14, 309–24.

Taylor, Jerry (2015), "Examining Cato's Case Against a Carbon Tax," https:// niskanencenter.org/blog/examining-catos-case-against-a-carbon-tax/, accessed September 27 2017.

Thaler, Richard H. and Sunstein, Cass R. (2008), *Nudge*; New York: Penguin.

The Economist (2013), "Carbon Copy," *Economist*, December 14.

Thompson, Don and Elliott, Dan (2017), "The Costs to Fight the Deadly Wildfires in the West Are Spiraling Out of Control," http://www.businessinsider.com/ ap-us-states-struggle-to-pay-spiraling-cost-of-fighting-fires-2017-10, accessed January 17, 2018.

Trachtman, Joel P. (2017), "WTO Law Constraints On Border Tax Adjustment and Tax Credit Mechanisms to Reduce the Competitive Effects of Carbon Taxes," *National Tax Journal*, 70 (2), 469–94.

US Bureau of Labor Statistics (2018), *Employment, Hours, and Earnings*, May.

US Department of Energy (2005), "Hurricane Katrina Situation Report #28," (Washington, DC: Office of Electricity Delivery and Energy Reliability).

——— (2007), "Deliveries of Coal from the Powder River Basin: Events and Trends 2005-2007," (Washington, DC: Office of Electricity Delivery and Energy Reliability).

——— (2017a), "U.S. Energy and Employment Report," (Washington, DC: DOE).

——— (2017b), "Staff Report to the Secretary on Electricity Markets and Reliability," (Washington, DC: DOE).

US Department of State (2015), "U.S. Cover Note, Intended Nationally Determined Contribution, and Accompanying Information," (Washington, DC: State Department).

US Energy Information Administration (2017), "Assumptions to the Annual Energy Outlook 2016," (Washington, DC: EIA).

——— (2018), "Monthly Energy Review," March 2018 (Washington, DC: EIA).

US Environmental Protection Agency (2018), "Inventory of U.S. Greenhouse Gas Emissions and Sinks: 1990–2016," (Washington, DC: EPA).

US Interagency Working Group on the Social Cost of Carbon (2016), "Technical Support Document: Technical Update of the Social Cost of Carbon for Regulatory Impact Analysis Under Executive Order 12866," (Washington, DC: EPA).

van der Ploeg, Frederick and Rezai, Armon (2017), "The Agnostic's Response to Climate Deniers: Price Carbon!" (Oxford: OxCarre).

Wald, Matthew L. (2012), "An Argument Over Wind," *New York Times,* September 14.

Watson, Paul (2017), "A Melting Arctic Could Spark a New Cold War," *Time Magazine*, May 12.

Weitzman, Martin (1974), "Prices vs. Quantities," *Review of Economic Studies*, 41 (4), 477–91.

Wolozin, Harold (1970), "Pollution, Property, and Prices: Book Review," *Journal of Economic Literature*, 8 (1), 103–105.

World Bank Group (2016), "State and Trends of Carbon Pricing," (Washington, DC: World Bank Group).

——— (2017), "States and Trends of Carbon Pricing 2017," (Washington, DC: World Bank Group).

Yamazaki, Akio (2017), "Jobs and Climate Policy: Evidence from British Columbia's Revenue-Neutral Carbon Tax," *Journal of Environmental Economics and Management*, 83, 197–216.

Yuan, Mei, et al. (2018), "The Revenue Implications of a Carbon Tax," *European Economic Review*, forthcoming.

INDEX

Tables and figures are indicated by an italic *t* and *f* following the page number

carbon price floor and state policies,
110–111
carbon tax. *See also* design of carbon tax;
rates for carbon tax; revenue from
carbon tax
advantages , policy, 54
appeal of using markets, 45
British Columbia, 49, 52
carbon tax reform distributional
impact, 95–98
cost of emission reduction, 58
costs of, 116–118
enacting, 129
EU rejection, 77
highest rates, 84
history of, 48–49
how proceeds are used, 47
lowering distorting taxes, 48
measuring distributional
impact, 93–98
measuring the costs, 46–48
as most efficient strategy, 3
opposition to, 4
pocketbook argument, 3–4
practical political argument, 4
in practice, 48–52
proportional to one's carbon
footprint, 90
public attitudes measured, 51–52
rates, setting, 111–112
recent congressional initiatives, 138
robust tax needed, 136–137
second benefit of, 48
study of distributional impacts,
93–95, 94*f*
Sweden, 49
things to avoid in designing, 112–113
upstream or downstream, 102
urgency of issue, 1
carbon tax regimes, existing, 148n14.
See also Canada
Canada, 124
carbon trading, 69
catastrophic events, 11–12
cement production, 105
certification service for offsets, 68–69
Chicago
floods, 29, 146n7
negative electricity prices, 151n23
University of Chicago, 42–43

China
air conditioning, 30
border tax issue, 108, 109
cap and trade policy, 77, 124
carbon dioxide emissions, 2, 19*f*, 19
GDP per capita, 20
steel exports, 109
trade question, 122–125
citizen group action, 139
Citizens' Climate Lobby (CCL),
131–132, 139
clathrates, 12
CLC. *See* Climate Leadership Council
Clean Air Act, 54–58
Amendments of 1990, 73, 149n5
best system of emission reduction, 55
CLC plan for emission reduction, 135
1977 Amendment, 56
clean energy
policies, 3
subsidies, 63–64
Clean Power Plan
as mandate, 54, 118–119
Trump rollback, 118
climate action tax credit, 50–51
climate change. *See also* scientists on
climate change
accelerating, 12
calculating future costs, 25–27
damages not shown in GDP growth
rates, 117–118
differing geographic impact, 91
events of 2017, 1–2
human-induced or fluke, 16, 33–34
impacts of, 2
inherent uncertainties about, 115–116
quantifying the damages from, 115
random weather fluctuations vs., 16
Trump, Donald J. on, 130
"climate club," 137, 162n15
climate deniers, 34
Climate Extremes Index (CEI), 10
Climate Leadership Council (CLC), 97,
131, 135, 137, 143n7
Republicans supporting a carbon
tax, 138
climate policy
clean energy policies, 3
criteria for, 53–54
opposition to, 129

developed and developing countries
    accounting for emissions by source or
        destination, 161n23
    carbon dioxide emissions, 19–20
    carbon pricing policies, 124
discount rate, 26
distributional impacts, 54. *See also*
        fairness criterion, in taxation
    carbon tax vs. carbon tax
        reform, 157n13
    damages from pollution, 90–91
    electric vehicles, 151n25
    exemptions, 112–113
    exposure to chemicals, 146n13
    fuel economy standards, 62,
        66, 150n16
    hybrid car policies, 66
    OTA carbon tax study, 93–95, 94f
    per capita rebate, 157n16
    of recycling carbon tax revenue, 95–
        98, 96f, 97f
double dividend, 47–48
    economic impact of carbon tax, 116
    weak double dividend, 159n2
drought, 7–11
    California, 8
    Dust Bowl, 11
    examples , 7
    groundwater, 9
    New York, 8
Drought Monitor, 8
Dust Bowl, 11

Earth Summit, 155n5
The Economics of Welfare (Pigou), 44
efficiency criterion, in taxation, 87–89
electricity
    access to, 30, 146n12
    for air conditioning, 30
    carbon price needed to reduce
        emissions, 154n22
    from coal, 102, 158n6
    cost-of-service regulation, 56–57
    deregulation of sector, 120
    feed-in tariffs, 150n18
    negative prices, 64, 151n23
    renewable energy credits (RECs), 63
electric vehicles, 134, 151n25
emission reduction
    attaining significant, 136–137

benchmarks, 137
carbon prices related, 137
in climate policy, 53
complementary policies, 84–85
defining "progress," 135
targets, 137
tax burden related, 90–91
Emissions Assurance Mechanism
        (EAM), 126, 159n22
emissions intensity, 20
emissions trading, 74–76
Emission Trading System (ETS), 77,
        83, 124
    theft of emission allowances, 82
employment impact, 51
    automation, 121, 123
    coal miners, 119–121
    manufacturing sector, 123
    overall trends, 123, 148n20
    for service station workers, 92, 93
    transitional assistance to workers,
        121–122, 133, 155n6
    worker productivity, 123
    zero-carbon economy jobs created,
        121, 132–133
enacting a carbon tax, 129
energy company R&D, 71
energy efficient windows and
        appliances, 65, 151n24
energy intensity, 20
Energy Policy Act of 2005, 64
Energy Policy and Conservation Act
        (1975), 58
energy policy incoherence, 3
energy-saving habits, 67
Environmental Kuznets Curve, 148n18
Environmental Protection Agency
        (EPA), 2, 111
    Clean Air Act standards, 55
    fuel economy standards, 60, 151n26
    future phase-out of carbon
        oversight, 135
    Pruitt carbon pollution rollback,
        118–119
ETS. *See* Emission Trading
        System (ETS)
European Union (EU), 2
    allowance prices, 80
    cap and trade policy, 77, 83
    Paris Agreement, 143n4

exemptions
  carbon capture and storage, or CCS, 106–107
  in design of carbon tax, 112, 158n14
  grandfathering existing power plants, 149nn2, 4
externalities, 36
  Coase Theorem, 43
  Jefferson Memorial, 73
  Pigou's approach, 44–45
  positive, 152n35
extreme weather
  "business as usual" path, costs of, 23
  costs from damages, 24
  extreme weather event days, 10

fairness criterion, in taxation, 88, 89–91
  economic incidence, 92
  in green tax reform, 132–133
  how fairness is measured, 89
falsification in scientific inquiry, 147n16
federal deficit, 126, 155n1, 161n4, 162n18
federal leadership assessed, 3
fee and dividend proposal for a carbon tax, 131–132, 137
feed-in tariffs, 150n18
fires
  Alaska, 14
  Arizona-California, 15
  California, 2, 15
  financial and other costs, 15–16
  fire season in the West, 15
  fluke or climate change?, 16
  Forest Service fire suppression costs, 15
  increased size and severity, 15
  New Mexico, 14–15
  statistics, 143n3
floods
  Chicago, 29, 146n7
  Florida, 29
  Hurricane Sandy, 24–25, 28
  Louisiana, 8
  New York, 28
  sea level rises, 11–12
  storm-surge barrier system, 25, 27, 28
  Tax Day Flood, 8–9
Florida
  flooding, 29
  sea level rises, 30–31
fluorinated gases, 105–106, 158n12

fossil fuels. *See also* coal; fracking revolution; oil and gas production; petroleum
  British Columbia vs. rest of Canada, 51, 148n21
  "business as usual" path, costs of, 23
  carbon tax impact on buyers and sellers, 93
  costs of burning, 36
  costs of climate change in price of, 3
  costs of consumption, 24
  design of carbon tax, 102
  firm fiduciary responsibility, 37
  full social costs, 45
  other impacts of burning, 147n3
  polluter pays principle, 90
  public opinion on carbon tax, 130
  subsidies, 3
fracking revolution, 120, 155n6, 157n3
  methane emissions, 136
framework for reform, 130
Friedman, Milton, 43, 156–157n12
fuel economy standards, 58–60, 151n26
  average efficiency, light duty vehicles, 149n8
  battery storage for electric vehicles, 134
  credit trading, 150n15
  distributional impacts, 150n16
  law of unexpected consequences, 60
  older vehicles on the road, 61, 150n14
  rebound issue, 60–61
  subsidies interacting with regulations, 66
full social costs, 45
future costs of climate change, calculating, 25–27

gas service stations
  New York, 24, 145n1
  as small emitters, 112
  workers, 92, 93
GDP growth rates
  with carbon tax, 116–117, 117f, 160n4
  damages from climate change, 117–118
  declines related to rise in global temperatures, 118
GDP per capita, 20
  growth rates, Sweden and US compared, 49, 50f
  Pascal's climate wager, 32t, 32–33

glacier melting, 14, 145n23
global warming. *See also* heat spells;
    temperatures rising
  historic record, 18
  impact of methane emissions, 12
God, existence of, 31–32
The Grapes of Wrath (Steinbeck), 11
Great Barrier Reef, 12–13
greenhouse gases. *See also* methane
    emissions
  California measures, 78
  cement production, 105
  challenges, 21
  climate sensitivity parameter, 20–21
  Coasian bargaining at the individual
    level, 43
  coverage under a carbon tax, 106
  effect of accumulation, 17
  effect of switching from coal to other
    sources, 20
  fluorinated gases, 105–106
  four factors producing, 20
  historic emissions impact, 21
  irreversible action, 147n17
  measuring stock of, 17
  Pascal's climate wager, 32t, 32–33
  past versus future, 21, 23
  reasons for recent increase, 19
  risks to property and life, 24–25
  sea level rises, 14
  taxing other sources, 105–106
Greenhouse Gas Protocol
    (1998), 159n20
Greenland ice sheet, 11
green tax reform, 4–5. *See also* British
    Columbia
  differential impacts, 98
  fairness, 132–133
  framework overview of, 131
  revenue neutrality, 131
  significant emission reductions,
    136–137
  streamlining climate policy, 133–136
  Sweden, 49
groundwater drought, 9

Halstead, Ted, 137
Hansen, Jim, 132
Harris County Flood Control District, 9
head tax, 88–89, 155n3

heat spells, 10–11
  "business as usual" costs, 29
  Dust Bowl, 11
  reef corals, 12–13
  residential air conditioning, 29
Highway Trust Fund, 138
Holcomb, Kansas coal-fired plant,
    120–121
Hurricane Harvey, 1–2, 9, 14
  Weather Channel, 143n1
Hurricane Katrina, 14, 30
Hurricane Maria, 143n2
hurricanes, 1–2
  allowance prices and, 79–80
  costs of storms, 24–25
Hurricane Sandy
  costs of, 24
  damage risk, 28
hybrid cars, 60–61, 64–66
hybrid systems, cap and trade, 81, 154n16

import taxes, 107, 158n7
incidence, tax, 92
income tax
  multiple layers, 110
  no good measure for ability, 89
  paid in 2015, 155n3
income tax rates, 47–48
  British Columbia reforms, 51
  fairness in green tax reform, 132
India, 30
information to reduce energy
    consumption
  businesses, 67–68
  consumers, 66–67
innovation, in climate policy, 53
  carbon tax providing incentives for,
    124–125
  increased R&D investment, 134
  low allowance prices, 85
  patent protection, 134
insurance, 15, 28, 146nn5
interest rate and future costs, 26
Intergovernmental Panel on Climate
    Change, 118
internal carbon pricing, business
    use of, 67
Internal Revenue Service (IRS), 106
investment tax credit, 64, 150n21
irreversible action, 147n17

Jefferson Memorial, 73
Journal of Law and Economics, 42

Keeling, Charles (Dave), 16
Keeling Curve, 16–18, 18f, 19
    usefulness of, 21
Kentucky, coal miners and carbon
    pricing, 118–122, 132
Kyoto Protocol, 77–78, 155n5

Larsen C ice shelf, 12
leakage. *See* carbon leakage problem
light truck loophole, 58, 59, 149n8
The Logic of Collective Action (Olson),
    147–148n9
Louisiana floods, 8

mandates, 54–55
    problems with, 56–57
    technology, 56–57
manufacturing sector
    competitiveness, 123–125
    employment, 123
    high emissions sectors, 123
    impact of carbon tax on, 123
    output and jobs, 123
Marcellus Gas Basin, 103
marginal analysis, 147n5
marginal utility of income, 155n4
market solutions, 3–4
    appeal of carbon tax, 45
    Pigou approach, 44–45
Marshall Wind Energy project, 64,
    150–151n22
Massachusetts
    drought, 8, 9
    Renewable Portfolio Standard (RPS)
        programs, 62–63
Massachusetts ClimateXChange, 139
Mauna Loa Observatory, 16, 139
melting sea ice, 13–14
methane emissions, 12
    coalbed methane, 135
    dangers of, 135
    leakage in oil and natural gas drilling
        and pipelines, 105
    from livestock, 105
    minimizing leaks, 136
    regulatory proposal to reduce
        emissions withdrawn, 105

surface coal, 135–136
taxing natural gas, 104–105
Miami, 30
Microsoft, 67–68
Min-Max Regret Criterion, 147n18

National Ambient Air Quality Standards
    (NAAQS), 149n3
National Highway Transportation Safety
    Administration, 151n26
National Oceanic and Atmospheric
    Administration (NOAA), 10
    Monthly Climate Update, 10–11
National Park Service, 73
natural gas, 3
    carbon dioxide emissions, by source,
        99–100, 100t
    coal job loss and, 120–121
    fracking revolution, 120
    local distribution companies (LDCs),
        104–105
    points of taxation, 103–105
    prices, 120
    processing plants, 104, 158n8
New Jersey, 101, 108, 157n3
New Mexico fires, 14–15
New York
    adaptations with storm-surge barrier
        system, 25
    cost of continued emissions, 26–27
    costs of Hurricane Sandy, 24
    gas service stations, 24, 145n1
Nigeria, 101, 108
Nordhaus, William, 137, 162n15
North American Free Trade Agreement
    (NAFTA), 122
North Dakota, 101, 133, 153n3
Norway, 13
nuclear power plants, 138
nudges, 151n27

oceans. *See also* sea level rises
    melting sea ice, 13–14
    ocean seabed formations, 12
OECD countries, 137. *See also* European
    Union (EU)
Office of Tax Analysis (OTA), 93–98,
    156nn9, 11–12
off-road diesel, 159n24
offsets, 69–70

Regional Greenhouse Gas Initiative
(RGGI), 78, 81, 84, 110, 153nn9, 10
regional instability and conflict, 2
regressive subsidies, 66
regressive taxes, 89–90
revenue from carbon tax and
corporate tax cuts, 96–97, 97f
regret avoidance approach, 33–34
regulation, 54–62
current emphasis on, 4
price-based approach vs., 149n7
utility deregulation, 160n11
renewable energy credits (RECs), 63
Renewable Portfolio Standard (RPS)
programs, 62–63, 150n18, 19
Microsoft, 68
republicEn group, 138
research and development (R&D), 70–71
battery storage, 134
Department of Energy spending
on, 162n9
patent protection, 134
as positive externality, 152n35
private sector shortfall, 133–134
societal benefits, 134
residential solar installers, 121
Resources for the Future (RFF), 61–62,
116–117
revealed preference, 150n13
revenue from carbon tax
corporate income tax and, 96–97,
97f, 138
dependability of, 126–127
distributional impact, 95–98, 96f, 97f
long-term trends, 126–127
state uses of, 110
what to do with, 87–88, 126
revenue neutrality, 4
AAF proposal, 162n18
British Columbia tax reform, 52
definition, 87
green tax reform framework, 131
risks to property and life, 24–25
interest rate and future costs, 26
paying to avoid, 27–29
Russia, 13, 14

scientific inquiry, 147n16
scientists on climate change, 31
data accumulating, 34
nature of scientific inquiry, 32

scrubbers, 120
example, 56–57
sea level rise, 11–12, 145n23
adaptations for, 14
climate-resilient infrastructure, 14
costs and adaptations, 24
Florida, 30–31
greenhouse gases, 14
historically black neighborhoods
impacted, 30
measuring dollar value of
disruptions, 47
melting glaciers, 14, 145n23
risks to property and life, 24–25
small emitters, 112–113
smart meters, 66
Smith, Adam, 45
snowpack, 9–10
social costs, 36–37, 111, 147n1
solar energy, subsidies, 63–64
Solar Holler program, 132–133
solar technology, 121
in coal mining areas, 132–133
South Korea, 77, 124
Spain, 85
special interest opposition, 129
spending programs, 87
Sport Utility Vehicles (SUVs,) 58–60
Staggers, Harley O., 160n10
Staggers Rail Act of 1980, 120
Stanford University, EMF24 study,
136–137, 162n14
state leadership, 3
steel imports, 109
storm-surge barrier system, 25
damage risk, 28
related damages, 27
strong double dividend, 48, 116
Sturges v. Bridgman, 35–42
negotiation costs, 43
Pigou approach and, 44–45, 47
private and social costs, 37–42, 38t
subsidies, 62–66
clean energy, 63–64
energy efficient windows and
appliances, 65, 151n24
hybrid vehicles, 64–66
impact on consumer prices, 54
oil and gas production, 150n20
regressive, 66
RPS programs, 62–63

University of Chicago, 42–43
US Climate Alliance, 3
US Interagency Working Group
    on the Social Cost of Carbon
    (2016), 159n21
utilitarian social welfare
    construct, 155n4
utility deregulation, 160n11

value added tax (VAT), 107
    destination basis VAT, 107
vampire appliances, 66
VAT. *See* value added tax (VAT)
voluntary programs, 68–70

weak double dividend, 159n2
weather. *See also* drought; floods
    climate change or weird
      weather, 14–16
    extreme weather event days, 10
    extreme weather example, 11
Weather Channel, 143n1
Weitzman, Marty, 153–154n14
West Virginia, 119–120, 160n10
    Solar Holler program, 132
wildfires. *See* fires

wind energy
    tax subsidies for, 64
    technology, 121
    zero-carbon electricity, 69
workplace environment, right to, 40–41
World Business Council for Sustainable
    Development, 159n20
World Resources Institute, 159n20
Worlds in the Making (Arrhenius), 20–21
World Trade Organization (WTO),
    109, 159n19
worst outcome decision-making
    criterion, 31–32, 33
    as Max-Min criterion, 146n15
    Min-Max Regret Criterion, 147n18
Wyoming, 132. *See also* Powder
    River Basin

zero-carbon economy, 70
    distributional impact, ameliorating,
      132–133
    incentives for, 69
    increasing profitability of, 124–125
    jobs created, 121
    need for new technology, 133–135
    political will for, 137